THE THEOLOGICAL ANTHROPOLOGY OF DAVID KELSEY

The Theological Anthropology of David Kelsey

Responses to Eccentric Existence

Edited by

Gene Outka

William B. Eerdmans Publishing Company
Grand Rapids, Michigan / Cambridge, U.K.

Published 2016 by
Wm. B. Eerdmans Publishing Co.
2140 Oak Industrial Drive N.E., Grand Rapids, Michigan 49505 /
P.O. Box 163, Cambridge CB3 9PU U.K.

Printed in the United States of America

22 21 20 19 18 17 16 7 6 5 4 3 2 1

Library of Congress Cataloging-in-Publication Data

The theological anthropology of David Kelsey: responses to Eccentric existence /
edited by Gene Outka.
pages cm
Includes bibliographical references.
ISBN 978-0-8028-7243-2 (cloth: alk. paper)
1. Theological anthropology — Christianity.
2. Kelsey, David H. Eccentric existence.
3. Kelsey, David H. I. Outka, Gene H., editor.

BT701.3.T45 2016
233.092 — dc23

2015032354

www.eerdmans.com

Contents

Editor's Preface vii
Gene Outka

Methodological Choices in Kelsey's *Eccentric Existence* 1
John E. Thiel

A Response to *Eccentric Existence* 16
Charles M. Wood

Humanity Before God; Thinking Through Scripture:
Theological Anthropology and the Bible 31
David F. Ford

Eccentric Existence and the Catholic Tradition 53
Cyril O'Regan

Eccentric Ecclesiology 91
Amy Plantinga Pauw

A Trinitarian Grammar of Sin 107
Joy Ann McDougall

For God's Own Sake: *Eccentric Existence* and the
Theological Education Debate 127
Barbara G. Wheeler and Edwin Chr. van Driel

From Narrative to Performance? 147
Shannon Craigo-Snell

David H. Kelsey Publications and Presentations 172

Contributors 177

Editor's Preface

The route leading to this volume has proven circuitous, beyond my imaginings. Serene Jones, who was our colleague at Yale at the point of origin of this project, first broached with me the idea of a Festschrift on David Kelsey's various publications, and it generated my enthusiasm. The time was propitious. Kelsey's long-awaited two-volume work, *Eccentric Existence: A Theological Anthropology,* totaling over a thousand pages, had become available. Jones and I agreed to serve as co-editors of such an undertaking. We consulted with Kelsey about a list of suitable contributors, and we followed his lead on this score. He chose a group of colleagues, former students, and others with whom he had collaborated on various relevant scholarly projects over the years.

However, before we sent the initial letters of invitation, Jones assumed her new responsibilities as president of Union Theological Seminary in New York, and because of that increased responsibility she has been unable to participate in the editorial process. As this became clear to me, I decided to go forward on my own, and not abandon an undertaking that seemed an important one. I will always be grateful for the impetus Jones originally provided. Invitations were issued; various delays occurred; I was involved over many months with letters to and fro, and the receipt of drafts of various sorts. Two additional restrictions were subsequently imposed. First, *Eccentric Existence* became the center of gravity. We had originally envisaged discussions of earlier parts of Kelsey's corpus as well (e.g., *Imagining Redemption*). While this proved in the end unworkable, the present essays contain various references to Kelsey's earlier publications. Still, this restriction makes the present volume less than a Festschrift on conventional reckonings. Yet I hope it constitutes a properly "celebratory volume" of many of Kelsey's contributions. Second, I had planned initially to include an individual chapter in which I assessed his depictions of the two love commandments. But ongoing preoccupation with another manuscript of my own had to take priority. Rather than delay the appearance of this present volume, I am content to wear here simply an editor's hat. May this attest to a long friendship.

Several of the contributors in the pages that follow register their conviction that *Eccentric Existence* will require years to assess fully. It seems best to try to take some of its measure earlier rather than later in the process of its reception. I find all of the chapters below to be accessible and deeply considered, and I am delighted to promote their distribution.

GENE OUTKA
Dwight Professor Emeritus of Philosophy and Christian Ethics
Yale University

Methodological Choices in Kelsey's *Eccentric Existence*

John E. Thiel

I begin an article on David Kelsey's *Eccentric Existence: A Theological Anthropology* by noting that this is a long-awaited book.[1] There is a sense in which one can find traces of a recent work in many of a consistent author's earlier writings. Kelsey's contributions to the Hodgson-King collection *Christian Theology* in 1985 and to the Festschrift for Hans Frei in 1987 are the first explicit literary announcements of his interest in this theological locus.[2] So dated, Kelsey's work on the project of theological anthropology spans more than twenty-five years. During this time, Kelsey's friends and students (in many cases, the same people!) have known that he was at work on a book-length treatment of the theme. Even though Kelsey published two important monographs in these years, his readers have ever anticipated the appearance of his theological anthropology. Now that this work has been published — in two large volumes comprising more than one thousand pages — the expectations of those who have learned so much

1. David H. Kelsey, *Eccentric Existence: A Theological Anthropology,* 2 vols. (Louisville, KY: Westminster John Knox Press, 2009). This article first appeared in a review symposium on *Eccentric Existence* in *Modern Theology* 27 (January 2011): 1-13. I am grateful to the editors of *Modern Theology,* Jim Fodor and William Cavanaugh, for inviting me to contribute this piece, and to Wiley-Blackwell for permission to publish it here. It is a great honor for me to be able to engage the work of David Kelsey, as I have, very much to my benefit, throughout my theological career.

2. David H. Kelsey, "Human Being," in *Christian Theology: An Introduction to Its Traditions and Tasks,* ed. P. Hodgson and R. King (Philadelphia, PA: Fortress Press, 1985), pp. 167-94; David H. Kelsey, "Biblical Narrative and Theological Anthropology," in *Scriptural Authority and Narrative Interpretation,* ed. G. Green (Philadelphia, PA: Fortress Press, 1987), pp. 121-44.

from his writings have been abundantly exceeded. *Eccentric Existence* is a theological *tour de force* that defies categorization. Although its subtitle announces that it is a theological anthropology, it redefines that theological genre in a host of ways. In spite of Kelsey's intention to engage in the genre of systematic theology "unsystematically," the work could verily be described as a Trinitarian systematics. And especially in the second volume, though in subtle ways throughout, *Eccentric Existence* unfolds as a practical theology of the Christian life.

In these few pages, I would like to consider some of the methodological choices that Kelsey made in writing the theological anthropology he did. Method has been an abiding interest of Kelsey's throughout his career. His second book, *The Uses of Scripture in Recent Theology* (1975), was "not an exercise in 'theological methodology,'" but instead a "study of theologians' methods" that, he modestly claimed, offered "a series of notes and observations about what theologians are actually doing as they pursue their craft."[3] In that first book on theological method, Kelsey did not construct a theory whose application he commended for the proper conduct of theology. But if theological method is broadly construed as attention to the practiced ways in which acts of theological imagination issue in theological proposals, then Kelsey's first book on that topic was early testimony to a life-long interest in method. On the face of it, *To Understand God Truly: What's Theological About a Theological School* (1992) is an essay on the authentic goals of theological education.[4] Here too, though, between the lines, the reader finds methodological concerns voiced generally in Kelsey's exploration of the nature and responsibilities of theological reflection. Kelsey's more recent *Imagining Redemption* (2005) is a practical theology that reflects on the theme of its title through a particular case study of tragic family circumstances.[5] Yet it ends, as does *Eccentric Existence,* with a "coda" that considers in retrospect what its author was and was not venturing in the preceding pages.

The very form of *Eccentric Existence* as a publication reflects its author's attention to method throughout. Many of the book's chapters are presented in A and B versions, the former continuing the argument and the latter, physically different in smaller font, detailing "more technical,

3. David H. Kelsey, *The Uses of Scripture in Recent Theology* (Philadelphia, PA: Fortress Press, 1975), p. 7.

4. David H. Kelsey, *To Understand God Truly: What's Theological About a Theological School* (Louisville, KY: Westminster John Knox Press, 1992).

5. David H. Kelsey, *Imagining Redemption* (Louisville, KY: Westminster John Knox Press, 2005).

in-house-academic-theology discussions." One could argue that all of the B version chapters are concerned with methodological issues, at least in the sense that some rehearse scholarly debates on which Kelsey comments with respect to his actual proposals. Kelsey, however, acknowledges that Chapters 1B, 2B, and 3B, which appear in the work's extended introduction, are presented "for readers who are interested in where the author stands on relevant methodological issues in academic theology."[6] This would be a good place to begin our inquiry.

What Kelsey's Project Is and Isn't

The significant methodological choices in Kelsey's magnum opus are a function of his comprehensive decision to develop the locus of anthropology in light of the Christian background belief that God relates to what is not God, and more specifically to human persons, in three "complexly interrelated but distinct" ways: "to create us, to draw us to eschatological consummation, and, when we have alienated ourselves from God, to reconcile us."[7] These three ways are, of course, expressions of the Christian tradition's belief in the Trinitarian God, and these three ways describe the particular activities of the Trinitarian persons — respectively, the Father, the Spirit, and the Son — in the plot of the biblical narrative and its doctrinal interpretation. God, in this tradition of Trinitarian belief, is relational in God's very manner of being, immanently, in the perichoretic relations of the persons in the divine unity *in se,* and economically, in God's graceful outreach to what is not God *ad extra.* Kelsey is committed to doing a theological anthropology under the auspices of this most particular of Christian beliefs. Indeed, in Kelsey's judgment, Christian beliefs about the three ways that God relates to human persons are "non-negotiable for Christian faith"[8] and define the context for a Christian particularism out of which a theological anthropology best proceeds. The consequence of this choice is that Kelsey offers three distinctive anthropological presentations in the three principal sections of this very large work, each of which parses the human condition from the perspective of one of the three ways that God relates to human persons in Christian belief.

6. Kelsey, *Eccentric Existence,* p. xiii.
7. Kelsey, *Eccentric Existence,* p. 5.
8. Kelsey, *Eccentric Existence,* p. 8.

This is an extraordinarily interesting way (or ways!) to write a theological anthropology. God is at the center of Kelsey's anthropology and, as the title of his book declares, human beings are not. To many contemporary theologians, Kelsey's decision to make human persons "eccentric" even to a theological anthropology will have a Barthian ring, and will be especially reminiscent of Barth's judgment that anthropology is properly Christology.[9] The Barthian resonances in a certain Yale style of theology during the last several decades, to which Kelsey has contributed significantly, might encourage that identification as well. But Kelsey assumes that this approach to what he calls "secondary" theology — the intentional, disciplinary practice of criticizing and revising Christian claims and warrants — cannot be reduced to the work of an individual theologian or to a local "school." Premodern theology itself was guided by the question, "What is the logic of the *beliefs* that inform the practices composing the common life of communities of Christian faith?"[10] This Christian particularism makes the tradition's central beliefs the norms for all Christian practices, including the practice of secondary theology, and Kelsey's approach to theological anthropology advances his judgment, so difficult to dispute, that the doctrine of the Trinity articulates the tradition's most basic belief whose logic is implicated in all beliefs and practices, including those surrounding the human person. "Anthropological questions," Kelsey observes,

> did not constitute a *locus* of their own in premodern secondary theology. Anthropological questions were scattered among discussions of various ways in which God relates to all that is not God, and especially to human beings. Consequently, anthropological proposals were made as answers to questions that were raised by proposals made, in the first instance, about God.[11]

Thus, "such anthropological proposals, even when they were controversial in their day and opposed to one another, had in common that their internal logic was theocentric."[12]

Kelsey does not think that post-Enlightenment theology has outgrown this traditional conception of theological responsibility. He is keenly aware,

9. Karl Barth, *Church Dogmatics,* III/2, ed. G. W. Bromiley and T. F. Torrance (Edinburgh: T&T Clark, 1960).

10. Kelsey, *Eccentric Existence,* p. 27.

11. Kelsey, *Eccentric Existence,* p. 28.

12. Kelsey, *Eccentric Existence,* p. 29.

though, that so many modern theologians have come to exactly the opposite conclusion, particularly with respect to the locus of anthropology. The Enlightenment "turn to the subject" valorized the human person in ways that led theologians to venture an analysis of humanity apart from its God-relatedness, as though this distinctly Christian understanding of the human person would first need to be "bracketed"[13] in order to achieve a relevant analysis of the human condition. Only then, in possession of such a meaningful understanding, would the theologian have information with sufficient interpretive power to bring the tradition to contemporary life. Although he appreciates the many insights that this theological approach has garnered, Kelsey does not consider this methodological orientation to be the best for the task at hand. God's relatedness to humanity, in the three distinct ways that the Trinitarian God relates to human persons, is the time-honored approach that Kelsey adopts here, and, given the anthropocentricity of modern theology, this requires that he "argue . . . that such theocentricity is a major *desideratum* in theological anthropology."[14]

What Kelsey's project is not, then, is an exercise in general apologetics. While Kelsey understands his project as an exploration of the question of the "logic of the *beliefs* that inform the practices composing the common life of communities of Christian faith," he consistently eschews any responsibility to the question "What is the logic of coming to belief, or of coming to faith in God . . . ?"[15] Although this latter question about the logic of *coming* to belief is perfectly legitimate and has been asked and answered throughout the Christian tradition, it has tended to eclipse the former question of the logic of the beliefs themselves in modern theologies. Kelsey insists that "it is a profound conceptual and methodological mistake to conflate any theological project that attempts to answer the question of the logic of Christian beliefs with a theological project that attempts to answer the question of the logic of coming to faith."[16] So many modern theologies, he believes, have accorded a theological primacy to the task of explaining the logic of coming to faith because this endeavor allows them to find meaningful connections to the culture at large, typically by adopting some cultural account of how one lives a meaningful human life and then demonstrating how that account is compatible with the Christian

13. Kelsey, *Eccentric Existence,* p. 29.
14. Kelsey, *Eccentric Existence,* p. 29.
15. Kelsey, *Eccentric Existence,* pp. 27, 80.
16. Kelsey, *Eccentric Existence,* p. 113.

life of faith. In one way or another, the logic of coming to faith is portrayed as a function of, and so consistent with, authentic self-actualization, and this demonstration hopes to justify Christian belief before the cultural court of modernity in which the Christian tradition is on trial and presumed guilty of rational incoherence and so contemporary irrelevance. In twenty-five stellar pages, Kelsey summarizes the prominent accounts of self-actualization in the nineteenth and twentieth centuries — the anthropologies of Kant, Romanticism, Hegel and Marx, and Existentialism — and how they have been theologically appropriated in various modern theologies.[17] Kelsey reverses this theological trajectory, pursuing a method that makes basic beliefs about the Trinitarian God the point of departure for any and all acts of theological parsing.

The methodological conflation of the logic of beliefs with the logic of coming to belief has, in Kelsey's judgment, resulted in several deleterious consequences for theological anthropology, the most interesting of which will allow us to consider the scriptural warrant he chooses for the kind of anthropology he develops.

Narrative Choices

Kelsey's methodological argument to this point is that modernity's "turn to the subject" encouraged theologians to accord primacy to the question of the logic of coming to belief, which eclipsed theology's premodern commitment to the question of the logic of the beliefs themselves. In theological projects devoted to the locus of anthropology, the logic of coming to belief offered an apologetical venue to engage modern philosophical accounts of self-actualization, which portrayed the human condition as a struggle to become fully one's self out of an initial state of deficiency. Typically, these philosophical accounts and their theological appropriations are understood to be claims for human empowerment. With ironic flair, Kelsey argues that theological projects committed to the "turn to the subject" lead "to a theological anthropological denigration of human beings and a correlatively utilitarian and functionalist trivialization of God's relating to human beings."[18] In order to cohere apologetically with modern philosophical accounts of self-actualization, modern theological anthro-

17. Kelsey, *Eccentric Existence,* pp. 82-110.
18. Kelsey, *Eccentric Existence,* p. 113.

pologies must assume that human nature initially finds itself in a problematic state that requires resolution. This, in turn, has led modern theological anthropologies to represent the human condition as problematic "in the sense of a weakness, a damaged integrity needing to be restored, a lost freedom needing to be liberated, or a disease needing to be healed." The struggle for self-actualization in the modern philosophical accounts becomes a template for the theological representation of the struggle with sin "in the passage from unfaith to faith," an identification on which "the apologetic force of such theological anthropologies depends."[19]

The consequence of this framework is what Kelsey calls a "'God's grace/humans' sin' structure" so typical of modern theological anthropologies. This structure determines the manner in which the Christian story is read and the way in which the scriptural plot is narrated in theological interpretation. In such theological anthropologies, and to the degree that modern theology is largely anthropological in orientation, in such modern theologies,

> [t]he central Christian claim about God is that God relates to reconcile in the very odd mode of incarnation leading to crucifixion and resurrection . . . ; therefore, the central Christian claim about human beings is that they must be in a condition of weakness, damaged integrity, lost freedom, or disease so profound . . . as to require such an astonishing mode of divine relating for it to be overcome in the full actualization of human subjects. The apologetic force of this sort of anthropological project requires this structure. It has, however, the systematic consequence that Christian claims about other ways in which the triune God relates to all that is not God — for example, to create and to draw to eschatological consummation — are theologically marginalized.[20]

Once God's relating to reconcile an otherwise irretrievable human fallenness is placed on theological center stage, then God's relating to create and to bring humanity to eschatological consummation are relegated to the position of shadow beliefs that, at best, enhance God's reconciling activity. The unbounded power of the Trinitarian God finds itself procrusteanized on the bed of human sin so desperately in need of grace.

19. Kelsey, *Eccentric Existence,* pp. 113-14.

20. Kelsey, *Eccentric Existence,* p. 114. Later in his presentation, Kelsey refers to this structure as the "conventional binary structure of secondary theology." See Kelsey, *Eccentric Existence,* pp. 468f.

This typically modern way of structuring the anthropological project not only diminishes the Trinitarian fullness of God's ways of relating to human creatures but also misrepresents the tradition's most basic beliefs about the kind of created reality human persons are. Attention to the creation story reveals that the tragic dimensions of human sin lie not in humanity's own distortions but in the degree to which sin distorts a creature who magnificently reflects God's glory. The Christian belief that "God relates to create all that is not God entails the claim that what God creates, including human creatures, are good in virtue of God relating to them creatively." Human creatures, Kelsey avers, "in particular are a mysteriously complex mix of creaturely fragility and amazing resources of many kinds of strength,"[21] a traditional belief that the modern accent on human fallenness obscures. This modern "God's grace/humans' sin" structure also obscures this theological affirmation of created goodness by so highlighting the divine activity of reconciliation that it eclipses the basic belief that God draws all to final consummation, which "entails that the goodness of human creatures is confirmed by the eschatological glory for which they are destined and in which in some way they already participate."[22]

Christian secondary theology warrants its claims by appeal to Scripture, specifically what Kelsey calls "canonical Christian Holy Scripture." There are several features of the biblical writings that make them canonical. The canon, a specific collection of various writings, is judged to be inspired divine revelation by the community of believers who are committed to its practice in their lives. This judgment conveys the authority that believers accord to canonical Holy Scripture for measuring their lives. Moreover, canonical meaning is shaped especially by the texts that are stories, to the point that the entire canon can be read, and is read, as one story with a particular plot. We have seen, by implication at least, that Kelsey wishes to highlight the three distinguishable but interrelated versions of this plot that are layered in the canon — a plot in which God relates to what is not God in "creative blessing, in eschatological blessing, and to deliver and reconcile those who are alienated in some sort of bondage."[23] In the modern period, these three versions have largely been overshadowed by the plot of reconciliation, and in such ways that the creation plot has been reduced to a function of it and the eschatological plot largely ignored.

21. Kelsey, *Eccentric Existence,* p. 115.
22. Kelsey, *Eccentric Existence,* p. 115.
23. Kelsey, *Eccentric Existence,* p. 187.

Kelsey enlists the work of the biblical scholar Claus Westermann in order to defend this judgment.

In his magisterial studies of the book of Genesis, Westermann argued that Genesis 1–11 was redacted by its Yahwist and Priestly editors as an introduction to the story of God's deliverance of Israel at the Reed Sea. More specifically, Genesis 1–3, the story of God's creation of the universe, of humanity, and the story of the first sin, provided a context for that later deliverance story by explaining the need for deliverance, as humanity betrayed its primordially created state of faithfulness to God. Genesis 1–3, then, for Westermann, is not first and foremost a story of creation but an introductory premise to the Old Testament story of reconciliation. If, in Kelsey's judgment, Christian readings of Scripture are obliged to appreciate the Trinitarian emplotment of canonical Holy Scripture, then privileging Genesis 1–3 as the normative site for understanding how God relates to humanity in creative blessing will be problematic since, as Westermann has shown, this story actually stands within the narrative of reconciliation. Kelsey seeks to warrant his theological anthropology scripturally with "the distinctive literary features of creation stories whose narrative logic is their own, and is not bent under the pressure of the narrative logic of another class of stories about God relating to what is not God."[24] Kelsey finds such stories in the Hebrew Wisdom literature.

The canonical Wisdom literature — Proverbs, Ecclesiastes, Song of Solomon, and Job — does not, of course, offer a creation story, but rather a theology of creation that envisages the human person in created relationship to God. The Wisdom literature reflects on the human person's God relatedness in the most ordinary, day-to-day situations, what Kelsey calls the "quotidian,"[25] in order to appreciate God's ongoing providential activity and the trust in God that is the believer's proper response. Unlike traditional Christian readings of Genesis 1–2, which understand humanity to be created in a state of perfection, Wisdom literature accepts the only state of humanity to be its created finitude here and now, which is "not an evil," nor "a problem to be solved, nor a predicament from which we need to be saved."[26] The Wisdom literature encourages its interpreters "to describe the quotidian in terms of human practices" enacted by " '*personal,* living human bodies' " whose flourishing unfolds in the ultimate context

24. Kelsey, *Eccentric Existence,* p. 188.
25. Kelsey, *Eccentric Existence,* p. 190.
26. Kelsey, *Eccentric Existence,* p. 212.

of God's ever-present creativity and in the proximate ways in which that creativity originates and fosters human persons in their concrete actuality. This Wisdom construal of theological anthropology, Kelsey believes, provides an alternative to the "God's grace/humans' sin" structure of modern theological anthropologies. It refuses to assume some original state of human ideality now lost to realistic sinfulness, for in that construal the single narrative logic of Christian reconciliation typically explains graceful human rescue only by marginalizing God's creative and eschatologically consummating activities.

Kelsey's choice of Wisdom literature as a narrative warrant for his theology embraces a biblical account of the human person understood completely and authentically in his or her relatedness to God, as an extraordinary creature who knows, in faith, that he or she lives on "borrowed breath" and is called to repay this loan by wise action that responds to God's creative blessing. Kelsey's anthropology offers very insightful accounts of human sinfulness as failure to live in the three ways that God relates to human persons. But his Wisdom-based anthropology does not begin from an account of the human person in sinful loss. Rather, he considers persons in the full range of their created powers who always already stand within the ambit of God's relationality and who are thus shouldered with the responsibility of trust, hope, and love toward God and neighbor that mirrors the divine glory itself.[27] Indeed, Kelsey's choice of a Wisdom construal of theological anthropology conveys his appreciation for what we might call the "gifted worthiness" of the human person that one finds in these scriptural texts. His commitment to such an anthropology of gifted worthiness, in fact, is a function of his decision to expound the locus from a fully Trinitarian perspective and explains why the structure of his presentation of the three ways of divine relating departs from the creedal order of Father, Son, and Spirit, in favor of respective reflections on God's relating to create, God's relating to draw to eschatological consummation, and, "*when* [and only when!] we have alienated ourselves from God,"[28] God's relating to reconcile us. Human worthiness originates in the divine act of creation and is confirmed in the drawing of that worthiness into eschatological consummation, which, as a divine activity, is not logically dependent on God's reconciling activity. "Stories about God delivering and reconciling," Kelsey states, "generally presuppose stories about God draw-

27. See Kelsey, *Eccentric Existence,* pp. 316f.

28. Kelsey, *Eccentric Existence,* p. 5. Italics mine.

ing to eschatological consummation, but the converse does not hold."[29] Thus, a most contemporary theological anthropology charged with traditional sensibilities offers a corrective to the odd ways in which modern theologies have tried to satisfy and convey the Enlightenment claim for human empowerment.

Systematically Unsystematic Theology

Before raising some critical questions about Kelsey's argument, I would like briefly to consider one other methodological matter that the author raises occasionally in his presentation, namely, his understanding of his work as a systematically unsystematic theology. Early in the book, Kelsey concludes his chapter-length discussion of the aims of his project by stating:

> An account of the logic of Christian anthropological beliefs aiming to exhibit them as a "system" may turn out itself to be a systematically distorted account of human being. Focusing on the apparently unsystematic, conceptually shaped practices that constitute the common life of ecclesial communities as the faith that is to be understood serves, I propose, to make this a project in systematically unsystematic secondary theology.[30]

This, of course, is an intentionally provocative and paradoxical way of defining his methodological goal, and Kelsey leaves this formulation undefined as he introduces it. Readers of his previous book, *Imagining Redemption,* will recall that it was first introduced there, no doubt out of the concerns of this larger work, which could not help but to contextualize this earlier discussion.

Kelsey brings *Imagining Redemption* to conclusion with a chapter-length "coda" that includes a sectional heading identical to the one immediately above. What makes his presentation "systematic" in its reflections on redemption is that it "tries to move from thought to thought in a systematic way, and it traces out systematic connections between Christian beliefs about redemption and a number of other Christian beliefs." But

29. Kelsey, *Eccentric Existence,* p. 187.
30. Kelsey, *Eccentric Existence,* p. 45.

Kelsey rejects any aspirations to the systematic that would make some "philosophical doctrine . . . the intellectual framework that will explain the meaning of Christian beliefs most profoundly or demonstrate their truth most persuasively."[31] This rejection of philosophical theorizing as a grounding for theological reflection is Kelsey's understanding of systematic theology's rightful commitment to be "unsystematic." As such, this position is an iteration of Kelsey's concern in *Eccentric Existence* that the modern conflation of theological questions about the logic of beliefs with questions about the logic of coming to belief leads theology down an apologetical path on which Christian beliefs will be accommodated to non-Christian theories of human nature. Kelsey, however, goes further in his penultimate book.

Theory, Kelsey notes, can be understood simply as a statement that "proposes a set of general principles that can explain an event or situation of which there may, in principle, be an indefinite number of others of the same type."[32] Some Christian beliefs, like God's providential relation to the world, are subject to this kind of theorizing since there are so many possible applications of the principle that God providentially relates to the world. There are, however, other Christian beliefs "about absolutely unique situations or events that *in principle* cannot have more than one instance," such as the belief "that God created from nothing *all* reality" or the belief in "the incarnation in this world of the Second Person of the Trinity" or the belief that "God's actualization of the eschatological kingdom will bring a new creation."[33] These beliefs cannot be theorized since they express " 'singularities' "[34] rather than general principles capable of multiple possible applications. Their content possesses an integrity shaped through an actual, particular tradition of Christian belief and practice, and this integrity in itself requires no application or translation into some other kind of meaning. "If the beliefs explicated by systematic theology include beliefs of both of these types," Kelsey avers, "then *systematic theology* cannot be defined as the enterprise of developing a single, rigorous, systematic, internally coherent, comprehensive body of 'theory' of Christian faith."[35] It must remain "unsystematic" in order to be faithful to its tradition of basic beliefs.

31. Kelsey, *Imagining Redemption,* p. 88.
32. Kelsey, *Imagining Redemption,* p. 89.
33. Kelsey, *Imagining Redemption,* p. 90.
34. Kelsey, *Imagining Redemption,* p. 94.
35. Kelsey, *Imagining Redemption,* p. 90.

Eccentric Existence brings these earlier reflections to bear on its subject matter. Kelsey cites approvingly Kierkegaard's observation that existence is not a system, and so "there can be no systematic, comprehensive taxonomy of the variety of existential hows" that might be enlisted theologically to explain faith in God, or any of the ways that God relates to what is not God.[36] The traditional, and exegetically dubious, distinction between the creation of humanity in the "image" and "likeness" of God in Genesis 1 itself inclines theology to "systematize" by making "image" into an anthropological principle of created ideality and "likeness" a set of realistic existential applications, now in sin but searching for redemption. A "systematically systematic" theology, then, would be one that proceeded from the assumptions of modern apologetics, making humanity the center of its theological exposition and typically in a way that accords a rather exclusive primacy to the biblical plot of reconciliation.

The first "coda" to *Eccentric Existence* considers in a positive fashion how the Trinitarian template of the book specifies its unsystematic quality. That theology be "systematically unsystematic," Kelsey maintains, is a "methodological imperative . . . reflected in the three-part structure of [the] project."[37] There is a sense in which the biblical narrative of God's relating to create possesses a kind of logical priority to the narratives of God's relating to bring to eschatological consummation and God's relating to reconcile, since these narratives presuppose the existence of what is not God. Yet, Kelsey insists that the image of a triple helix best captures the relationships between and among these three narratives in his argument. Each of the three sections of his work offers theological-anthropological insights by putting the questions of "what," "how," and "who" to the mysterious reality of the human creature as his or her life transpires in its ultimate and proximate contexts. The order and reasonable coherence of this approach are what make *Eccentric Existence* a "systematic" theology. What makes the work a "systematically unsystematic" theology is its assumption that human existence as *imago Dei* can only be properly and fully appreciated in light of the three forms of divine relationship, perichoretically interwoven in reality, Kelsey believes, and thus properly too in theological explanation. Only from the perspectives of this explanatory triple helix can a theological anthropology account for what it means for human persons

36. Kelsey, *Eccentric Existence,* pp. 12, 421. The context for these words is the doctrine of sin. But they certainly would apply in Kelsey's judgment to any other theological context.

37. Kelsey, *Eccentric Existence,* p. 897.

to be the *imago Dei.* Only from these three perspectives may the *imago Dei* be unsystematically, theocentrically explained in ways that mutually "sharpen it, complexify it, and deepen it in an open-ended way that resists every drive to systematize human existence, which is 'mystery' in part just because it is not 'a system.'"[38] And if humanity in its mysteriousness eludes system, how much more does the divine mystery who is the proper object of all theology, including theological anthropology?

Some Questions to the Author

I hope that I have been able to do some justice to the theme of methodological choices in this remarkable book in the space allotted to me. I would like to conclude with a few questions from which the author may choose the best avenues for continued conversation.

First, is the author's nonfoundationalist, or unsystematic, or anti-apologetical approach to theology truly as methodologically normative as he claims? Certainly Kelsey is correct that premodern theology pursued this traditional approach. But given the fact that theology has passed through the fire of the Enlightenment, has not, in fact, theology's proximate context changed in a way that calls for an appropriate methodological response? We usually do not think of method as a theological locus, but Kelsey makes a fine case for doing so. Yet, historical research clearly has shown that Christian doctrine develops. Why should this not be true for the "doctrine" of theological method? At the very least, would there not be a richer spectrum of theological options available for Christian appreciation if "systematic" and "unsystematic" styles of method were to flourish side by side as different, but both normatively acceptable, ways to elucidate the mysteries of God and human person?

Second, as a Roman Catholic interpreter of Kelsey, I especially appreciate his commitment to an anthropology of human strength and responsibility before God and even in the midst of sin, so powerfully expressed in the relations he develops between God's creative and eschatological blessings and in his unwillingness to settle on the fallenness of human nature as his anthropological point of departure. Indeed, Kelsey seems perfectly at ease with a Franciscan style of Christology, which so appreciates the created goodness of humanity that it affirms the occurrence of the incar-

38. Kelsey, *Eccentric Existence,* p. 900.

nation even if humanity had not sinned. But is this anthropology faithful to the classical Reformation heritage captured in the great Lutheran and Reformed confessions of faith of the sixteenth and seventeenth centuries? Or, is it not important that a contemporary Protestant theology that heralds traditional assumptions be faithful in that way?

Third, and finally, does the choice for Wisdom literature as the scriptural warrant for the creation narrative do justice to the social dimensions of human sinfulness that post-Enlightenment liberation theologies have exposed, analyzed, and theologically addressed so brilliantly? Granted, the argument of the book unfolds with attention to three scriptural narratives. Yet, as the author notes more than once, there is a kind of logical priority to the creation narrative and so one might expect to find its effects in the theological-anthropological proposals that issue from the other scriptural plots. More, might the Wisdom orientation, with its attention to the quotidian, encourage an approach to the human that puts the ordinariness of human life too exclusively in focus, an ordinariness that elicits the question "Whose?" and that is subject to all the critiques of false universalism that liberation theologies have directed to traditional theologies? Or, does Kelsey think that this narrative commitment, made to open a theological space for the fullness of God's Trinitarian ways of being in relation to humanity, offers a perspective on humanity that can be appropriated in all the socially particular ways about which liberation theologies would be concerned?

I look forward to seeing the author's answers in print[39] and, as personal, living human bodies in a fairly proximate context, to continuing our conversation about the God who relates to create, to bring to eschatological consummation, and to reconcile us when we have alienated ourselves. Until then, I will be grateful, as I always am, for the creative blessing of his remarkable theological wisdom!

39. David Kelsey responded most effectively to these questions in the *Modern Theology* symposium. See David H. Kelsey, "Response to the Symposium on *Eccentric Existence,*" *Modern Theology* 27 (January 2011): 72-74.

A Response to *Eccentric Existence*

Charles M. Wood

In his review of Eberhard Busch's biography of Karl Barth, Hans Frei offers an interesting explanation for the vastness of Barth's *Church Dogmatics* and for its evident resistance to effective summary — an explanation, that is, beyond both Barth's customary loquaciousness and his love of the subject matter: In the *Dogmatics,* Frei said, Barth was engaged in a work of "conceptual description" requiring him "to recreate a universe of discourse" that he believed had been largely lost, and to "put the reader in the middle of that world" in order to show the reader how the concepts worked.[1] That is to say, there was a pedagogical reason for the prolixity.

Something similar might be said about the length of David Kelsey's *Eccentric Existence,* though the reason is not quite the same. In this case, the underlying cause for the fact that we are confronted here with over a thousand pages on theological anthropology is Kelsey's constitutional aversion to reductionism. It is an aversion that translates into published work that is both methodologically and substantively important, if also at times a challenge to the reader's powers of endurance. Kelsey is, one might say, a practitioner of slow theology; and that is a reference not so much to the considerable amount of time he has devoted to this book as

1. Hans W. Frei, "Eberhard Busch's Biography of Karl Barth," in *Types of Christian Theology,* ed. George Hunsinger and William C. Placher (New Haven, CT: Yale University Press, 1992), pp. 158-59.

A briefer version of this chapter appeared in the *International Journal of Systematic Theology* 13, no. 3 (July 2011): 313-22.

to the way the book itself (at least as I understand this) is meant to work. The author is intent not, as Frei's Barth was, on socializing the reader into a forgotten Christian universe of discourse, but rather on imparting a discipline of thought, principally by exemplifying it. We are witness here not only to the results of his thinking but also to a large extent to the process of reflection itself.

What I have just been describing is an aspect of the book Kelsey himself characterizes as its "tone of voice," a tone that is not assertorial or "dogmatic" in the popular sense of that word, but conversational. Throughout the book, the recurring address to the reader is: "Here is an important theological question; try looking at it this way" (p. 9). An account of Kelsey's typical way of looking at theological questions, ordered toward the particular subject of this book, occupies the introductory section, but we never lose sight of the way this methodology is deployed as we move through the remainder of the work.

The overall structure of the book can be quickly summarized. There are six chapters of "introductions" (or two introductions of three chapters each — more on this in a moment). These are followed by the three main parts of the book, each devoted to one of the three distinct ways in which, as Kelsey understands matters, God relates to us human beings: as creator, as consummator, and as reconciler. Each of these parts includes a good deal of exegetical work on relevant scriptural material. Each includes some reflection on the appropriate form of human response to that aspect of God's active relating — called faith, hope, and love, respectively — as well as on the ways that our refusal or distortion of that response manifests itself in particular forms of sin. The book concludes with a set of "codas" in which the theme of the "image of God" — a theme Kelsey has deliberately avoided up to that point — receives some constructive attention, as Kelsey considers the relations among these three strands of investigation with the help of the image of a triple helix.

There are thirty-six chapters, not counting the three unnumbered codas. Of these thirty-six chapters, eleven are designated "B" and set in slightly smaller type than the corresponding main chapters, which in these cases are designated "A." The "B" chapters, Kelsey tells us, are "more technically-oriented, in-house-academic-theology discussions" (p. xiii), set apart in this way from the main constructive work. The introductory section contains three of each sort of chapter (1A and 1B, etc.), amounting, in Kelsey's judgment, to two distinct introductions; thereafter, the Bs are clearly outnumbered (three of eleven in Part One, two of eight in Part Two, three of eleven in Part Three) and are concerned with specific exegetical or conceptual issues arising from the main exposition.

The discipline to which this entire study belongs is one Kelsey calls "secondary theology." Kelsey's way of distinguishing between primary and secondary theology differs from some others, and one must be careful not to assimilate his usage to another. "Primary theology," in his usage, is the self-critical moment in which a community of faith examines its practices in the light of its own explicit standards for those practices, standards usually formulated in the community's normative doctrines. This is an aspect of the ordinary activity of the community and its members, built into their engagement in the practices of worship, education, witness, mutual care, and so forth as a "self-critical dimension" of each of these practices. "Secondary theology," growing out of primary theology, is a community's reflection upon those standards themselves. Such reflection may be prompted by difficulties arising in the practice of primary theology (e.g., the apparent inability of existing doctrinal formulations to offer adequate guidance in a new cultural situation), or by new knowledge that seems to call existing doctrines into question, or simply by the community's own commitment to ongoing self-examination. In any case, the effective pursuit of secondary theology normally requires more extensive knowledge and training in relevant disciplines than can (or should) be expected of most members of the community. This need for a cadre of theological specialists — mainly housed these days in a variety of academic institutions — should not, in Kelsey's view, lead us to think that secondary theology is "academic" while primary theology is "ecclesial." Both are ecclesial; both are part of what Kelsey, like Karl Barth, would regard as the church's own responsible testing of the adequacy of its talk about God. The main difference is that while primary theology tests the church's everyday talk and action in the light of its doctrinal formulations, secondary theology tests those doctrinal formulations themselves. In both cases, the aim is a constructive one.

To my mind, this is a welcome distinction. A distinction between "first-order" and "second-order" theology, in which the former is what people say about (or to) God and the latter is a kind of critical reflection upon the former, is a more common, and certainly important, distinction. It is one to which Schubert M. Ogden, among others, has given a good deal of productive attention, and conversations with Ogden over the years of our colleagueship on a theological faculty have informed my own thinking on the matter.[2] But what Kelsey offers here is a further distinction within the latter, reflective sense of the term, regarding both what is reflected upon and the criteria governing the critical judgments reached. In the move from Kelsey's primary to Kelsey's secondary theology, the subject matter shifts from the church's everyday talk and practice to the church's normative doctrines; and at the same time the criteria for judgment shift from the church's normative doctrines to whatever it is that ultimately validates (or invalidates) them. The boundary between primary and secondary theology is porous in more than one respect. For one thing, as noted, a person engaged in the first may be prompted by difficulties arising there to move into the second; for another, the theological aptitude acquired by a member of a community (and taught by that community) as a constitutive element of its piety may well include an openness to the kind of self-critical examination secondary theology represents;[3] and for a third, the normative doctrines of a religious community ordinarily contain what William A. Christian, Sr., calls "governing doctrines," or teachings about how the primary doctrines themselves should be formed and assessed, a fact that may introduce an element of secondary theology within the doctrinal corpus itself.[4] One value of Kelsey's distinction is in its calling attention to the self-critical moment ingredient in all responsible Christian life and witness, the *metanoia* that inevitably undercuts any simple bifurcation of faith and reason, piety and intellect.

At the same time that it is an explicitly ecclesial discipline, Christian secondary theology as Kelsey describes it may have more promise as a discipline of the modern university than many current alternatives. As will be evident from the account to follow, the theology that Kelsey commends is both tradition-specific, in that it attempts to identify what is normative in and for actual religious communities, and publicly accountable, in that the intelligibility and truth of the claims it advances are subject to examination and testing by whatever the relevant standards may be. Christian theology needs the university — or, at least, it needs the intellectual resources and

2. See, for example, Schubert M. Ogden, *On Theology* (San Francisco: Harper & Row, 1986) and *Doing Theology Today* (Valley Forge, PA: Trinity Press International, 1996); Charles M. Wood, *Vision and Discernment* (reprint edition, Eugene, OR: Wipf & Stock, 2002).

3. On this, see Kelsey's remarks on academic freedom and the capacity for self-critique in *To Understand God Truly* (Louisville, KY: Westminster John Knox Press, 1992), pp. 184-86.

4. William A. Christian, Sr., *Doctrines of Religious Communities: A Philosophical Study* (New Haven, CT: Yale University Press, 1988).

the forms of disciplined reflection the university provides — if it is to fulfill its own task effectively. If Kelsey is correct that "[t]he overarching aim of a research university is inquiry leading to the mastery of the truth about whatever is studied,"[5] and that "[f]or the research university . . . critical inquiry requires that no alleged authoritative source of truth, either sacred or secular, be exempt from rigorous testing of its veracity,"[6] then there is nothing in this understanding of Christian theology that would prevent its taking a role in that enterprise, and much that would encourage its seeking one. At the same time, the university needs theology, on something like Kelsey's understanding of it, in order to provide its students and faculty the resources for a responsible critical understanding of the life and practices of Christian communities, and also to help them take account of the vision these communities may offer about (to use William A. Christian's language) "the setting of human life and about the conduct of life in that setting."[7] Much the same might be said concerning the disciplines of self-critical inquiry within religious communities other than Christian, and something analogous to Kelsey's kind of theology for, e.g., Muslim and Buddhist communities might well eventually find a more prominent role, along with Christian theology, in the university of the twenty-first century. For lack of a better generic term, we might call this mode of tradition-specific yet publicly accountable scholarship "normative religious inquiry."[8] I should say that in this brief excursus I have been taking Kelsey's ideas in directions in which, so far as I know, he has not taken them himself, at least in print; but I hope to be making a legitimate use of them.[9] My aim has been only to suggest that his approach to theological inquiry and to theological study might assist in a useful reframing of the issues surrounding the question of the place of Christian theology — along with analogous forms of reflection specific to other traditions — in the university.

5. Kelsey, *To Understand God Truly,* p. 83.

6. Kelsey, *To Understand God Truly,* p. 84.

7. Christian, *Doctrines of Religious Communities,* p. 1.

8. Something like this argument is foreshadowed in a brief essay by one of Kelsey's teachers, the historical theologian Robert Lowry Calhoun: "The Place of Religion in Higher Education," in Jacques Maritain et al., *Religion and the Modern World* (Philadelphia: University of Pennsylvania Press, 1941), pp. 63-71, reprinted as No. 2 of The Hazen Pamphlets (New Haven, CT: The Edward W. Hazen Foundation, various dates).

9. His review essay on three recent books on the subject offers some relevant comments, but it would be unwise to attempt to construe his own constructive position from them. David H. Kelsey, "Theology in the University: Once More with Feeling," *Modern Theology* 25, no. 2 (April 2009): 315-27.

To what tests, then, are Christian doctrinal formulations subject, and by what criteria are they to be evaluated? Kelsey's treatment of these questions is a substantial contribution to theological prolegomena in its own right. Some of the preparation for it, especially on the theological uses of the Bible, has been undertaken in earlier publications such as *The Uses of Scripture in Recent Theology* (recently reprinted as *Proving Doctrine*) and several shorter exploratory essays; but tackling these methodological issues more constructively in close proximity to a particular doctrinal locus is particularly advantageous.

Kelsey's general approach here is again akin to Karl Barth's on the main point that Christian talk about God and the God-relatedness of things is to be normed decisively by the canon of Holy Scripture. The kinship may have more to do with a common lineage in the Reformed tradition than with any specific dependence of Kelsey on Barth. It appears to me that it is in Kelsey's development of this point that he makes his major contribution to theological method, and that the outworking of the method yields in turn his major contribution to theological anthropology. In what follows, I want to identify and discuss these two key contributions, and also to raise some critical questions about them. In focusing on these matters I will inevitably be neglecting a great deal of importance in these volumes.

Attention to the role of Scripture in secondary theology is not the sum of Kelsey's methodological reflections, but it informs the entire discussion in ways that I will attempt to indicate shortly. First, however, a sketch of the broader methodological context is in order. In a very brief overview of the "standards of excellence" of secondary theology (pp. 23-24), Kelsey distinguishes between formal and substantive standards of excellence. The formal standards are those "to which all forms of reasoned reflection are subject" (p. 23) such as clarity, consistency, transparency in procedure, and appropriateness in argument. However, Kelsey learned long ago from Stephen Toulmin and others that what counts as appropriateness in argument will vary from one field of discourse to another, so that at this point the generic, formal standards need some specification. Here, Kelsey makes a special point of noting that those involved in secondary theology often incorporate (or borrow from, to use a phrase from Schleiermacher) a variety of other disciplines or fields of inquiry in their work, and that

> [w]hen they incorporate an argument from another kind of argument-making practice, the standards of what counts as a good argument must be those of the practice from which the argument is appropriated and

> not necessarily the standards of what counts as a good argument in secondary theology. For example, when a proposal in secondary theology is defended as a historical proposal (say, "Jesus of Nazareth was crucified by the Romans"), the arguments advanced in support of the proposal must count as good arguments in the practice of history (e.g., arguments based on what count as good evidence in the practice of history).

The ways that theological claims and arguments relate to the claims and arguments of other realms of discourse — not only history, but also metaphysics, the natural sciences, and everyday life — is a question that receives attention throughout this work. Kelsey's understanding of the responsibility of secondary theology to the formal standards of excellence incumbent upon any "communicative practice" has a great deal to do with the shape as well as the content of this theological anthropology.

The substantive standards are more inquiry-specific, and are four in number. These derive from Christian communities' own general understanding of what they are about. The first is that theological proposals about *who God is* "must comport with the person of Jesus." The second is that theological proposals about *how God relates* "must comport with Holy Scripture's accounts of the ways in which God relates." The third is that theological proposals "must either be shown to comport with relevant theological formulations in the communities' theological traditions or be shown to be preferable to them"; that is, insofar as a community's existing doctrines have served over time, the burden of proof is upon the innovator. The fourth is that theological proposals must indicate how and why a community's existing formulations are inadequate to its present cultural context. The intention here, as Kelsey later puts it (p. 44), is "to avoid dehistoricizing faith." Christian communities are always located in particular sociocultural contexts that are always undergoing some change, however gradual or dramatic, and good secondary theology will display an attentiveness to the fit between a community's discursive practices and its actual context. How "fit" is to be determined is, of course, another question, and one to which Kelsey gives relatively less explicit attention in these volumes. He observes that Christian communities throughout history have borrowed "practices, iconography, gestures, music, rhetorical forms, beliefs, technical terms, and concepts" from their host cultures, often reshaping these in the process of borrowing; but that these adapted items do not always transfer very successfully to another culture, or even to a different era within the same one. (He might have included dress, architecture, social organization, gender identity and relations, and a number of other culture-specific phenomena on the list, though many of these can be included under the general terms "practices" and "concepts.") In any case, the question of what "adequacy" to a particular sociocultural context amounts to, and how it is to be determined from instance to instance, is at least flagged here for further attention. In this regard, the relation between this fourth substantive standard and the first two seems crucial. As Kelsey frames the issue elsewhere, the goal is perhaps better described not as adequacy to the context, but rather as faithfulness to the gospel *within* the context: "What types of speech and action in the practices [of Christian communities] seem to you the inquirer to be, in their cultural context, faithful, and which ones unfaithful, to the Christian thing?"[10]

The relationship between the first two substantive standards themselves also merits some examination. One might ask about the relationship between the two questions implicit in them, namely, "Who is God?" and "How does God relate to us, and to all else?" Kelsey tells us that these, "the fundamental questions in Christian theology" (p. 15), arise from Christian communities' efforts to be faithful to their own identity, and that they are distinct, if inseparable, questions. One might also ask about the relationship between "the person of Jesus" and "Holy Scripture's accounts of the ways in which God relates." According to Kelsey, it is by coming to understand (via Scripture) the ways in which God relates to us that we come to understand who God is; furthermore, both — the "how" and the "who," the ways of relating and the identity of the one relating — center in Jesus Christ. Do we have in these first two substantive standards of excellence, then, something akin to the classic "material and formal principles" of the Reformation (perhaps with *solus Christus* rather than the usual *sola fide* as the material, and *sola scriptura* the formal)? There is something to this suggestion, but it would not do to reduce Kelsey's meaning to this point, especially if it were taken as an endorsement of a stereotypically Lutheran over a stereotypically Calvinist hermeneutics. There is an important sense in which Kelsey would wish to avoid a "Christocentric" reading of Scripture, precisely for the sake of a more adequate understanding — or, better, apprehension — of Jesus Christ. Kelsey follows Hans Frei in arguing that the hermeneutical force of the Gospels, Christianly understood, is to render Jesus' personal identity.[11]

10. Kelsey, *To Understand God Truly,* p. 206.

11. There is a sensitive critical exposition of Frei's proposal in the context of contemporary Christological alternatives in the second volume of *Eccentric Existence* (pp. 680-93).

But the Gospels require the full canonical context for the realization of their meaning; and Kelsey's conviction (see below) is that modern theology has found a number of ingenious ways to avoid dealing with the full canon. If "the person of Jesus" seems to play a role throughout this work that is as elusive as it is crucial, it may be because of the centrality of a living apprehension of who Jesus is (rather than a set of statements about him) to the entire project.

As I look at this overall scheme for the accountability of secondary theology to standards of excellence, one of the things that strikes me is its comprehensiveness. Like the "Wesleyan quartet" of my own Methodist tradition — Scripture, tradition, reason, and experience — Kelsey's proposal has the advantage of acknowledging that there are several things to keep in mind, and several questions to pursue, in fulfilling our theological responsibility. (There is even, I suppose, a rough correlation between the "Wesleyan" four and Kelsey's standards: Scripture, tradition, and experience might with some ingenuity be correlated with the second, third, and fourth of his substantive standards, respectively, while reason might lend itself to explication along the lines of Kelsey's formal standards for theology as a reflective and communicative practice. Again, the import of the first substantive standard in its relation to the second, and in fact to all the other standards, may require some further exploration.)

Now to the more specific topic of Scripture, or of "Christian canonical Holy Scripture," as Kelsey would have it. In a dense chapter (3B) on this concept, Kelsey offers some important distinctions among terms often used more or less synonymously and then works with these distinctions to lay the conceptual groundwork for his own proposal as to what precisely it is that is to give Christians their understanding of how God relates. Kelsey moves from "Bible" to "Scripture," then to "Holy Scripture," and finally to "canonical Holy Scripture," to build a rich account of the various (and not mutually exclusive) ways this body of texts can be approached and interpreted. His chief interest here is in Scripture as canon, that is, "as an authoritative collection of texts, not merely a collection of authoritative texts" (p. 148, citing Bruce Metzger). How is the wholeness of this collection to be construed, and how is it to be brought to bear authoritatively upon the life of the community and upon theological proposals? The thoroughness and sensitivity of this discussion would make it apt reading for anyone seeking a better grasp of the Christian uses of Christian Scripture.

In a subsequent chapter (12B), he returns to the concept of canonical Scripture in order to make explicit his own proposal for its construal and reading and for its application to secondary theology. In between these two chapters, we have been given the whole of Part One of the book, on God's relating to us as Creator: a *tour de force* that provides some compelling support for the canonical construal he now offers. His argument is that most influential construals of the "wholeness" of Christian canonical Scripture in the history of Western theology have been either "unitary" or "binary," focusing upon one or, at most, two modes of divine relating, and neglecting or distorting whatever material does not fit the chosen pattern. As Kelsey sees it, this simply cannot be done; or, at least, it cannot be done while doing justice to the integrity of the material. His suggestion is that if one attends closely to the content of the canon one will see not one or two but rather three major "plots" or sets of stories, corresponding to three distinct ways that God relates to all that is not God. He is convinced that these three cannot successfully be harmonized into a single story line; all known attempts to do so have only succeeded in making one of the three dominate the other two. Kelsey's counterproposal is not to give up on the idea of canonical wholeness or on the idea that this wholeness has a narrative form, but rather to envision the "canon-unifying narrative" in a way that allows for a "concurrently triple" copresence of the three major plots and their distinctive portrayals of creatures' God-relatedness (p. 476). A corollary proposal for the structuring of works of secondary theology holds, not surprisingly, that these works should display in their own organization the same triplex pattern. The figure of a triple helix is introduced at this point to symbolize the relationships to be discerned within the scriptural canon and mirrored in constructive theological accounts.

As Kelsey sees it, a major casualty of the dominant binary pattern of modern theology and its reading of the canon is our understanding of God's relating as Creator, and all that this involves. This is largely because the pattern of canonical reading that the dominant construals have encouraged has compelled theologians to derive their understanding of God's creative relating from portions of the canon whose main interest is actually elsewhere, i.e., in reconciliation or redemption rather than in creation as such. They have been led to neglect for this purpose, in particular, that large portion of biblical material that is conventionally characterized as Wisdom literature — in which, as Kelsey shows us in Part One, some of the most profound and pertinent "wisdom" concerning the God who creates, the character of creation, and the appropriate response of creaturely reality to its Creator may be found. "In modern systematic theology, 'doctrines of creation' do remarkably little work," Kelsey observes; "much talk about 'creation' and 'creaturehood' is terminally abstract" (p. 160). He turns, then, to the Wisdom literature[12] and its "witness to creation" as the key resource for a richer, more concrete and detailed, and finally more realistic portrayal of creaturehood, human and otherwise. "[S]tories of God's creating have their own narrative logic which should not be ruled by the narrative logic of stories of God's drawing creation to eschatological consummation or by stories of God's reconciling alienated creation. Wisdom's witness to creation firmly backs just that move" (p. 162). Because it is "conceptually independent" of the logic of these other canonical plots, Wisdom allows us to linger with the implications of creaturehood.

A significant methodological consequence of Kelsey's turn to Wisdom should be noted. In contemporary scholarship, the Wisdom literature is generally known not only for its own realism about the human condition — its worldliness, or secularity, one might say — but also for its openness (or the openness of its authors and redactors) to the wisdom and insights of surrounding cultures. It is often described as a "cosmopolitan" literature in this regard. It might be seen, then, as providing a sort of canonical warrant for a theologian's receptivity to the wisdom and insights of her or his host culture (and other cultures) as potential resources for theological formulation, even when those resources may pose serious challenges to the community's received understandings. That is to say, Kelsey's formal standards of excellence for secondary theology would seem to be required not only by theology's standing as a reflective and communicative practice among others (e.g., as an academic discipline) but by the same scriptural canon that governs its understanding of how God relates to creation. This may not be (and likely is not) the only part of canonical Scripture that provides such a warrant, but it is an important one, as Kelsey's own explorations of scientific and social-scientific accounts of aspects of human reality in Part One would indicate. He expresses the point with admirable clarity this way (p. 66):

> Indeed, so far as I can see, it is not necessary for most of the material content of Christian theological claims about human personhood to have any privileged source such as revelation, whether in Jesus Christ or elsewhere — though, of course, some of it may do so. Having a religiously privileged source for its content is not what makes an anthropology "theological."

12. Specifically, Proverbs, Ecclesiastes, Song of Solomon, and Job (p. 188).

> Rather, what makes anthropological claims Christianly theological is that the selection of their contents, and the way that they are framed, are normed by claims about God relating to us, when God is understood in a Trinitarian way.

It is canonical Wisdom that gives support to Kelsey's misgivings about certain features of "standard" Christian theological anthropologies, such as their continuing — if sometimes inadvertent — indebtedness to a notion of original human perfection and of a catastrophic "fall" therefrom, and the legacy of metaphysical dualism, and that enables him to develop a rich, complex, and cogent alternative account. This account dwells at some length on creaturely ambiguity, vulnerability (we are accident-prone, he notes), and neediness, not as the results of any defection from an original state of integrity, but simply as marks of our finite creatureliness. If Christians (and Christian theologians) were to allow themselves to absorb more fully Wisdom's witness to creation, they might find themselves thinking quite differently about a number of things, and responding to both God and creatures in some unaccustomed ways. Kelsey's patient attention to what Wisdom has to teach, and his exemplification of its strategies, make these chapters some of the most original and potentially fruitful in recent theology.

They are also some of the most demanding. This work is not "terminally abstract"; it comes close to being terminally concrete. The author marshals resources from a variety of modes of reflection on the human, and pursues his points often in great detail. Further, Kelsey's search for adequate terminology to characterize human reality leads him to coin and then repeatedly employ some very cumbersome locutions, chief among them being "human living personal bodies" as his favored term for the subject of Christian theological anthropology. The repetition does serve to keep the point in mind, but it also wears on the reader's patience, particularly if the reader is not entirely convinced that the chosen wording is, in fact, the most accurate and serviceable that might be thought of.

This brings me to the first of three questions I would like to put to Kelsey concerning this treatment of the human as creature, and of the Creator-creature relationship. (These are three of many that could be raised, of course.) Kelsey arrives at the designation "human living personal bodies" through some sustained reflection on each of the component concepts and on how they might be most properly related. These discussions of, e.g., personal identity and embodiment are important aspects of the overall portrayal he is presenting, and the phrase does capture the results of this reflection and remind us of it. But as a way of referring to the anthropological subject, is this really a felicitous alternative to, say, "human beings" or (in a theological context) "the human creature"? The latter, in particular, would seem to have a lot going for it in terms of Kelsey's own interest in recovering the canonical witness to human creatureliness. It does, in a way, privilege one of the ways God relates to us (and thus privilege the idea of humans *qua* created over humans *qua* redeemed or reconciled); but Kelsey observes rightly that there is an asymmetry to these ways of relating so that our being created is presupposed by our being brought to consummation or reconciled from estrangement. Whatever else may be said of us, we are creatures; and whatever else is said of us theologically must not violate that status and relationship. A further advantage of "the human creature" (one possibly shared with some other candidate terms) over "human living personal bodies" is that it might invite more reflection on the human *species* than is found in Kelsey's work, and thus on human history and prehistory, human adaptation to environments, migration, cultural differences, the construct of "race," and a variety of other considerations, many of which come under the general purview of anthropology in the more generic sense. There is a way in which "human living personal bodies," despite its values, draws one's attention toward one set of considerations and away from others. But this may simply mean that Kelsey's accomplishment has not left future theological anthropologists with nothing to do.

My second question is this: When Kelsey turns in Part Two to eschatology, he aims to offer an account of what God's relating to us "consummatingly" amounts to. He has already articulated an important principle governing any such account: "The desideratum here is not that it be shown how the conceptuality of contemporary anthropological proposals comports with the conceptuality in which biblical eschatological texts [are] articulated, but how it comports with the narrative logic of canonical accounts of how God relates to all that is not God" (p. 39). And he has also made it clear that the understanding of creation he proposes "entails no theological claim that having created human living bodies, God is thereby committed to preserving them in being indefinitely" (p. 284). And yet, in his treatment of biblical testimony to the resurrection of the body, he appears to assume that God's *eschatological* promise does in fact involve a commitment to humans' ongoing bodily existence, that is, to their ongoing subjective life, aware and self aware, in relationships with others, having some kind of bodiliness (though not carbon-based), and forever immune to damage or suffering (cf. p. 539). He recognizes the great conceptual challenges that such an affirmation faces on several fronts, and warns that speculation in this area runs the risk of lapsing into "theological science fantasy" (p. 541). Further, he acknowledges that any fully worked out account of this postmortem state would have to rely on "additional, probably metaphysical claims whose warrants lie outside the convictions by which the set of theological claims are warranted — namely, that the triune God actively relates to all that is not God in a peculiar threefold way" (p. 561). But he does not seem to entertain the possibility that (to use Karl Rahner's phrase) the hermeneutics of eschatological assertions might be differently framed, and that creaturely consummation Christianly understood might not entail any sort of experienced survival of our physical death.[13] Given Kelsey's general commitment to the testing of inherited theological positions, I find it puzzling that his eschatological reflections have taken the form they have.

My third question concerns the intended Trinitarian logic of the overall project. In turning from introductory matters to the anthropology proper, Kelsey writes (159):

> The root question for this theological anthropology is, What does the specifically Christian conviction that God actively relates to us imply about what and who we are and how we are to be? The structure of the overall answer that I am proposing is grounded in the three-part specifically Christian background belief that the triune God actively relates to us in three interrelated but distinct ways: as One who creates, grounding our reality, and its value and well-being; as One who promises us an eschatological consummation and draws us to it; as One who reconciles us in our multiple estrangements.

The "concurrently triple" pattern of divine relating that Kelsey discerns in the canon of Christian Scripture is grounded in God's triunity. Recall Kelsey's methodological declaration that what makes something Christianly theological is its being "normed by claims about God relating to us, when God is understood in a Trinitarian way" (p. 66). (He adds that such Trinitarian understandings of God are "cognitively Christocentric.")

13. For some thoughts along this line, see e.g. Kathryn Tanner, "Eschatology Without a Future?" in *The End of the World and the Ends of God,* ed. John Polkinghorne and Michael Welker (Harrisburg, PA: Trinity Press International, 2000), pp. 222-37.

My question concerns the adequacy of the term and concept of "reconciliation" to designate one of the three ways of God's relating. Unless creatures are *inevitably* estranged — that is, unless estrangement is a constituent feature of creaturehood, as Paul Tillich would have it — the God who acts triunely *ad extra* need not be acting to reconcile. We would seem to need, then, some more comprehensive term for the aspect of God's relating that is "appropriated" to the Son — or else suppose that this aspect of God's relating is an option actualized only in the instance of estranged creatures, in which case God cannot be said to relate *triunely* to "all else." Certainly, we human creatures in our "multiple estrangements" — our manifold failure in faith, hope, and love — experience God's relating to us in Christ as (among other things) reconciliation. Just as certainly, reconciliation is the theme of a substantial portion of what Kelsey describes as the canonical witness. Reconciliation is the specific shape this aspect of God's "concurrently triple" way of relating takes when it encounters estranged creatures. In the context of anthropology the concept has a definite and indispensable role. However, at the level of an apt characterization of the triune God's relation to all that is not God, it would seem to need opening out to a broader range. One way to pursue this possibility would be to ask what aspect or dimension of God's eternally triune activity has, for us estranged creatures, the effect of reconciliation. What in God's relating to all that is not God takes the form of reconciliation when it runs across estrangement? One might, for example, consider a wider view of the "priestly" dimension of the *munus triplex Christi,* conventionally associated with the work of reconciliation (cf. the Westminster Shorter Catechism, q. 25). In the scriptural matrix in which the concept is found, is reconciliation the sole intent or effect of the office of priesthood? Does the aspect of the divine work that is expressed in a particular way in the priestly office not have to do with *fostering* relationship (i.e., enabling relationship to flourish, preventing estrangement between Creator and creation) as well as with restoring relationship in the event of estrangement? Reconciliation, then, could be seen as a more need-specific, contingent instance within a larger pattern of activity. If to be created is to be estranged (the Tillichian route), then "all else" is indeed in need of reconciliation, and this query is moot; but if not, perhaps some such reflection within the context of a Trinitarian understanding of providence would be useful.

On these and many other points, Kelsey's work stimulates further reflection. *Eccentric Existence* deepens our understanding both of human creaturehood and of the discipline of theological inquiry. It is a welcome gift to theological scholarship.

Humanity Before God; Thinking Through Scripture: Theological Anthropology and the Bible

David F. Ford

It is a privilege to contribute to this volume in honor of David Kelsey. I remember arriving in Yale with a letter of introduction to Hans Frei, and discussing with him which courses I should take. Regarding the first course I mentioned, he made quite clear, without saying anything directly, that it would not in his opinion be worth doing; the first course he himself mentioned was one by Kelsey, which I joined. I had never before been in a class like this: very close reading of a contemporary text (the most memorable for me was Paul Ricoeur's *Symbolism of Evil*); intensive discussion of biblical, hermeneutical, philosophical and theological issues together; and, presiding over the intimidatingly bright and eager students, someone who continually questioned and commented in ways that combined technical expertise and conceptual clarity with a strong theological interest. It has been a special delight over thirty years later to see in *Eccentric Existence: A Theological Anthropology* the mature fruit of that extraordinary theological mind, heart, and imagination.

Eccentric Existence is an astonishing achievement. It is a feast of high quality thinking that requires a good deal of chewing but rewards with theological nourishment that is hard to equal in recent Christian thought. It distills more than three decades of work and tackles some of the most difficult questions in theology in a thorough, coherent, and culturally alert way. The result is a rich, habitable conception of what it is to be human in relation to God and the whole of creation, a "generous orthodoxy" that deserves to become a benchmark by which to assess contributions to theological anthropology for many years to come.

This essay began as a contribution to a symposium on *Eccentric Exis-*

tence, published in *Modern Theology,* to which David Kelsey responded.[1] I have revised what I wrote there, taking Kelsey's and other responses into account, together with some further reflection on a work that will take many more years to assimilate with any thoroughness.

Within recent theology the obvious location for it is the "Yale school" (seen as a set of colleagues who for decades engaged with each other and with each others' students), especially as represented by Hans Frei and George Lindbeck. Their work (together with Kelsey's earlier books on the theological interpretation of Scripture and the shaping of theology as a discipline) has been widely influential but so far had not been worked out in systematic doctrinal form. *Eccentric Existence* is "scholastic" in the best sense: It takes rich texts, ideas, and approaches, focuses them around key questions, and orders the answers in recurrent patterns. The overarching purpose is to think theologically and constructively. It might be seen as the theological culmination of the Yale school, but its scope is far wider than that.

There are two main directions in which it reaches out in order to construct coherence around its leading questions concerning the "what," "how," and "who" of humanity. One is toward Reformed theology, notably Calvin and Barth. These are not simply followed, and there are serious disagreements with each, but they are key reference points and dialogue partners (in ways not true, for example, of Aquinas, Luther, or any twentieth-century Roman Catholic thinker, and Balthasar does not appear in the index), and above all they are models in being thoroughly biblical.

The other direction is towards the world of contemporary thought and especially the secular aspects of its culture. There is a simultaneously Christian and secular sensibility (such as Frei discerned in Barth) at work here. Kelsey is often strongly critical of his theology's "host culture," and extremely wary of allowing it to dictate terms, assumptions, and frameworks. It is a typically Yale school ad hoc approach, taking the Bible as framework and norm for his theological anthropology (in ways to be explored below). Yet it is a rigorous, well-argued engagement with the non-theological, genuinely open to the insights and findings of the natural and human sciences, historical and literary inquiry, and philosophy. The

1. David F. Ford, "The What, How and Who of Humanity Before God: Theological Anthropology and the Bible in the Twenty-first Century" and David H. Kelsey, "Response to the Symposium on *Eccentric Existence*," *Modern Theology* 27, no. 1 (2011): 41-54 and 72-86 respectively.

intellectual atmosphere of the work, for all its reference to continental European theology and biblical scholarship, is largely North American (or, perhaps, Anglo-American). It might even be seen as the coming of age of North American systematic theology after Barth, using a distinctive, sometimes idiosyncratic, idiom in order to move critically beyond him and engage with a culture very different from his. It would be most instructive to compare Kelsey's two volumes with Barth's *Church Dogmatics,* especially exploring the divergences from volume III in method, contemporary dialogue partners and conclusions, and the resonances with volumes IV.1, 2, and 3 and their three Christological ways into the doctrine of reconciliation.

There are two further preliminary remarks relevant to my main theme of Kelsey's biblical interpretation. First, regarding theological substance, the most obvious comment is that this is an utterly God-centred, Trinitarian anthropology. Its consistent theocentricity exceeds any other anthropology I know. As such, the earlier work of Kelsey (in *Proving Doctrine*) is relevant, analyzing how various theologians have used Scripture, and arguing that the doctrine of Scripture is best seen as part of the doctrine of God.

Second, there is Kelsey's strong statement that the whole work is secondary, hypothetical theology. It is an invitation to "try seeing things this way," a thought experiment that he offers to other "secondary theologians" and to those engaged in the primary theological work of direct Christian Bible study, teaching, preaching, ethical and political discernment, prayer, and pastoral counseling. I have elsewhere discussed the importance of the subjunctive mood (of "perhaps," "maybe," "what if . . . ?" and experimenting with possibilities) in theology, along with the indicative, imperative, interrogative, and optative moods.[2] I see *Eccentric Existence* as being most fruitful if its hypothetical, subjunctive mood is acknowledged. It is a set of suggestive and well-ordered ideas with which to think about being human before God. This is Kelsey's safeguard against some dangers in the worthwhile enterprise of scholastic systematizing, especially against scholastics' tendency to fight passionate theological battles over secondary matters. The main forms of disagreement with Kelsey should rather, I suggest, be to put forward preferable hypotheses, to ask him questions (one gets the impression he will have anticipated many of them, and this was confirmed by

2. David F. Ford, *Christian Wisdom: Desiring God and Learning in Love* (Cambridge: Cambridge University Press, 2007), especially Chapter 1; David F. Ford, *The Future of Christian Theology* (Malden, MA: Wiley-Blackwell, 2011), Chapter 4.

his responses to the *Modern Theology* version of this essay), or to develop his ideas or scriptural references in ways that differ from his. He is, above all, a theologian in the Christian mainstream trying to make sense of being human, and he invites others to join the enterprise by offering something comparably rich and convincing as food for thought and practice.

In line with this reading of him, what follows is largely suggestive and interrogative. It is also very tentative and to be taken as only an interim report. This work of decades deserves far more than the hours of reading and rereading that I have been able to give it so far. Thinking through repeated rereading is perhaps the single most important element in sound interpretation and judgment. I have been left pondering many matters, some of them so fundamental that even preliminary conclusions on them are only likely to be arrived at in the course of years. Indeed, the main challenge of Kelsey to other theologians is, while thinking through him, to try to do justice to his important subject matter in ways that improve on his. His intellectual and imaginative synthesis is daring and well argued in its architectonic scope, its basic theological moves, its engagement with contemporary thought and culture, its conceptuality, and its interpretation of Scripture. Of those, the latter (which, of course, has implications for the others) will be the lens for the following provisional remarks.

I. The Canon and Its Three Narratives

Two fundamentally important scriptural dimensions of Kelsey's two volumes are his concept of the Christian canon of Holy Scripture and his discernment of three narrative logics within it.

On the canon I do not want to dwell long. Kelsey's earlier work had prepared the way for his position here, and he makes what I consider a sound and nuanced case for Christian theology appealing primarily to the canon understood as he describes it. This is a matter of considerable theological significance, and there are well-supported alternative approaches to the Bible (e.g., reading it primarily as literature, or as a historical text, or as a religious phenomenon); but the main conclusion to which he comes is in line with the practice of many Christian academic theologians. He takes the canon as authoritative in ways that are open to taking other approaches into account too. Kelsey's theology is in fact at many points influenced by literary, historical critical, and other ways of reading the Bible, and he frequently names the scholars whose conclusions help shape his theology.

More controversial and distinctive is Kelsey's claim that there are "three irreducible plotlines" in the Bible. He structures his whole work around the plotlines of creation, consummation, and reconciliation.

The first narrative, that of creation (discovered more as the background to the Wisdom literature than through the creation stories of Genesis), is the presupposition for the other two, but definitely independent of them. This supports his wisdom-centered approach to creation being both directly and indirectly related to God and having its own integrity quite apart from eschatology or salvation history. This has great advantages in allowing a separate account of creation (yet fully in relationship to the Trinitarian God) and an engagement in many ad hoc ways with the sciences and other accounts of the "what" of humanity without reference to eschatology or salvation (though on this they also have their contributions to make).

The second narrative, that of eschatological consummation, is seen as oriented to a blessing over and above the blessing of the creation, and especially related to the "how" of human living in time. God has a distinct purpose for creation that is distinguishable from its historical flourishing and well-being (two terms to which Kelsey gives his own definitions), and since the resurrection of Jesus the situation is an inaugurated eschatology of "already" and "not yet." Kelsey's exploration of the implications of this for future-oriented action in society is one of several high points in the work — a rich wisdom for practices of joy and hope.

The third narrative, that of reconciliation, addressing the "who" question of human identity before God in the face of estrangement from God and the sinful distortions of faith, hope, and love, culminates in the crucifixion and resurrection of Jesus. Here Kelsey relies heavily (and, in my judgment, with justification) on the work of Hans Frei, who saw the realistic narratives of the Gospels rendering the unsubstitutable personal identity of Jesus as the one who has died in our place and is alive now. This is another high point, the most creative and convincing appropriation and elaboration so far of Frei's seminal work, which Kelsey supports with extensive interpretation of the Synoptic Gospels and fills out with existential content through an original interpretation of the Sermon on the Mount.

The main thing to be said about this three-plot account of the Bible is that, whatever its problems, it is a hypothesis that is remarkably fruitful to think with. It allows the reader to think intensively through each of the three parts of the book, exploring the particularity of creation, consummation, and reconciliation in succession before bringing them together in the "triple helix" of the book's coda. Whatever my eventual conclusions about it, this triple pattern is now deeply imprinted on my thinking and, I am sure, will be regularly recalled while doing theology in the future. At the very least it has heuristic value in assessing how far justice has been done to the distinct concerns of the doctrines of creation, eschatology, and reconciliation, and ensures that no single, totalizing grand narrative is allowed to claim a systematic overview.

Yet it is (like all the other ways of trying to discern the coherence of the canon) underdetermined by the texts to which it appeals. Some of the issues I am still wrestling with include the following five.

First, does Kelsey make the plotlines too distinct from each other? I am still ruminating on the advantages and disadvantages of his way of distinguishing the plots of creation and consummation from each other, rather than seeing creation as more straightforwardly oriented towards consummation. Kelsey's response to this worry about too great distinctiveness is that his position

> does not distinguish them in order to separate them from one another. To the contrary, it insists on their inseparability (hence the image of the triple helix). However, it urges that the ways in which the three narratives are related to one another in theology need to respect the distinctive plotline or "narrative logic" of each, or else one or two of them will be misrepresented. The emphasis on distinctness is in service of clarity about their inter-relations.[3]

The adequacy of this response is indeed better grasped through a rereading of the coda on Introduction A, "*Imago Dei* as Triple Helix." This also applies to concerns about his way of distinguishing the plotlines of consummation and reconciliation in the story of Jesus: He sees them as separable yet converging in the resurrection.[4] The issue of distinctness is helped by recalling the hypothetical, secondary status of this theology. Yet further questions arise.

Second, a major set of criticisms of alternative ways of construing the canon is that those others "conflate" two or three of the plotlines, or allow

3. Kelsey, "Response to the Symposium on *Eccentric Existence*," p. 82.

4. His line here also calls for a discussion of his divergences from Hans Frei on the narrative logic of the Synoptic Gospels in Hans W. Frei, *The Identity of Jesus Christ: The Hermeneutical Bases of Dogmatic Theology* (Philadelphia: Fortress Press, 1975). Does he here see himself in line with Frei, adding something to him, or diverging from him?

one or two of them to "absorb" the other(s). One of the most original, radical, and controversial methodological sections is Chapter 12B, "The Unity of Canonical Holy Scripture and the Structure of Secondary Theology." This argues that practically every other Christian theology fails to do justice to the three distinct plotlines, resulting, for example, in "all-too-easy harmonization of the canonical accounts," at the risk of "domesticating in dangerously misleading ways the complexity, ambiguity and fierceness of God" (p. 468). Such a drastic critique deserves thorough debate, which needs to explore how so many could have got it so wrong for so long, and what their responses to the critique might be. Kelsey has responded by noting how the history of theological controversies, "in which the relation between different ways in which God relates to all else has regularly been framed in a binary way,"[5] with every resolution generating further problems, suggests that binary approaches are inadequate. Instead, his approach through distinguishing three narratives allows for the complexity to be clarified, and he convincingly demonstrates this in several instances.

Yet his identification of other approaches as binary may fail to do justice to their complexity. His accusations of conflation and absorption do not take account of classic ways of distinguishing yet interrelating biblical narratives (and other genres) through levels of meaning and, specifically, through typology, allegory, and other sorts of figuration (I think, for example, of work in dialogue with the Yale school, such as that by John David Dawson on Origen and Frei[6]). Kelsey pays little attention to premodern forms of biblical interpretation or to the reception history of particular scriptural texts: To have done so might have revealed how the tradition has often tried by different means to achieve similar ends to his. He acknowledges that "in a more fully developed doctrine of Scripture" explicit attention would need to be given to such aspects as figurative reading,[7] but does not recognize these as part of an interpretative strategy for coping with complexity, ambiguity, and plurality, serving the need to distinguish between diverse dimensions of Scripture and avoid over-systematization.

Third, regarding over-systematization and "all-too-easy harmonization," I am very sympathetic to his concern to resist their domestication of Scripture, but not yet fully convinced that his three distinct yet interrelated

5. Kelsey, "Response to the Symposium on *Eccentric Existence,*" p. 82.

6. John David Dawson, *Christian Figural Reading and the Fashioning of Identity* (Berkeley and Los Angeles: University of California Press, 2001).

7. Kelsey, "Response to the Symposium on *Eccentric Existence,*" p. 81.

plotlines are the right principal way to achieve this. There are other ways, besides the figurative approaches just mentioned, of trying to do so. To put in succinct and hypothetical form a constructive suggestion that would need to be worked out in detail, what if one were to try to combine the following elements: first, Dawson on figurative reading (combining Origen and Frei); second, Ben Quash's critical appropriation from Hegel and Balthasar of the categories of drama, lyric, and epic[8] — Kelsey's category of narrative could benefit from being differentiated into epic and dramatic, the former tending towards totalizing, the latter towards the sort of polyphony that Kelsey's plurality of plots aims to preserve; third, Ricoeur's account of the many genres of Scripture (such as narrative, law, hymn, prophecy, wisdom) as a complementary way of resisting totalization without over-dependence on discerning three distinct plotlines[9]; and fourth, learning from Jewish scriptural interpretation, especially its use of midrash and other forms, and, in general, its ways of resisting systematization and sustaining argument and disagreement around particular interpretations?[10]

Regarding Jewish interpretation, Kelsey does recommend that Christians and Jews read their Scriptures together. I would be interested in what he thinks Christians might learn from doing so, but one cannot find out without doing the joint reading. More fundamentally, the question is whether a scripturally-sensitive Christian theology today ought to engage with Jewish readings — not only of the Tanakh and the Christian Bible but also of Christian theology.[11] More broadly, interreligious reading of scriptures and other religious texts is a growing practice that, in a global perspective, might be considered as important an accompaniment for Christian scriptural interpretation as forms of secular understanding.[12]

8. Ben Quash, *Theology and the Drama of History* (Cambridge: Cambridge University Press, 2005).

9. Paul Ricoeur, *Figuring the Sacred: Religion, Narrative and Imagination,* ed. Mark I. Wallace, trans. David Pellauer (Minneapolis: Augsburg Fortress, 1995).

10. Cf. Michael Fishbane, *Sacred Attunement: A Jewish Theology* (Chicago: University of Chicago Press, 2008), which is structured around four levels of interpretation of Jewish Scriptures and liturgy, maintaining a coherence without systematization that is not centered on narrative.

11. A perceptive recent Jewish response to Christian postliberal theology (including that of George Lindbeck) is Peter Ochs, *Another Reformation: Postliberal Christianity and the Jews* (Grand Rapids: Baker Academic, 2011).

12. The practice of Scriptural Reasoning, in which Jews, Christians, and Muslims study their scriptures together is one example. See Peter Ochs, "Reading Scripture Together in Sight of Our Open Doors," *The Princeton Seminary Bulletin* 26, no. 1 (2005): 36-47; David F.

Fourth, with regard to creation in particular, is narrative the right lead genre through which to approach it? Kelsey's understanding of creation depends largely on Job and Proverbs, rather than on the narratives of Genesis 1–2: Should this shift the lead genre of creation from narrative to something else more appropriate to Wisdom? He does not acknowledge that Job and Proverbs are actually largely written in different types of poetry (including, of course, some narrative, but with much else too). I think, for example, of the superb commentary by Ellen Davis (a former colleague of Kelsey at Yale) on Proverbs, Ecclesiastes, and the Song of Songs in which the importance of their varieties of poetry is fully recognized.[13] Kelsey's response is that narrative is especially appropriate to "the doctrine of God, God's active relating to all else insofar as that bears on theological anthropology" and to the doctrine of Scripture, and that at least since Irenaeus "the sort of 'wholeness' ascribed to the Canon is a wholeness rooted in the coherence of a narrative of God's ways of relating to all else. In these respects *Eccentric Existence* is very traditional."[14] That is so; but one question, as in the second and third points above, is whether the tradition is more plural and nuanced than this allows. But there is also

---

Ford and C. C. Pecknold, eds., *The Promise of Scriptural Reasoning* (Malden, MA: Blackwell, 2006); Basit Bilal Koshul and Steven Kepnes, eds., *Scripture, Reason, and the Contemporary Islam-West Encounter: Studying the "Other," Understanding the "Self"* (New York: Palgrave Macmillan, 2007); Peter Ochs and William Stacey Johnson, eds., *Crisis, Call, and Leadership in the Abrahamic Traditions* (New York: Palgrave Macmillan, 2009); Mike Higton and Rachel Muers, *The Text in Play: Experiments in Reading Scripture* (Eugene, OR: Cascade, 2012); David F. Ford, "Scriptural Reasoning: Its Anglican Origins, Its Development, Practice and Significance," *Journal of Anglican Studies*, 11, no. 2 (2013): 147-65. Another example is Comparative Theology — see works by Francis X. Clooney, SJ, including: *Comparative Theology: Deep Learning Across Religious Borders* (Malden, MA: Wiley-Blackwell, 2010); *Beyond Compare: St. Francis De Sales and Sri Vedanta Desika on Loving Surrender to God* (Washington, DC: Georgetown University Press, 2008); *Seeing Through Texts: Doing Theology among the Srivaisnavas of South India* (Albany: State University of New York Press, 1996); *Theology After Vedanta: An Experiment in Comparative Theology* (Albany: State University of New York Press, 1993); and Clooney, ed., *The New Comparative Theology: Thinking Interreligiously in the 21st Century* (London: T&T Clark/Continuum, 2010). For a discussion of both practices see Michael Barnes, SJ, "Reading Other Religious Texts: Intratextuality and the Logic of Scripture," *Journal of Ecumenical Studies* 46, no. 3 (2011): 389-410; David F. Ford and Frances Clemson, eds., *Interreligious Reading After Vatican II: Scriptural Reasoning, Comparative Theology and Receptive Ecumenism* (Malden, MA: Wiley-Blackwell, 2013).

13. Ellen F. Davis, *Proverbs, Ecclesiastes and the Song of Songs* (Louisville, KY: Westminster John Knox Press, 2000).

14. Kelsey, "Response to the Symposium on *Eccentric Existence*," pp. 81 and 82.

a question regarding Kelsey's own radical shift to the priority of Wisdom literature in his doctrine of creation: Might this doctrine in particular call for a rebalancing of genres in line with Kelsey's own position, with less emphasis on narrative?

Finally, I wonder whether overall, somewhat ironically, the very means Kelsey uses to prevent over-systematization end up failing to do full justice to the particularities of the Bible. He relies too much on narrative, and in particular on distinguishing three plotlines, whereas I have suggested plural means to sustain plurality. He says that "in a more fully developed doctrine of Scripture explicit attention would certainly need to be given to different Scriptural genres, to figurative reading, and to the history of the reception of Scripture. . . . One way each of these additional proposals would need to be tested would be to probe how far each of them goes either to ward off or to invite either sort of over-systematization [i.e., in reading Scripture or in theological construction]."[15] I suggest that such proposals do indeed pass the test of helping to avoid both sorts of over-systematization, and that Kelsey's project would be enriched by them.

II. Key Interpretative Moves

Within the framework of the canon and its three plotlines, Kelsey makes some major interpretative moves that deserve to be noted. I will select some from the three parts, each of which I consider largely successful and of long-term importance for theological anthropology, and will make a brief comment on the culminating coda.

Creation

In Part One, "Created: Living on Borrowed Breath," there is his shift of the scriptural center of gravity in the doctrine of creation from Genesis 1–3 to Proverbs and Job. There have been others who have emphasized the importance of Wisdom literature for a biblical understanding of creation, but there has been nothing quite like this with regard to its intra-scriptural and scholarly rationales and its consistent working through of the theological implications. The consequences for traditional theologies of creation are

15. Kelsey, "Response to the Symposium on *Eccentric Existence*," p. 81.

serious, not least in what it means for positions on the fall and original sin. Another implication that is developed at length, and convincingly, is the primary focus in Kelsey's theology of creation on God's immediate involvement with the whole of creation and, as regards human existence, on God's mediated involvement in ordinary life — or "the quotidian," as Kelsey calls it.

This central concern for ordinary living, grounded not only in the Wisdom literature but also in the Bible's "realistic narrative" perspective (people and events in interaction, rather than private interiority or large-scale overviews and generalization) is present throughout the two volumes. It is closely tied to a pervasive preoccupation with practices. What he means by "practice," as something socially established, interactive, partly formed through concepts and beliefs, and being done to some end but not necessarily having a product, is defined early in the work (Chapter 1B) and then recurs throughout. The church and other communities, organizations, and social bodies are identified primarily through their public practices; theology itself is an ecclesial practice; right orientations of living before God are described mainly through practices (gathered under the rather awkward label of "existential hows," but often managing to sum up powerfully and richly what is involved in Christian living — gratitude, praise, wonder, delight, perseverance, joy, hope, contemplative prayer, and a passion for communion in love with God and neighbor); and sins are distorted practices. This allows him to offer a thorough alternative to conceptions of human existence that are more centered on consciousness, interiority, or various versions of the self's relation to itself. There are lengthy, often very technical, discussions of modern concepts of identity and person, all guided by the insistence on being true to the primacy of social practices as portrayed in the Wisdom literature and scriptural narratives, especially those of the Synoptic Gospels.

Overall, the way Kelsey focuses scripturally on wisdom allied to realistic narrative has the effect of opening up discussion of creation to other discourses (especially the sciences and philosophy) without losing sight of his scriptural norm. The normativity is, of course, above all centered in the scriptural witness to God and the relating of all else to God. The considerable ad hoc freedom Kelsey exercises in drawing critically and constructively on other discourses is grounded in his most essential claim: that human existence is "eccentric" because it is centered on God, and this God warrants seeking wisdom in such ways. His *tour de force* of biblical interpretation is the two chapters devoted to Job chapter 10, and any more thorough treatment of his exegesis would have to discuss this at length. It could have considerable influence on discussions of the nature of human personhood, the importance of bodiliness in human identity, decisions about when human life begins, the theological understanding of disability, and much else.

However one assesses his specific conclusions, this theocentric and scriptural search for theological wisdom while also energetically seeking wisdom beyond Scripture is exemplary for twenty-first-century theology. The wisdom-seeking could, of course, always go further. I have already mentioned the lack of engagement across religious traditions and Kelsey's Protestant focus within the Christian tradition. But, looking at the current theological scene (which Kelsey rarely does — his range of explicit reference[16] within theology of the past fifty years is very limited, and almost totally North American and European), there are few works that can match this in its combination of being profoundly centered in God, imaginatively and intelligently scriptural, consistently social in relation to both ordinary and public life, wisdom-seeking in many directions, and rigorously argued throughout.

Consummation

In Part Two, "Consummated: Living on Borrowed Time," the key interpretative move is not, as in Part One, an attempt to refocus theology around different Scriptures from those traditionally used. Rather, Kelsey takes the classic tension in eschatology between the "already" and "not yet," centers it on the Holy Spirit conceived as "circumambient," and works it out in ways well supported by a range of standard scriptural texts. His biblical argument for "circumambience" as a leading metaphor for the Spirit is well made, and critical of conceptions of the Spirit that get caught in binary oppositions such as inside/outside, within/without, interior/exterior. He

16. Kelsey's case for not explicitly mentioning many conversation partners is persuasive: To discuss predecessors and contemporaries in depth not only makes the work much longer but also risks these interpretations, rather than the constructive theological proposals, becoming the center of the conversation. "The alternative is simply to advance one's own proposals, with reasons for agreeing with them, and, without dishonoring the achievements of others, to leave it to the reader to compare and contrast that proposal with others to see where the differences fall and what are the relative theological strengths and weaknesses of the fresh proposal." (Kelsey, "Response to the Symposium on *Eccentric Existence,*" p. 81).

avoids, on the one hand, primarily invasive or heteronomous concepts of the Spirit, and, on the other hand, individualist, subjective, or privatized concepts. The circumambient Spirit is first of all a gift from beyond us and involved with the whole of our natural and social environment, but it is also intimately involved with us in our interiority. This combination of the public and the intimate does justice to the complex biblical testimony and its diverse metaphors, especially the different stories of the giving of the Spirit in Acts 2 and John 20.

But more important than the spatial metaphors is the language of time and eschatology. I do not think his metaphor of "borrowed" (in relation to time or breath) is theologically felicitous — it implies an act of borrowing and appears to compromise the language of "gift." That aside, his handling of the temporality of humanity is another high point in the work. His relating of the "ultimate context" of "the Spirit sent by the Father with the Son" to our "proximate contexts" in which we may live now, hoping in God's promise or living at cross grain to that hope (Chapters 13, 14, 16, 17), is a masterpiece of theology that reads like a working out of Bonhoeffer's key insights into the interrelation of the ultimate and penultimate (though Kelsey does not seem to have Bonhoeffer in mind here). The description of those proximate contexts in terms of temporality, public life, ambiguity, tensions and conflicts, promise, and the relativization of values offers a conceptual grid through which to think richly about historical existence in the ambience of God's Spirit who draws all into eschatological blessing. Kelsey grapples theologically with optimism and pessimism, continuity and discontinuity, and what it means to avoid the many possible distortions of hope. It is a wise inaugurated eschatology, its key texts being perhaps Romans 8 and Ephesians 1, and it is not afraid of loose ends and open questions (on which there is a chapter). It is here, appropriately, that Kelsey especially makes good his claim to be writing a systematically unsystematic theology.

Reconciliation

Part Three, "Reconciled: Living by Another's Death," has four main exegetical elements: on the narrative logics of the Synoptic Gospels, on "in Christ," on "love," and on the Sermon on the Mount. I have already above affirmed Kelsey's development of Frei's understanding of the unsubstitutable identity of Jesus Christ as rendered by the Synoptic Gospels, and also raised an open question about his way of distinguishing between the narrative logics of consummation and reconciliation. The fairly routine discussions of existence "in Christ" and of "love" convincingly support his theological points. The extended discussion of the Sermon on the Mount is an appropriation of Ulrich Luz's exegesis. In this case Kelsey makes fascinating use of the work of a biblical scholar, though in some other cases in both volumes his tendency to follow closely a particular scholar (usually North American or German) makes one long for him to engage more directly and freshly with the scriptural text for himself. At times there seems to be an inhibition regarding such engagement, as if he is reluctant to trespass on the territory of the guild of scholars. Yet some of his most illuminating insights into texts come when he risks his own interpretations, which often happens outside the big "set pieces" and in the context of discussions of the shaping of human life through "existential hows" and their sinful distortions.

It is always interesting to note a theologian's "canon within the canon," in the sense of the aspects or books of Scripture to which he or she pays special attention. Kelsey is a master analyst of the basic moves theologians make in this regard. So what about Kelsey himself in Part Three? Kelsey's personal canon there is mainly the Synoptic Gospels and Paul, supported by Exodus and Deuteronomy. These figure in a theology of reconciliation that is essentially in line with that of Frei, Barth, and Calvin (though I would be interested also to explore the less explicit resonances with Tillich). I am sympathetic to the main ways he interprets both the Synoptics and Paul, but wonder what the result might be of enlarging his operative canon. In other words, there are questions raised from within the larger canon that might lead to his theology being enriched and in places challenged or at least rebalanced. I select just three texts as the lens through which to question him.

1. John

First, there is the Gospel of John. It is not a text that he habitually thinks with. This need not be a problem — having myself written a monograph largely focused through two verses from 2 Corinthians I have no objection to such "journeys of intensification."[17] Kelsey's three such journeys into Job

17. See David F. Ford, *Self and Salvation: Being Transformed* (Cambridge: Cambridge University Press, 1999).

10, the Synoptic Gospels, and Paul (especially his "in Christ") are right at the core of his anthropology. Yet he also tries to justify his comparative neglect of the Fourth Gospel by contrast with the Christian tradition. I think this is unfortunate and theologically impoverishing.

The main relevant discussion is an excursus on "Narrative in John and Jesus' Identity" (pp. 635ff.), backed up by Chapter 19B "Christological Reflection and the Gospels' Narrative Logics." These deserve far fuller discussion than is possible here, but I offer three points to be explored.

First, is it true that "John's narrative cannot be read as rendering Jesus' personal identity" (pp. 636-37)? Kelsey sees John using anecdotes, symbols, and abstract terms in order mainly to commend Jesus as a teacher, with the main question John answers being not "Who are you?" but "Where do you come from?" On the unsubstitutable personal identity of Jesus, John, for Kelsey, has nothing to add to the Synoptics. An alternative reading (which would need to be substantiated at length, not least in debate with certain Johannine interpreters whose influence one might detect behind Kelsey's position) might see John as indebted to the Synoptics or their traditions, but crafting his narrative so as to take us even deeper into Jesus' identity and into the narrative that renders it, with the "who?" question utterly central, indicated not least through the use of "I am." It is possible (and I would take this line) to read John as a thoroughly dramatic and simultaneously theological Gospel whose demotion on the grounds Kelsey gives is unwarranted. For Christian theology a great deal hangs on indwelling John's Gospel — as did (in extremely diverse ways) not only premodern theologians such as Origen, Augustine, and Aquinas but also Luther, Calvin, Schleiermacher, Barth, Bultmann, Balthasar, and the later Moltmann.[18] There are gains in Kelsey's Synoptic and Pauline journey of intensification, but I would like to see him now take a similar journey into John. Why not? His own commitment to the whole canon would seem

18. Moltmann's own reflections on coming later in life to appreciate John are instructive (see Jürgen Moltmann, "God in the World — the World in God: Perichoresis in Trinity and Eschatology" in *The Gospel of John and Christian Theology,* ed. Richard Bauckham and Carl Mosser [Grand Rapids: William B. Eerdmans, 2008], pp. 369-81). He discovered that the Gospel of John does not appear in his works published between 1960 and 1980 but is increasingly referred to after 1980. "The Fourth Gospel is no longer for me a book closed 'with seven seals,' suspect in Marburg of a certain Gnostic heresy. It has become an open and inviting book full of new insights for a curious and hungry systematic theologian" (p. 369). One suspects that Kelsey too was affected by tendencies in both biblical scholarship and systematic theology to marginalize John.

to make this desirable. He responds that John would play a larger role "in a fully developed Christology" and that "the selection of Scripture to be discussed, Part by Part in *Eccentric Existence,* was always an ad hoc judgment about what sorts of text seem most clearly to bear on the theological issues central to the discussion at hand. Selection was never made so as to underwrite a sketch of '*the* overall Biblical view' nor to represent the full range of different Biblical views of any topic in particular."[19] This does not quite answer the neglect of a text that is so important for the Christian theological tradition and not least for those to whom he is especially close. And would the fully developed Christology still support the view of John given in *Eccentric Existence*?

Second, Kelsey's comparative neglect of John is especially unfortunate because this would seem to be the Gospel that best suits his overall enterprise. It is above all the "eccentric" Gospel, centered on God yet constantly concerned with who Jesus most fundamentally is as a human being in relation to God. This claim does, of course, need to be argued with those who read it differently, but it is not short of advocates.[20] His view of the canon (and also, I would argue, a good deal of scholarly opinion) should relieve him of many concerns that some others have about it (on grounds, for example, of it being late or questionably historical). His strong emphasis on existence "in Christ" is based on Paul but could just as well draw on John.

Third, and more speculatively, I wonder whether there is a symmetry between what Kelsey is doing in relation to the Yale school and what John does in relation to the Synoptic tradition. Just as Kelsey is synthesizing some of the key themes of colleagues with whom he has been in conversation over decades, yet also is being far more systematic in his theological thinking about them and is adding both material and theological judgments of his own, so John might be seen as doing something

19. Kelsey, "Response to the Symposium on *Eccentric Existence,*" p. 81.

20. For example, among the contributors to Bauckham and Mosser, eds., *The Gospel of John and Christian Theology,* advocates would include (taking into account their essays in this volume and their other writings): Richard Bauckham, Stephen C. Barton, Miroslav Volf, Rowan Williams, Andrew Lincoln, Marianne Meye Thompson, Alan J. Torrance, Martin Hengel, Murray Rae, and Jürgen Moltmann. See also Edwyn Clement Hoskyns, *The Fourth Gospel,* ed. Francis Noel Davey (London: Faber and Faber, 1940); Dorothy Lee, *Flesh and Glory: Symbolism, Gender and Theology in the Gospel of John* (New York: Crossroad, 2002); Craig R. Koester, *The Word of Life: A Theology of John's Gospel* (Grand Rapids: William B. Eerdmans, 2008).

similar in relation to his predecessors. Both can be read as the outcome of decades of indwelling texts, traditions, communities of prayer and discourse, and, above all, Christ himself. Kelsey's extraordinary theocentric anthropology is in many ways as daring as John's theology (exemplified most directly in his Prologue), and I hope the former will draw more on the latter in future.

2. *Isaiah*

Second, there is the book of Isaiah. It does not appear in the index (though I may have missed some references — one of the serious problems faced by students of the book interested in tracing its engagement with Scripture is the lack of a Scripture citations index, and the general index itself has many omissions). Again, as with John, this may only serve to underline Kelsey's legitimate concentration on his canon within the canon and his journeys of intensification that rely on a limited number of biblical texts, and he has welcomed the idea that Isaiah could play a part in a fuller Christology.[21] Yet it does prompt some further questions.

First, what is the relation of Kelsey to the Christian tradition's interpretations of Isaiah? Isaiah has been called "the fifth gospel" because of its pervasive influence on both the New Testament and the whole Christian tradition. What does it mean that Kelsey can virtually ignore it? Is it enough to say that it could be a later supplement to what is already said in *Eccentric Existence*?

Second, might Isaiah be a good test case for the distinctness of Kelsey's three plotlines? There, in a largely poetic, prophetic genre, the authors (scholars usually identify a first, second, and third Isaiah) might be read as profoundly concerned with creation, eschatology, and reconciliation in ways that resist Kelsey's overall thesis. So how might he read Isaiah? And might some of the theologies he criticizes with regard to their unsatisfactory interrelating of the three plotlines be indebted to Isaiah?

Third, and closely connected with the second point, is the question of typology and figuration already mentioned above. Isaiah revels in such hermeneutical moves in ways that the New Testament authors and later tradition developed further, and many contemporary exegetes and theo-

21. Kelsey, "Response to the Symposium on *Eccentric Existence*," p. 81.

logians have been critically appropriating and further improvising upon.[22] These moves are less systematic than Kelsey's three pervasive plotlines and his consistently "plain sense" readings, but are more ad hoc, context-sensitive, improvisatory, and pneumatological.

3. *Song of Songs*

Third, there is the Song of Songs (or Song of Solomon), to which there is one passing reference as being part of the Wisdom literature (p. 188). Three questions are raised by this neglect.

First, why is it mentioned but not otherwise discussed along with Proverbs, Job, and Ecclesiastes in Kelsey's shift from Genesis to Wisdom as the main exegetical base for his doctrine of creation? The commentary by Ellen Davis referred to above shows clearly how appropriate it is to include the Song alongside the others — the ancient Israelite young men at whom they were all aimed needed to have their desires of many sorts educated. Moreover, she shows the resonances with other creation themes, making the Song a specially suitable example for Kelsey's shift.

Second, sex and gender are obviously major concerns of the Christian tradition and of Christians and many others today. Kelsey rarely engages with sex and gender issues directly despite laying down as a "substantive standard of excellence" for his sort of theology that it "provide analyses of the relation between received — that is, traditional — theological formulations and relevant features of the current culture of the ecclesial community's host society that show in what ways and why the former are inadequate in that cultural context" (p. 24). Why do sex and gender issues not figure more prominently in his anthropology, and why is the Song, alongside much else in the canon, not allowed to prompt such attention? Kelsey's response is that this was

> a function of the distinction between human creatures' "basic personal identities" and their "quotidian personal identities." The former, constituted by their incorporation into Jesus Christ, are theologically more

22. They have long been staples in the Catholic tradition, and have been renewed through the *ressourcement* that helped to inspire the Second Vatican Council, but they have also been increasingly appropriated within Protestant biblical interpretation, as seen in many of the entries in Kevin J. Vanhoozer et al., eds., *Dictionary for Theological Interpretation of the Bible* (Grand Rapids: Baker Academic, 2005).

basic than the latter. The latter are, in varying proportions, partly ascribed to them by their cultures, and partly are self-scribed. A host of theologically fraught issues attend the ways in which those quotidian identities are formed. Issues about gender, sex, and race are generated in large part by the ways in which quotidian personal identities are socially and culturally constructed, and are underdetermined by biological reality. Without in the slightest denigrating the importance of those issues, I judged them to be topics for another time and another project.[23]

In the context of his whole project, this is to me a persuasive position.

Third, there is a huge amount of commentary on the Song in the Christian tradition of prayer and spirituality, especially contemplative prayer, in which the allegorical interpretation is dominant. Davis, Ricoeur,[24] and others have shown how fruitful that tradition can be through giving fresh contemporary improvisations on it. Kelsey has a short but rich commendation of "prayer as contemplative adoration of God" (p. 748), but it seems odd that the only figures from the tradition mentioned in this regard are Calvin and Charles Wesley. Do the several streams of Christian theology and practice connected with contemplative prayer play no part in his conception of contemporary Christianity?

The Triple Coda

Finally, there is the triple coda, drawing the three parts together in a triple helix around the idea of Jesus Christ as the image of God and human beings as imaging the image. I find the amount of exegesis here somewhat excessive in view of the basic, fairly simple point. I also wonder whether there might be theological mileage in taking "word" alongside "image," and culminating with the Gospel of John as a dramatic triple helix of creation, consummation, and reconciliation. In this coda, Jesus might be the Word of God creating all, drawing all to himself on the cross, and having the words of eternal life, with human beings, by virtue of being and having human bodies, wording the Word.

23. Kelsey, "Response to the Symposium on *Eccentric Existence,*" p. 80.

24. André LaCocque and Paul Ricoeur, *Thinking Biblically: Exegetical and Hermeneutical Studies,* trans. David Pellauer (Chicago: University of Chicago Press, 1998).

III. Concepts and Contexts

There is a huge amount more to be said about the biblical interpretation in this marvelous work. Before concluding I want to highlight two further matters.

First, there is the relationship between biblical and non-biblical concepts and categories. Kelsey develops a large technical apparatus of terminology and then uses it rigorously. Likewise he distills from Scripture some leading concepts and categories. There is scope for a great deal of debate about each type and their relationship to each other, but there is not space to pursue that important discussion now. Kelsey's own style will be found too technical and abstract for some, but I would defend him in opting for as much precision as is appropriate to the topics he is handling. Much of the book is not easy reading, and it should be seen as especially aimed at academically trained theologians — though I see no reason why anyone educated to university level should not be able to gain a great deal from reading it.

Second, there is the social context in which he has written this book, as suggested by what it contains. He is clearly an academic, and in his biblical interpretation this shows in the number of biblical scholars he mentions. He is also clearly a Protestant who has strong affinities with the Reformed tradition. There will no doubt be discussion about the level of reference to the church. Explicitly there is not much, but this is actually an utterly ecclesial theology, emphasizing Christian communal practices throughout. Yet this will not please those for whom ecclesiology should (for various reasons) be made explicit in such a wide-ranging anthropology as this. Had he been more explicit he would have had to be even more "particularist" than he is already. Perhaps more serious is the fact that quite large tracts of the wider Christian tradition (even within Protestantism) do not figure much within his horizon. Put in terms of scriptural interpretation, this means that his engagement with the reception history of the Bible is patchy. From his standpoint, to have had a more explicit engagement would have greatly lengthened the work and also risked diverting attention onto secondary matters of interpretation. This is understandable, but it is also the case that those rooted in other traditions would be likely to make different decisions as regards what to omit.

As regards the "host society" to which he refers, beyond his concern with the church, his main interest in it, as stated above, is in its secular aspects. With these his mode of theological engagement is, I consider, exemplary even when I would differ from some of his conclusions. There is a notable lack of concern with other religions than Christianity, with the partial exception of Judaism. It feels like a book whose main lines were laid down before the late twentieth-century resurgence of religion in the public sphere. But in this, as with many other areas of omission, one can immediately think of ways in which *Eccentric Existence* could inspire further relevant work.

Conclusion

This book is a massive achievement, and the above remarks are only the beginning of my reception of it. I hope it will be discussed widely and put on the reading list of every research student in Christian theology and in biblical studies. I hope it will be taken up by pastors and practical theologians, and that its ethical, political, and interreligious implications will be worked through. I doubt whether this theological anthropology will be matched for a long time to come.

What are its major substantive contributions likely to be? Besides those already mentioned, I would suggest the following: the ways Kelsey interrelates key doctrines, especially Trinity, creation, sin, eschatology, reconciliation, and Christian living; how ultimate and proximate contexts are related in each part; the way he escapes spirit/body and other dualisms; the distinction between the logic of belief and the logic of coming to belief; the critiques of a broad range of concepts of person in Christian theology and beyond; the realism about death, finitude, and ambiguity; the resistance to anthropocentric accounts of creation; the distinction between being and having a living body; the speculative account of resurrection bodies; the accounts of faith, hope, and love; the distinction between evil and sin, and the thorough account of the latter; the culminating idea of the triple helix image of God in Christ.

It is noteworthy how many of those contributions involve conceptual distinctions and interrelations. So my final thought takes up again the earlier insistence that Kelsey be taken very seriously when he says this is secondary theology "in the hypothetical mode" (p. 9). It is supremely a thought experiment. The prime locus of Kelsey's wisdom and creativity as a theologian is not so much in the comprehensiveness of his retrieval of the Bible and the tradition, nor in the literary quality of his writing, but in a powerful combination of two elements: on the one hand, his theological (and strongly biblical) engagement simultaneously with God, Christian community, secular society, and the physical creation, and, on the other hand, his brilliant, thorough, and deeply Christian thinking. *Eccentric Existence* is above all an invitation by a superb thinker and teacher to undertake in his hospitable company the hard and joyful work of theological thinking.

Eccentric Existence and the Catholic Tradition

Cyril O'Regan

There have been a number of theology texts of true excellence produced this past decade. Even so, it is not clear that any rival David Kelsey's magisterial *Eccentric Existence* in scope, erudition, methodological sophistication, the ability to make Scripture count theologically, and analytic finesse.[1] And it is patently clear that none has remotely the level of fittingness. *Eccentric Existence* represents at once a capstone to a brilliant career in publishing and teaching at Yale, while also exceeding it. It is the exclamation point to theological production that could only have been hoped for rather than anticipated. It is justly a cause of celebration that a major theologian has provided us with two volumes that are the fruit of a half century of pondering and that will take the reading public a number of years to digest. Despite an almost untoward level of accomplishment that leaps off every page, *Eccentric Existence* does not pretend to definitiveness. *Eccentric Existence* is an exercise in systematic theology that is contextually embedded and ecclesially specified. Kelsey understands himself to be writing theology in an early twenty-first century context and to be writing it out of and for (a) the Protestant tradition in general and (b) the Reformed tradition in particular. Encyclopedic knowledge of the Protestant tradition and complete mastery of its major thinkers are necessary, but not sufficient, conditions for a theology that is always in process even as, or especially as, the discourse of theology obeys rules for Christian speech and prescribes action that has guided the church for

1. David H. Kelsey, *Eccentric Existence: A Theological Anthropology*, 2 vols. (Louisville, KY: Westminster John Knox Press, 2009).

almost two millennia. Obeying a grammar is not simply constraint, but also freedom, and specifically, it gives the theologian the responsibility of saying anew, of performing a non-identical repetition of the theology that has gone before, which is regarded as relatively adequate to the God who is the transcendental signified. In the sense that *Eccentric Existence* is just one more attempt to speak God truly,[2] it cannot claim to be the whole truth.

Nor, despite its copiousness, does Kelsey claim that his book is comprehensive. More than modesty is involved here, and more than looking over one's shoulder at Barth's herculean performance in his *Church Dogmatics. Eccentric Existence* is much more than your standard theological anthropology in that it insists on the necessity to articulate the background beliefs that make a properly theological anthropology possible.[3] An adequate theological anthropology supposes articulating a general systematic theology frame that will not beggar reflection on God as "the One with whom we have to do," which is Kelsey's translation of the Calvinist, and specifically Barthian, notion of God as the unique object of veneration. These qualifications, or rather disqualifications, of definitiveness belong to the order of the *de facto.* Belonging to the order of principle rather than fact is Kelsey's judgment that there can be no single monolithic story about God's relating to us. God's mystery eludes that, which means that there can be no single monolithic story to tell about what and who we are and how we ought to be.[4]

Kelsey may sound postmodern here, and even seem to evoke Jean-François Lyotard's asseverations about the obsolete nature of metanarratives,[5] but his discourse is as formally theological as its meaning. He is not making a philosophically invariant statement taken to be regulative of and for theology. Kelsey goes on to summarize the results of the text, which up to that point has argued that there are three inflections of the biblical narrative: one in which the articulation of creation proves both primitive and regulative, another in which the consummation serves this role, and another again in which reconciliation plays this role. While these variations can be related, they cannot be fully synthesized. This point is too important

2. I am here evoking Kelsey's *To Understand God Truly: What's Theological About a Theological School* (Louisville, KY: Westminster John Knox Press, 1992).

3. Kelsey, *Eccentric Existence,* p. 8.

4. Kelsey, *Eccentric Existence,* p. 130.

5. Jean-François Lyotard, *The Postmodern Explained: Correspondence 1982-1985,* ed. Julian Pefanis and Morgan Thomas; trans. Don Barry, Bernadette Maher, Julian Pefanis, Virginia Spate, and Morgan Thomas (Minneapolis: University of Minnesota Press, 1992), esp. pp. 17-37.

not to pay attention to, and I will do so in section one when I provide an overview of the text, which performatively casts itself as the very failure to synthesize the elements of which it speaks. In providing such an overview, I will attend to three particular points: (i) the governance of Trinitarian discourse in theology and its non-synthesizable complexity and, relatedly, the debt owed by *Eccentric Existence* to the theology of Karl Barth; (ii) the coherence of *Eccentric Existence* with Kelsey's previous work and its coherence with Hans Frei's form of biblical interpretation and Christological figuration; (iii) the question as to whether the most basic structural point of the text, the undecidability and compossibility of inflections of the canonic narrative, and the concomitantly different relations between the Trinitarian hypostases, is totally without precedent. For pragmatic as well as necessary reasons, I will be entirely schematic.

My most basic concern is the two-sided one both of acknowledging and opening up dialogue between *Eccentric Existence* and Catholic theology for the mutual benefit of both, but especially the latter. Kelsey's theology in itself is neither systemically open nor closed to Catholic thought. Given its own charge of articulating a specifically Reformed theological anthropology, *Eccentric Existence* is formally indifferent to Catholic theology. This indifference is not contradicted by the fact that especially in part one of *Eccentric Existence,* which concentrates on the canonic narrative as inflected by creation and focused on the triune God's relating creatively to the world, there are implicit and explicit criticisms of transcendental types of theology, influentially illustrated by Karl Rahner. In section two I trace a pattern of criticism of Rahnerian-style theology/anthropology, even as I remain convinced that the theological method exhibited by *Eccentric Existence* discourages polemic. Contrariwise, although Aquinas is not a major interlocutor in the text, not only is it the case that Aquinas's Trinitarian doctrine of creation does not come under the same strictures as Rahner's theology, but, arguably, in significant ways is approved. To be satisfied with this, however, is to risk reducing Kelsey's work to an instance of a class, which would include George Lindbeck's *The Nature of Doctrine* and Kathryn Tanner's *God and Creation.*[6] I intend to go beyond the text by asking the question whether, in the two other areas of his theological articulation, those focused on consummation and reconciliation respec-

6. George A. Lindbeck, *The Nature of Doctrine: Religion and Theology in a Postliberal Age* (Philadelphia, PA: Westminster, 1984); Kathryn Tanner, *God and Creation in Christian Theology: Tyranny or Empowerment?* (Oxford: Blackwell, 1988).

tively, there are any obvious Catholic conversation partners. I suggest that taken cumulatively, Balthasar's biblical orientation, his affinity with Barth's Christologically focused systematic theology, as well as the fact that the doctrine of the Trinity essentially organizes his entire theology (and however high his Christology is, it is constructed from below), suggest that conversation between his theological elaboration and that of *Eccentric Existence* might be mutually beneficial. Accordingly, in section three I sketch the more important ways in which Balthasar and Kelsey correspond when it comes to a theological anthropology, as well as the Trinitarian theology that is its presupposition. Needless to say, theological register and inflection are different, and there are any number of substantive theological differences. But the differences that really matter are those differences that are a function of confessional allegiances. It is paradoxically the very proximity of Kelsey and Balthasar on the major issues of theological method and substance that illuminate Protestant-Catholic differences.

Trinitarian Horizon

Among the many gifts *Eccentric Existence* provides theology is perhaps the most fully fleshed out and coherent Trinitarian theology of the past few decades. Christian theology is necessarily Trinitarian, according to Kelsey, since the analysis of any foreground doctrine, for example, a Christian take on persons in relation, supposes the backdrop of the ultimate context or contexts of the activity of the triune God in creation, consummation, and reconciliation. Creation, consummation, and reconciliation pick out three variants of the canonic narrative, which is bedrock for the Christian community and bedrock also for Christian theology. The community of three persons is active in each of the constitutive acts in which God deals with what is other than God: the Father creating in the Son in the power of the Spirit; the Spirit, sent by the Father with the Son, drawing all to eschatological consummation; and finally the Son, sent by the Father, in the power of the Spirit, reconciling the world to God.[7] Creation, consummation, and reconciliation are modes of God's relation to what is other than God, and each is helpfully characterized by a different preposition: in the case of creation by the preposition "to," in the case of consummation by the preposition "between," and in the case of reconciliation by the

7. Kelsey, *Eccentric Existence,* p. 122.

preposition "among."[8] "To" indicates the radical otherness of the triune God, but perhaps also an asymmetry in terms of relation. Here transcendence is non-contrastive, since the triune God is absolutely near as well as absolutely transcendent.[9] "Between" also expresses the coincidence of transcendence and nearness, but suggests in addition a real difficulty in separating out the activity of the Spirit from that of human beings who are blessed with relative agency of their own. And finally, "among" speaks to an otherness and nearness that expresses itself in the passion, death, and resurrection of the unsubstitutable particular Jesus of Nazareth.

The overall slant of the Trinitarianism of *Eccentric Existence* is very definitely economic. Yet it is not reductively so, especially if one thinks of economic forms of Trinitarianism in the modern period as being beset by the Kantian problematic of how we know God. Of course, the Kantian or post-Kantian problematic not only tends to dictate the economic turn, it also functions to inhibit any form of Trinitarian thought gaining traction in theology. However much Schleiermacher goes beyond Kant's commitment to autonomy, the marginalization of the doctrine of the Trinity in the *Glaubenslehre* is a Kantian legacy, which Kelsey is interested in overcoming.[10] This is one of the more important ways in which Kelsey continues Barth. Kelsey repeats Barth's discussion of revealed, revelation, and revealedness of *Church Dogmatics* I/1 to establish the theocentric horizon of theology and to underscore that the triune God is a God who relates to us. But Kelsey gets even more traction from *Church Dogmatics* IV,[11] where

8. Kelsey, *Eccentric Existence,* pp. 125, 128, 129-30.

9. If Kelsey is not actually indebted to Tanner's articulation of "non-contrastive transcendence" in *God and Creation,* he most certainly is wholeheartedly in agreement with a view that proves foundational for all of Tanner's work. The notion of "non-contrastive transcendence" continues to play a role in Tanner's subsequent work. See *The Politics of God: Christian Theologies and Social Justice* (Minneapolis: Fortress Press, 1992) and *Christ the Key* (Cambridge: Cambridge University Press, 2010).

10. See Friedrich Schleiermacher, *The Christian Faith,* trans. H. R. Mackintosh and J. S. Stewart (Philadelphia, PA: Fortress Press, 1976), Conclusion #170-171 (738-50). In *Religion Within the Boundaries of Reason Alone* (1793), Kant had argued that the doctrine of the Trinity was an *adiaphora,* that is, marginal to Christian faith, which is reducible to experience of the discontinuity and continuity of the self.

11. Kelsey seems to appreciate that Barth's Trinitarianism is both prospective and retrospective, that is, it is spoken of in a mode of anticipation in *Church Dogmatics* I/1 (#8-10) and in the mode of retrospection only later when Barth has rendered his doctrines of creation and reconciliation. The full extent of the meaning of the Trinity is only available in the retrospective mode. Nonetheless, the contributions of *Church Dogmatics* I/1 to the full doctrine of the Trinity are inalienable. They include making the triune God the subject as

Barth provides a rich substantive analysis of the particular ways in which Father, Son, and Spirit relate to a world created, reconciled, and consummated. Barth's Trinitarian excursions provide a basic frame for Kelsey's much more focused, coherent, and argued Trinitarianism. Kelsey's vision is definitely in line with Barth's, which some have summarized as the "One who loves in freedom,"[12] but Kelsey has to be understood not only as integrating what Barth left unintegrated but also as developing and emending Barth along the Trinitarian axis or axes.

When it comes to the question of the identity of the method deployed by Kelsey, given the form of *Eccentric Existence* with chapters devoted to biblical exegesis that function as equivalent to Barth's excurses in *Church Dogmatics,* the insistence that theology is an independent discipline that draws from the resources of Scripture, especially the canonic narrative, and its overarching, if not fully developed, Trinitarianism, it seems safe to say that Kelsey's text belongs within the tradition of Barth. This still remains true even when one observes the amount of secular knowledge that Kelsey is prepared to accept into theology from the natural and human sciences and occasionally even from art. Certainly, Barth also adopted (and adapted) secular knowledge on an ad hoc basis. While Kelsey's theology goes down a totally different track than that of liberal Protestant theology, which is systemically apologetic, like Barth he thinks engaging in apologetics in ad hoc fashion does not compromise Christian theology. Compromise occurs if and only if another discourse or other discourses are allowed to regulate theological discourse. And this, no more than Barth, is Kelsey prepared to brook.

Even without appeal to Kelsey's own writing history and the influence of his Yale colleagues on his views, which I will rehearse momentarily, the substantive and methodological commitments of *Eccentric Existence* are sufficient to justify the ascription of "Barthian." Of course, as already indicated, the ascription can only work if the interpreter or commentator

---

well as the object of revelation, that revelation of the triune God is the revelation of God as incomprehensible, the revelation of the triune God as sovereignly free, and that while the triune God is known only in his works, the reality of God is not reducible to his works.

12. For this phrase, which has proved so influential even in very non-Barthian modes of theology, such as those of Jürgen Moltmann and Peter C. Hodgson, see, for Barth, *Church Dogmatics* II/1: *The Doctrine of God* (Edinburgh: T&T Clark, 1957), #28. For Moltmann, see his *The Trinity and the Kingdom: The Doctrine of God,* trans. Margaret Kohl (San Francisco: Harper & Row, 1981), pp. 52-56; for Hodgson, see *Winds of the Spirit: A Constructive Christian Theology* (Louisville, KY: Westminster John Knox Press, 1994), pp. 47ff.

takes account of the ways in which Barth is also developed and emended in Kelsey's text. Still, with this caveat, I see no compelling reason to refuse the ascription. Now, given the assumption of a binary between Barth and Schleiermacher, which assumes Schleiermacher to be a prime example of liberal Protestantism, maybe even one of its originators, it would be easy to conclude that *Eccentric Existence* represents an unequivocal No to the *Glaubenslehre.* I think this judgment precipitous and that the situation is more complicated in Kelsey's book. It is certainly true that Kelsey rejects Schleiermacher's appeal to religious experience and/or Christian consciousness or self-consciousness as the basis of Christian theology, which has as one of its many unhappy effects the marginalization of the doctrine of the Trinity. *Eccentric Existence* unfolds a theocentric paradigm on the other side of the modern turn to the subject, religious or otherwise. It is equally true that to the extent to which Schleiermacher is read as suggesting that other discourses (cultural or disciplinary) set the terms of Christian discourse, then this provides good grounds for his rejection. Nothing in *Eccentric Existence* suggests that the conventional reading of Schleiermacher can be blithely dismissed. Still, *Eccentric Existence* provides clues that matters might not be quite so simple. Some clues are literary: the shape and form of *Eccentric Existence* often reminds the reader more nearly of the *Glaubenslehre* than *Church Dogmatics* in its finely orchestrated movement from the horizon of creation to that of reconciliation, the linearity of its argumentative logic, and its brilliant economy despite seeming comprehensiveness. Granted the theocentric perspective required to speak of the relation between the God and human being throughout *Eccentric Existence,* which seems to go in the opposite direction to what one finds in the *Glaubenslehre,* it is interesting that in each of the three theological manifolds Kelsey articulates what the appropriate divine attributes are. This is one of the most conspicuous features of the *Glaubenslehre.*[13] There are other resonances. Kelsey rejects the tendency in Schleiermacher to-

13. For example, in theological reflection on Christian consciousness' experience of God's relation to the world, the appropriate divine attributes are eternity, omnipresence, omnipotence, and omniscience. Within theology's reflection on Christian consciousness of sin, the most appropriate divine attributes are God's holiness, justice, and mercy. Within theology's reflection on redemption, the appropriate attributes are love and wisdom. A reading of Kelsey's choices with regard to divine attributes provides as good a basis as any for a reading of his relation with Schleiermacher. Crucially, however, for Kelsey, as with Barth, reflection on divine attributes occurs within the precincts of God as revealed and thus God as Trinity.

ward experientialist foundationalism. Still, in his articulation of our condition characterized by a gap between the factual disposition of our lives in relation and divine intent regarding our disposition, like Schleiermacher, Kelsey favors a descriptive-presentist account rather than a genetic or quasi-genetic account. This comes through especially loudly in Kelsey's accounts of the contexts and mechanisms of sin.[14] There seem, then, to be some traces of the *Glaubenslehre* in Kelsey's text. How to account for this? One is forced to conjecture. It is possible that Kelsey entertains in tension two different readings of the *Glaubenslehre:* the conventional reading of the text as an exemplary instance of experiential foundationalism and an alternative reading that, if it brackets the appeals to Christian self-consciousness, finds a theology much closer to that of Calvin and much less disagreeable with a theology whose fundamental allegiance is to that of Barth. In this alternative construal Schleiermacher's theology then would begin with Christian biblical speech to which theology as second-order discourse would be entirely beholden, and the theological tradition would be the tradition of interpretation of Christian biblical speech governed by the canonic narrative, which Schleiermacher thinks moves from creation to reconciliation via sin. I want to suggest that this other Schleiermacher plays a not inconsiderable role in *Eccentric Existence.* Its effect is to inflect the Barthianism of the text, making it looser and more generous than it might otherwise be.

This brings me to my second point. *Eccentric Existence* is entirely consistent with Kelsey's previous work, even if it exceeds it. Kelsey's *The Uses of Scripture* endorses the canonic narrative,[15] while insisting that the narrative can be put to quite different uses and that use defines meaning. His short work on redemption gets echoed in both sections one and two,[16] in

14. Kelsey discusses sin in all three parts of his theological anthropology extended over two volumes. See in part one in *Eccentric Existence,* pp. 402-38; part two in *Eccentric Existence,* pp. 567-602; and part three in *Eccentric Existence,* pp. 847-94.

15. See *The Uses of Scripture in Recent Theology* (Philadelphia: Fortress Press, 1975). It should be stated that support of the canonic narrative is merely implicit in this text, since the real subject of the book is how scriptural authority functions in modern theological constructions. Kelsey's narrative predilection becomes more and more evident in the decades that follow. See, for example, "Biblical Narrative and Theological Anthropology," in *Scriptural Authority and Narrative Interpretation,* ed. Garrett Green (Philadelphia: Fortress Press, 1987), pp. 121-43; "Church Discourse and Public Realm," in *Theology and Dialogue: Essays in Conversation with George Lindbeck,* ed. Bruce D. Marshall (Notre Dame, IN: Notre Dame University Press, 1990), pp. 7-33.

16. See *Imagining Redemption* (Louisville, KY: Westminster John Knox Press, 2005).

the former in the emphasis on the fragility and vulnerability of selves, in the latter in the emphasis on an incapacity overcome. Finally, Kelsey' work on theological encyclopedias of the nineteenth century captures a moment in which there is a real stirring as to how to translate in synoptic theological fashion the givens of the Protestant tradition.[17] And, of course, the theological articulation of *Eccentric Existence* also remains consistent with the work of the two other Yale theologians who, if they did not quite form a school, nonetheless, constituted a constellation of theological thought in which theological traditions mattered precisely as modes of interpreting the canonic biblical narrative. If Kelsey in the end is closer to Frei than to Lindbeck, this is not to say that his own work has not internalized some crucial insights and adopted some common protocols. For Kelsey, as with Lindbeck, theological tradition is a history of scriptural reading that has grammatical rules that allow for variation in theological statement over time, even if there is a principled limit to such variation. However important doctrines are in the history of Christianity, Christianity is just as much about practices and forms of life. In the most decided way, here, as elsewhere, Kelsey sanctions Lindbeck's appeal to Wittgenstein's view of religion as a specific language game, not explicable in terms of another language game, and specific practices and forms of life that cohere with implicit and explicit belief, which are better described than explained.[18] In addition, while Kelsey shows himself aware that there are many ways in which the canonic narrative can be bracketed or marginalized in modern theology, he does think with Lindbeck (and also Barth) that one particularly totalitarian model is that of subjective experience, which permits itself a number of registers.

Still the relation between Kelsey and Frei is the closer of the two. A condition — but hardly an explanation of this — is that both Kelsey and Frei are theologians who command the entire history of modern Protes-

17. I am, of course, referring to *To Understand God Truly*. It is worth keeping in mind also Kelsey's approval of Edward Farley's work in this regard. See *Theologia: The Fragmentation and Unity of Theological Education* (Philadelphia: Fortress Press, 1983); also *The Fragility of Knowledge: Theological Education in the Church and the University* (Philadelphia: Fortress Press, 1988).

18. A possible difference between Kelsey and Lindbeck here is that Kelsey does not seem to think that language games and grammar have the same amount of integrity and coherence as Lindbeck seems to think. If "culture" is the metaphor for religion, then culture should be regarded as complex and mixed. Kelsey would perhaps be more comfortable bringing out the analogical character of "language game" and "grammar."

tant theology and are fully conscious of its trends, especially the ways it develops but also makes unrecognizable the premodern theological tradition of which the magisterial reformers are deemed to be an integral part because of, and not simply despite, their critique of the theological traditions and their attendant practices and forms of life. With the exception of the *Church Dogmatics,* no texts exert as much influence on Kelsey on *Eccentric Existence* as *The Eclipse of Biblical Narrative* and *The Identity of Jesus Christ.*[19] Kelsey's mode of discourse in *Eccentric Existence* is quite distant from the Frei of *The Eclipse of Biblical Narrative.* His is as constructively positive as the latter's is genealogical. Yet Frei's genealogical insights as to where biblical interpretation fails and what constitutes adequate interpretation is folded into the kind of exegesis the text practices. Frei's small text on Christology exercises an enormous influence in terms of style of biblical interpretation, which texts, especially New Testament texts, are privileged (Synoptic Gospels), and of the narrative rendering of "unsubstitutable" identity of Christ into which believers are inserted through faith. This allegiance is in evidence in part one of *Eccentric Existence.* It dominates in part three, which focuses on the canonic biblical narrative as rendering the unsubstitutable identity of Christ who enters into solidarity with us creatures as we define ourselves through behavior and quotidian practices at crosshairs to the triune God's intent.

Nonetheless, even as Kelsey displays important situational allegiances — Frei and Lindbeck were his long-time colleagues at Yale — the overall matrix of Kelsey's thought, which we have indicated is Trinitarian through and through, is provided by Barth. For what *Eccentric Existence* offers is neither a theological program, which one could argue is what *The Nature of Doctrine* does explicitly, and what *The Eclipse of Biblical Narrative* does implicitly, nor a systematic theology in miniature like *The Identity of Jesus Christ.* What it does supply is a comprehensively articulated theology of great subtlety and of real fidelity to and critical engagement with the theological tradition as well as an exhibition of interpretation that is at once copious and full of finesse and yet not without its surprises. Although Kelsey manages to persuade, and even to persuade totally, the role that Wisdom literature plays in *Eccentric Existence* is unrivaled in modern theology, and essentially has no precedent in contemporary Protestant theology. Kelsey

19. See Hans W. Frei, *The Eclipse of Biblical Narrative: A Study in Nineteenth Century Hermeneutics* (New Haven, CT: Yale University Press, 1974); also *The Identity of Jesus Christ: The Hermeneutic Bases of Dogmatic Theology* (Philadelphia: Fortress Press, 1995).

also puts his own unique stamp on this copiousness by making it as compendious as possible. *Eccentric Existence* is about as copiously rigorous a performance and as rigorous a copious performance as one will find in contemporary systematic theology.

Although I averred to it at the outset, it is worth tarrying awhile with my third and final point about Kelsey's reticulated text. This concerns what we referred to as the compossibility of and undecidability between narrative schematizations, which lead to both distinct theological and anthropological emphases. In the brief reception history of *Eccentric Existence,* for better or worse this has come to be regarded as perhaps the most "idiosyncratic" of the text's features.[20] But is this feature as idiosyncratic as it might seem? The history of modern Protestant systematic theology, especially along the Schleiermacher-Barth axis, suggest that *Eccentric Existence* is operating in the mode of development rather than innovation. There seem to be two major prompts. The first has to do with a reading of the *Church Dogmatics* that would emphasize its lack of archimedian point, and that the various topoi of creation, reconciliation, and consummation are performatively (if not reflectively) irreducible to each other. One might think of Kelsey making explicit what was merely intuitive in Barth and then building it into his theological performance. A second source, which reinforces Kelsey's relatively independent drawing out the implications of Barth's theological performance, is provided by Schleiermacher. This seems wildly implausible only if it is supposed that Barth and Schleiermacher are a true binary pair and that Kelsey's assumed support of the former would rule out of court any association with the latter, indeed make him forget a point about the *Glaubenslehre,* which Frei pondered as it seemed to trouble the all-too-easy distinction between Barth and Schleiermacher.[21]

20. Perhaps the two commentators who have accented this contribution most are John E. Thiel and David F. Ford. For Thiel, see "Methodological Choices in Kelsey's *Eccentric Existence,*" *Modern Theology* 27, no. 1 (2011): 1-13; Ford, "The What, How and Who of Humanity Before God: Theological Anthropology and the Bible in the Twenty-first Century," *Modern Theology* 27, no. 1 (2011): 41-54.

21. See, for example, Frei's discussion of Schleiermacher in *Types of Christian Theology,* ed. George Hunsinger and William C. Placher (New Haven, CT: Yale University Press, 1992), pp. 34-38, 70-78. Essentially Frei argues that Schleiermacher is not an apologetic theologian in the strict sense in that there is no faith-independent moment in Schleiermacher's mature work that functions as a foundation to secure argumentative traction with secular culture. In this respect, Schleiermacher's theology is closer to that of Barth than David Tracy (pp. 30-34).

Responding to criticisms of the *Glaubenslehre,* but recalling also his thoughts at the time of its production, in his *On the* Glaubenslehre: *Two Letters to Dr. Lücke* Schleiermacher wonders whether he might not have started with the antithesis of sin and redemption rather than with creation, or more specifically with the sense of absolute dependence on a divine whence.[22] Gradually, it turns out, however, that Schleiermacher is involved in more than second-guessing brought on by a pantheism charge; rather, he reflects on the way in which the concepts that initiate the operation of interpretation for the biblical narrative will inevitably overdetermine how we speak theologically about other parts of the narrative. Concretely, this means in the *Glaubenslehre* that sin and redemption get interpreted in the light of the analytic vocabulary for creation rather than the other way around. Matters would have been otherwise had one started with the antithesis of sin and redemption and the analytical vocabulary fashioned in this arena come to be presupposed by an analysis of createdness and creatureliness. What begins to dawn on Schleiermacher is that, with respect to theological articulation, nothing like Heraclitus's formula that "the way up is the way down" is apposite.[23] As far as I am aware, nowhere in the history of modern theology before Kelsey does a theologian grasp reflectively the compossibility of different theological schemes that, although not incompatible, are irreducible to each other. In terms of theological form then, *Eccentric Existence* is only relatively different; it is not truly eccentric. It has deep roots in the theologies of both Barth and Schleiermacher.

22. See Friedrich Schleiermacher, *On the* Glaubenslehre: *Two Letters to Dr. Lücke,* trans. James Duke and Francis Fiorenza (Oxford: Oxford University Press, 2000). In his letters Schleiermacher looks back at his choice of beginning with the feeling of absolute dependence upon a divine whence and wonders whether he could or should have started with the Christian experience of the antithesis of sin and redemption. In doing so, he reveals that he is not simply indulging in second guessing, but that this was a concern even as he wrote the *Glaubenslehre.* This "could have" or "should have" clearly influenced Frei's relative rehabilitation of Schleiermacher late in his career, such that, whatever their differences, Barth and Schleiermacher could not be regarded as antithetical and that Schleiermacher is in principle a more Christocentric theologian than he is usually given credit for.

23. The deeper issue of the systemic nature of the problem of beginnings and the losses that might be incurred by dint of having either of the starting points emerge in the second of the two letters. Schleiermacher seems to grasp that whichever of the two beginnings were adopted, the archeological primacy of the sense of absolute dependence, or the experiential primary of sin and redemption, would be consequent in terms of the sense of the canonic narrative. What is inchoate in Schleiermacher is developed by Kelsey who, if he is anticipated by Frei, goes beyond him here.

Actual Engagement with the Catholic Theological Tradition

Eccentric Existence is unequivocally a confessional text and takes its place in the great tradition of Reformed theology. Of course, for Kelsey, this means that his text takes its place in the great tradition of theology, for in his theological practice, as with Calvin and Barth, a proper Reformed theology represents a critical vetting of the received theological tradition, its formal and substantive priorities, and its modalities of biblical interpretation. There is no reason to suppose that Kelsey has anything other than an ecumenical sensibility, but being ecumenical is certainly not the point of this particular text. This does not mean, however, that non-Reformed theology is not engaged, or in particular that Catholic theology is not engaged. In fact, there is both direct and indirect engagement with Catholic theology, and this engagement takes positive and negative forms. Although the evidence is hardly on the surface, I think an argument can be made that there is something like an indirect and highly positive engagement with Aquinas's theocentric and specifically Trinitarian view of creation. By contrast, the evidence of engagement of a negative kind with modern Catholic theology is very much on the surface in Kelsey's recurring criticisms of Rahner and transcendental style theology throughout part one of his text. Given its considerably greater transparence, it only makes sense to pay more attention to this negative valance, and in significant ways to consider the implied more positive assessment of a thinker such as Aquinas as an indicator that the real problem with Rahner is not his Catholicism as such but rather his presumptive subscription to the modern turn to the subject.

It is legitimate to say that part one of *Eccentric Existence* bears a "polemical" relation to Rahner's transcendental theology as long as one supplies the requisite caveats. First, Kelsey's project is in a quite literal sense "constructive." This means that as his particular form of secondary theology attends to the biblical narrative and its various inflections, theological articulation does not proceed dialectically in and through a rejection of a position considered to be its foil, and it eschews a vetting procedure that finds a whole group of theologies inadequate in crucial respects. The underlying logic of the text is not negative in any of these ways, and again for theological reasons: theology is a response on behalf of a community to the superabundant triune God who is complexly rendered in Scripture. This responsiveness should be built into the very fabric of theological method. Second, in so far as possible, "polemical" should not carry any excess in tone beyond that of pointing to disagreement. One might cast this as an appeal to old-fashioned civility which is always in danger of going out of date. But I take it to be more than a matter of polite sensibility; rather, it expresses a commitment in Christian speech towards non-violent rhetoric as well as a recall of the way in which a theologian such as Schleiermacher both availed of and spoke of "polemic." If *Eccentric Existence* can be classed as it essentially classes itself, this means that its criticisms of other forms of theology, as well as borrowings from non-theological sources, are essentially ad hoc.

With the above two caveats in mind, it is accurate to say that Rahner, considered both in himself and as a metaphor for a post-Kantian form of foundationalism that has Protestant as well as Catholic exemplars, is a particular target in part one of *Eccentric Existence.* A crucial issue concerns theological method, with Kelsey essentially offering a conventional reading of Rahner, which for the purposes of taxonomy prioritizes *Spirit in the World* and *Hearers of the Word.*[24] Rahner, then, is thought to articulate a philosophical anthropology. Subsequently, this philosophical anthropology comes to function to justify particular theological claims, in the first instance claims about human being and derivatively an entire compendium of theological claims from the doctrine of the Trinity to the doctrine of the eschatological state. In *Eccentric Existence* there are essentially two areas of substantive criticism, the first concerning Rahner's articulation of God as triune,[25] the second focused on transcendentalist anthropology which in Kelsey's view consistently disembodies the person or community of persons called into being by the triune God. Beginning with the first area of criticism, at the very least *Eccentric Existence* suggests weaknesses in the following features of Rahner's Trinitarian thought: (i) the notion of mystery; (ii) the understanding of person as relation; (iii) the relation between immanent and economic Trinity: (iv) the subtlety or lack thereof in the use of Scripture. I concentrate here on (i) and (iii), but perhaps should say a brief word about (ii) and (iv).

As is well known, Rahner has reservations about thinking of Father, Son, and Spirit as persons given what he believes to be the chronic pastoral problem about the assumptions concerning person as a site of individual

24. See Rahner, *Spirit in the World,* trans. William Dych, foreword by Johannes B. Metz (New York: Herder & Herder, 1965); *Hearers of the Word: Laying the Foundation for Philosophy of Religion,* ed. Andrew Tallon, trans. Joseph Donceel (New York: Continuum, 1969).

25. See *The Trinity,* trans. Joseph Donceel, introduction by Catherine Mowry LaCugna (New York: Crossroad, 1997).

consciousness and self-consciousness.[26] Any number of Catholic theologians have repeated Rahner's diagnosis, although they are usually less happy with his proposed solution of "self-subsistent modes of existence."[27] Although Kelsey touches at best only very lightly on diagnosis, by and large he seems to have some general sympathy with Rahner on this point,[28] but not enough to revise the Nicene view of "one essence and three persons," which has established itself as an important expression of Christian grammar. Reflecting on the Nicene-Constantinople creed, Kelsey makes the point that the creed supports any number of doctrines of God. The creed, he writes, "functions meta-doctrinally, is a norm for asserting doctrinal proposals, not as such a proposal in its own right."[29] With respect to Kelsey's take on Rahner's view of the relation between the doctrine of the Trinity and Scripture, we are forced to argue from silence. Nonetheless, it seems safe to suggest on the basis of the centrality of Scripture throughout *Eccentric Existence* that Rahner's "biblical turn" comes across as purely stipulative and that in practice — if not necessarily in theory — Rahner's Trinitarian theology is divorced from Scripture in a way that far surpasses classical authors such as Augustine and Aquinas, both criticized by Rahner for their lack of rootedness in salvation history.

In part one of *Eccentric Existence* Kelsey thinks that assigning mystery to God follows naturally from the Christian consensus concerning the incommensurability of the creator to the creature. Barth's notion of incomprehensibility functions here more as an example of the broader

26. Rahner makes it clear that *The Trinity* constitutes a pastoral as well as intellectual intervention. If the intellectual intervention is intramural in that it suggests that the Catholic tradition, proximally in neo-Scholastic treatments of the Trinity and ultimately in the magisterial theological tradition, is flawed in that it forsakes the economy for speculation on God *in se,* the pastoral intervention has to do with Rahner's sense that there is little chance that "person" will not be identified with individual, and more specifically individual consciousness, such that the believer will hear three gods. Rahner is somewhat at odds with himself on the pastoral front throughout his essay. On the one hand, he is convinced that Christian believers are functionally monotheists while worrying that the language of three persons is making them tritheists.

27. Walter Kasper is a Catholic theologian who essentially agrees with Rahner's diagnosis of the pastoral problem but who is not in favor of his modalistic sounding and possibly substantively modalist solution to the pastoral problem. See Kasper, *The God of Jesus Christ,* trans. Matthew J. O'Connell (New York: Crossroad, 1986), pp. 289, 302.

28. Kelsey, *Eccentric Existence,* p. 616.

29. A fortiori the creed allows very different kinds of theological anthropological proposals over history, which have some relation but not necessarily a direct one with Trinitarian proposals. See Kelsey, *Eccentric Existence,* pp. 61-62.

Christian tradition rather than an individual theological position.[30] The register here is epistemic. Within this register there can be disagreement about whether the emphasis falls on the triune God as unknown (radical apophasis) or known as unknown (moderate apophasis). Kelsey supports the latter over the former and, arguably, worries whether Rahner belongs to the first dispensation.[31] Even if the worry is not justified by Rahner's own texts,[32] it may well be when it comes to Rahner's interpreters who seem to confound apophasis and agnosticism.[33] When God is known as the incomprehensible one, this is the fruit of divine disclosure in the orders of creation, consummation, and reconciliation.[34] Again, while the commitment to divine disclosure may not clearly distinguish either Barth or Kelsey from Rahner, given Rahner's repeated insistence on a positive rather than negative notion of mystery, it might point to the need to vouchsafe the given in more robust ways than found in his transcendentalist followers and his post-Kantian Protestant look-alikes.[35] It is Kelsey's third emphasis, however, which has its background in Calvin and Barth and its ultimate source in the Bible, which marks off Kelsey's Reformed view from that of Rahner. For Kelsey, to speak competently of the triune God

30. For divine incomprehensibility in Barth, especially in the context of the Trinity, see *Church Dogmatics* I/1, pp. 316, 320, 330.

31. Kelsey, *Eccentric Existence,* p. 59.

32. *Spirit in the World* and *Hearers of the Word* give evidence that Rahner has a positive rather than negative sense of mystery in mind. In *Spirit in the World* the orientation toward transcendence is after all orientation toward Being as *summum esse,* not toward emptiness. The crucial essay, of course, is "The Concept of Mystery in Catholic Theology," in *Theological Investigations* 4: *More Recent Writings,* trans. Kevin Smith (Baltimore: Helicon Press, 1966), pp. 36-73. See also "Being Open to God as Ever Greater: On the Significance of the Aphorism *'Ad Majorem Dei Gloriam,'*" in *Theological Investigations* 7: *Further Theology of the Spiritual Life 1,* trans. David Bourke (New York: Seabury Press, 1971), pp. 25-44; "The Hiddenness of God" and "An Investigation of the Incomprehensibility of God in St. Thomas Aquinas," in *Theological Investigations* 16: *Experiences of the Spirit: Sources of Theology* (New York: Crossroad, 1983), pp. 227-43, 244-54.

33. Rahner has not been well served here. Catherine LaCugna provides the clearest example of a self-consciously Rahnerian theology sliding from a positive notion of the Trinity as mystery to a negative notion of mystery as the limit of conceptual competence.

34. Kelsey, *Eccentric Existence,* p. 75.

35. A good example of a Protestant transcendentalist is Gordon Kaufmann. Here Kelsey has Frei as a precursor in diagnosing the problem in Protestant theology. Although Frei does not use the term "transcendental" to characterize Kaufmann in *Types of Christian Theology,* pp. 28-30, he is aware that the philosophical and rational commitments have their locus in Kant.

demands an emphasis on holiness and glory as well as mystery, and this is only possible in a systematic theology context in which God has disclosed Godself as the One with whom we have to do — to evoke Kelsey's own language in the first part of the book.[36] Of course, to speak of God's holiness and glory quite intentionally emphasizes the alterity of God and the corresponding creaturehood of human beings.[37] This creaturehood can and does take on an explicitly doxological form. Again, it is not that Kelsey and Rahner are worlds apart. Rahner after all defines freedom not in terms of autonomy but rather obediential potency. And in his essays on prayer as well as in his actual prayers, Rahner's thought heads in a doxological direction.[38] Still while this does lessen the distance between Kelsey and Rahner, it does not remove it altogether.[39] It would do so only if one could demonstrate that the doxological material has the same status as some of Rahner's more famous exercises in fundamental theology. Kelsey does not consider this option, but one suspects that were he to consider it, the presumption would be against equality.

Kelsey is also made anxious by Rahner's famous axiom that the immanent Trinity is the economic Trinity and vice versa because of the implication that it is otiose to consider the immanent Trinity to be in some relevant respect distinct from the economic Trinity.[40] Even as it is recognized that the immanent Trinity and economic Trinity are not two trinities but two aspects of one Trinity, and that the Trinitarian foundation of the world is accessed only in and through the Trinitarian economy, nonetheless, for Kelsey, it is a requirement of basic theological grammar to affirm that the immanent Trinity is the foundation of the economy since (a) Christian realism dictates that acts of creation, consummation, and reconciliation refer to the agency of the agent identified by the tradition as a Trinity of persons; and (b) one cannot intelligibly speak of the gratuity of creation,[41]

36. Kelsey, *Eccentric Existence,* pp. 73ff., 123ff., 309ff.

37. Kelsey, *Eccentric Existence,* pp. 75, 77.

38. See, for example, *The Need and the Blessing of Prayer* (revised edition of *On Prayer*), trans. Bruce W. Gillette (Collegeville, MN: Liturgical Press, 1997). See also *Encounters with Silence,* trans. James M. Demske, S.J. (Westminster, MD: Newman Press, 1965). See also in general, the numerous essays in *Philosophical Investigations* that are explicitly Ignatian in theme.

39. Even Walter Kasper complains that Rahner's Trinitarian thought is not especially doxological. He cites in particular Rahner's *Foundations of Christian Faith: An Introduction to the Idea of Christianity,* trans. William V. Dych (New York: Crossroad, 1978). See also *The God of Jesus Christ,* p. 302.

40. See Rahner, *The Trinity,* p. 22, and Kelsey, *Eccentric Existence,* p. 68.

41. Kelsey, *Eccentric Existence,* pp. 213-14, 122, 129, 163.

the "gracelike" nature of consummation,[42] and the real grace of reconciliation[43] without presupposing such as distinction.[44] Again, Kelsey is less interested in offering a proper interpretation of Rahner than a plausible one, whose influential history helps us to see how modern theology, both Protestant and Catholic, muddies the understanding of the Trinity. Indeed, Kelsey's laying bare the most basic desiderata for any relatively adequate theological view of Trinitarian mystery may more nearly indict a "Rahnerian" theologian, such as Catherine LaCugna whose *God for Us* exaggerates the Kantian element of Rahner's fundamental theology program and only pays lip service to the Thomistic realism, which, even in the earliest texts of Rahner, functions to qualify his Kantian-style transcendentalist commitments.[45] Of course, Rahner is but an instance of a broader tendency in modern Trinitarian theology, which, impressed by various objections to the classical formulation of the Trinity, dominantly but not exclusively existential in kind is prepared either to abandon the distinction altogether or to seriously qualify it. In addition to Rahner, this tendency is illustrated by forms of theology influenced by the Hegelian subversion of the immanent-economic Trinity distinction. The theologian who would most nearly fall under Kelsey's classical stricture would be Jürgen Moltmann, but others would fall under suspicion.[46]

42. Kelsey, *Eccentric Existence,* p. 526.

43. Kelsey, *Eccentric Existence,* p. 623.

44. The most important passage concerning the different senses of grace is the following: "Granted, as we have seen in parts 1 and 2, parasitic uses of 'grace' are also appropriate. God's relating in creative blessing and in eschatological blessing may appropriately be described as 'gracious' or 'gracelike.' . . . Strictly speaking, 'grace' should be used in the singular in reference to Jesus Christ — but only to him understood in the context of the triune God. . . ." Kelsey, *Eccentric Existence,* p. 623.

45. Catherine Mowry LaCugna, *God for Us: The Trinity and Christian Life* (San Francisco: Harper, 1991). On the (correct) basis that Christian believers only have access to God through divine self-communication in history, on more than one occasion LaCugna seems to draw the conclusion that nothing can be said about the Trinity *in se.* Here Rahner's functional apophaticism turns into agnosticism, his doubly ontologically modified Kantianism (Aquinas and Heidegger) into a pure Kantian epistemology in which the Trinity *in se* is on thither side of the screen that divides noumenon from phenomenon.

46. Moltmann is exposed to the objection of confounding the immanent and economic Trinity, despite Kelsey's appreciation of his view of *adventus,* which seems to imply that God cannot be reduced to the world and history (pp. 452-53). The degree of exposure bears a direct relation to the degree of Moltmann's Hegelian commitments, which is not something that Kelsey addresses in *Eccentric Existence.* Given Peter Hodgson's commitments to both Moltmann and Hegel, and his argument for the abolition of the classical distinction, it seems

The second and related area of contestation with Rahner, understood as an exponent of a transcendentalist style fundamental theology, concerns theological anthropology in the narrow sense of a theological conspectus on human being. Kelsey suggests the relation between both areas by means of the notion of mystery early on in volume one,[47] and he contends that while there is a formal similarity between his own view and Rahner's, there are marked differences. As Kelsey proceeds in the development of his constructive proposal in part one, the fundamental elements of his disagreement gradually unpack. Four are particularly worth mentioning: (i) Rahner's preference for speaking of the eccentric or ecstatic nature of human being as spirit; (ii) his notion of graced nature; (iii) the lack of clarity in Rahner's commitment to embodiness; (iv) finally, the ordered relationship between theology (God's relation to the economy) and anthropology (our relationship to the triune God as the ground of our being). I will deal with each of these in turn.

For Kelsey, theologies such as that of Rahner betray the given by suggesting a distinction between surface existence with its beliefs and practices and a depth dimension defined as spirit.[48] This esoteric-exoteric distinction opens a gap between those special believers who are able to access this depth dimension of the self (which is also a height) and those who are not. This kind of theology also routinely favors self-consciousness as an index of specialness. This is, however, to dissolve the theocentric into the anthropological paradigm: the unsubstitutabilty of each individual rests on divine call rather than on special religious properties or talents of human beings.[49] Needless to say, the early Schleiermacher is as much — if not more — implicated here than Rahner. On Kelsey's account there can be no organization into classes of religious persons, no more than one can divide a person into two histories.[50] In a person the surface is the depth, to invoke Goethe's phraseology, but to give it Kelsey's meaning. She lives her life in

---

clear that Hodgson (who is never cited) would fall under Kelsey's censure. It is an open question as to how the Trinitarian theologies of Eberhard Jüngel and Robert Jensen would fare. For information on Moltmann, see note 12.

47. Kelsey, *Eccentric Existence,* p. 75.

48. Kelsey, *Eccentric Existence,* p. 190.

49. Kelsey, *Eccentric Existence,* pp. 292, 525-26, 529, 532, 620.

50. In using this locution I am deliberately invoking Gilbert Ryle who spoke of mind and body in the Cartesian tradition as suggesting two collateral histories. Ryle is an indicative figure for both Frei and Kelsey. See his *The Concept of Mind* (Chicago: University of Chicago Press, 1949).

the quotidian and as quotidian. An inextricable aspect of the quotidian are practices that make for human flourishing.[51] Here Kelsey is taking to heart not only the lessons offered by Frei in *The Identity of Jesus Christ,* but also quite different correlative accounts that can be found in McIntyre and others. Human beings are mysterious not because of intrinsic inaccessibility, but because of a vertical relationship to God — established by God — unique to each individual.[52] Kelsey insists that a theological account of human mystery and a philosophical and/or phenomenological account should not be confused, although he does not deny that philosophy in general or phenomenology in particular might be capable of producing through its own resources an analogous account. Still, no such account or accounts can make the theological account redundant or displace its authority. Moreover, he argues there is a systemic skew in philosophical accounts — but also unfortunately in many theological accounts — toward viewing the human person in terms of adulthood.[53] This may seem innocent enough, but such a commitment at once reduces the radicality of Christian speech, which affirms the unsubstitutability of persons irrespective of levels of cognitive development, emotional maturity, and power of agency.

I come now to the second reservation in the specific area of theological anthropology. A constant refrain throughout *Eccentric Existence,* but especially in book one,[54] is the notion that creation is a gift. Being an existing creature is not something owed to one, nor does it belong to the order of logical or metaphysical necessity. Existence, however, is no brute fact, but rather indicates God's delight, solicitude, and affirmation of what is genuinely other to him. Still in line with Calvin and Barth, Kelsey shows himself disinclined to follow Rahner in asserting that the human creature is always already graced.[55] In a tone that is a little severe by his standards, Kelsey avers that strictly speaking "in the Gospels' narrative logic, grace is not a

51. Kelsey, *Eccentric Existence,* p. 197.

52. Kelsey, *Eccentric Existence,* pp. 75, 268, 284, 308.

53. Kelsey, *Eccentric Existence,* pp. 261-62. While this is not the only reason why Kelsey has reservations about the traditional notion of *imago Dei,* it is one of the major reasons. The other major reason has to do with the role Genesis 1:26 has played in the Christian tradition. First, Kelsey thinks that it has been made to bear too much theological freight, and that the Wisdom tradition is significantly superior in depicting our situation before God. Second, interpretation is almost always fighting against an essentialist strain.

54. Kelsey, *Eccentric Existence,* pp. 122, 129, 163, 278.

55. Kelsey, *Eccentric Existence,* pp. 213-14, 623.

transcendental cosmic structure nor a universally present divine dynamic. Nor is the incarnate one just one (perhaps narrative one) instantiation, illustration, or symbol in space and time of some such transcendental dynamic or structure."[56] Of course, Kelsey's theological situation with respect to the relation of nature and grace is quite different from that of Rahner, who has to deal with neo-Scholasticism's view of a "pure nature" to which not only Rahner, but almost the entire group of Catholic theologians that constituted the movement that came to be known as resourcement, took exception.[57] Nonetheless, however comprehensible Rahner's reaction is to the provocation of a dangerous rationalistic theological current, Kelsey worries whether it so generalizes grace that it seriously dilutes it when it comes to reconciliation.

A third reservation concerns embodiness. Kelsey's strong commitment to the bodily identity of human beings over time is not antithetical to Rahner's stated position, which, reacting against what he perceives to be the angelic view of human being that dominates Catholic thought in the modern period, insists on the bodiliness of the person by means of an appropriation of Aristotle's and Aquinas's hylomorphic theory. Kelsey worries, however, whether theologians such as Rahner, who after all emphasize spirit,[58] are insistent enough on the embodiness of human being, which not only specifies the human mode of finitude, but makes them publically accessible. While Rahner is not accused of having Cartesian tendencies, for Kelsey much more than a formal acknowledgment of embodiness is a theological desideratum. In a kind of orienting statement Kelsey says that God is no closer to spirit than he is to bodies.[59] This statement can stand alone, yet it also specifies Kelsey's general view that divine transcendence and immanence are best construed as being in direct, rather than inverse, proportion with regard to each other.[60] Fourth and finally, there is the issue of analogy between the triune God and human being.

56. Kelsey, *Eccentric Existence,* p. 623.

57. Of course, Henri de Lubac was one of the foremost of these theologians who challenged neo-Scholasticism on this point. Although there is no mention of de Lubac in *Eccentric Existence,* as a matter of fact Kelsey is sympathetic to his project. The lack of reference is probably explained by the fact that a theologian such as Tanner, who is close to Kelsey, has adopted and adapted de Lubac in her work. Kelsey can presuppose this adoption and adaption as he articulates his self-consciously Protestant systematic theology.

58. Kelsey, *Eccentric Existence,* p. 250.

59. Kelsey, *Eccentric Existence,* p. 256.

60. Kelsey, *Eccentric Existence,* pp. 255-56.

Kelsey acknowledges that such an analogy exists.[61] But the analogy is both different in kind and essentially weaker than what is found in the Augustinian tradition, from which it is not self-evident that Rahner gains sufficient distance. One is not able to come to know, even less demonstrate, the relations between the Trinitarian persons by attending to the structure of the self. The infinite qualitative difference between Creator and creature puts a block on such speculation and determines such speculation to be essentially idolatrous. What underlies this error is a hermeneutic decision, often explicit, but in the case of a theologian such as Rahner, merely implicit, to allow Genesis 1:27 to play a determining role in the construction of a theological anthropology.[62] Kelsey is fairly sure that it cannot and should not bear the weight. Obviously, this particular disagreement is different in kind than the other three, since it concerns how Trinitarian theology and theological anthropology can be weakly and strongly aligned.

In order to unfold the range of disagreement between Kelsey and Rahner I have had to extrapolate. The emphasis in *Eccentric Existence* falls so heavily on construction that contesting any theologian or even a particular theological regime represents something of a shadowside. No more than any other thinker with whom Kelsey disagrees does Rahner become an obsession. Perhaps even more importantly, the criticisms of Rahner do not seem to be intended as criticisms of Catholic theology *per se*. Rahner seems to function as a quintessentially modern theologian, that is, a theologian for whom the self-consciousness of the human subject is the lynchpin for theological reflection rather than an ecclesial theologian, that is, a theologian who speaks from and to a particular theological tradition. Kelsey does not attempt to justify this reading, and logically could modify it seriously if the textual evidence warranted it. What matters to him is how a Rahnerian-style theological method represents a danger to all Christian theological construction in the modern period and to a Reformed systematic theology in particular. Kelsey's interests, then, together with his view that the transcendental method is extra-territorial, justifies engaging with a somewhat ecclesially deracinated Rahner. Although Rahner admirers might reasonably object to this decontextualization, the good news is that the criticisms of Rahner are by no means transitive with regard to the broader Catholic tradition. This is true both logically and performatively. Logically speaking criticisms of Rahner do

61. Kelsey, *Eccentric Existence,* pp. 75-77.
62. Kelsey, *Eccentric Existence,* pp. 299, 302.

not apply to modern or contemporary Catholic theologies, which accept the grammar of Christian faith, are biblically grounded, and which eschew the transcendental method. In section three I will speak to Hans Urs von Balthasar as providing an example of a theology that operates more nearly on the same ground as Kelsey's and where in consequence the disagreements are finer, but also it turns out more perspicuous, from a confessional point of view. In terms of interpretive performance throughout *Eccentric Existence,* there is nothing to indicate specific hostility to the Catholic tradition. In light of this, but also taking into account Kelsey's association with such theologians as George Lindbeck, Kathryn Tanner, and Bruce Marshall, it is worth raising the questions whether and to what extent Aquinas's theological articulation is in principle approved. There are two attendant caveats: First, I am not suggesting that Kelsey expressly pursues these questions in *Eccentric Existence* and, second, only the barest outline is possible here.

Before I provide what amounts to the merest inventory of the positive correlation between Kelsey and Aquinas both in the areas of the doctrine of God and theological anthropology and also their relation, it is worth mentioning that structural features of Aquinas's thought support positive correlation. Aquinas's thought is theocentric both materially and formally; it self-consciously operates in terms of received grammar of God-talk, which serves as backdrop for theological anthropology; and if not biblical in the same way and to the same extent as Kelsey would enjoin following the Reformers, nonetheless, Aquinas's theology could not be judged to be unbiblical. Considered thus, Aquinas is a very different theologian than Rahner. Thus, the sets of reservations concerning Rahner's doctrine of God and his theological anthropology are not applicable to Aquinas. Sticking for the moment to the doctrine of God, we can begin by saying that Kelsey gives the reader no reason to suppose that when it comes to the Trinity that Aquinas is committed to anything like a form of radical apophasis. This is true even if the debt to Pseudo-Dionysius is fully acknowledged, for as a doctrine the Trinity belongs to *sacra doctrina,* that is, to what is possible to say about God in the context of God's salvific disclosure in and to the world.

While Aquinas is circumspect when it comes to unfolding the Trinity, the fact that a Trinitarian grammar is in operation allows him to say a considerable amount about persons, relations, and missions, while also making his own contribution both in terms of substance, for example, in terms of the characterizations of the Son and the Spirit, and in formal terms, that is, in his deployment of the logic of terms to police Trinitarian articulation.[63] There may be some significant component of negative theology when it comes to description of the Trinity — and this further specifies Aquinas's more general remarks about naming God — but the way of "remotion" in Aquinas is as distant from Kant's agnosticism as it is from the modern rationalist who knows God as if God were an object in the world or the biggest thing that is. This leads to a second and related point. Aquinas defines the persons of the Trinity in and through relations, even to the point of considering the persons as self-subsistent relations. But the persons are irreducible to each other, non-substitutable: The Son is not the Father and vice versa, and the Spirit is neither the Son or the Father. As with the major Trinitarian theologians, East and West, from the fourth century on, Aquinas, who is heir to these traditions and especially the Augustinian tradition, commences with an interpretation of the immanent Trinity as the ground of the missions, the economic activity of the Son and the Spirit in salvation history. For Aquinas, given primarily the Nicene-Constantinopolitan Creed and secondarily the witness of the magisterial theological tradition, the confession of the Trinity is part of the grammar of Christian speech, but, as he shows, and as Augustine and the Cappadocians had shown previously, while this sets restrictions on what can be said about the triune God, the space of interpretation remains open. And famously in the *Summa,* Aquinas articulates the Trinitarian ground of creation.[64] The created order, which in the treatment of the world within the realm of natural theology is given the placeholder status of contingency, now is interpreted purely as gift. The world is gift, if and only if the economy expresses a free action of God, however convenient or congruent this action is with our best expectations of how God might

63. Aquinas does not see himself as being an innovator, but rather someone who clarifies with the conceptual and grammatical tools at his disposal the common theological tradition. This intention is what undergirds his reflection on the Trinity in *Summa Theologica* I, Q. 26-43, although as good scholars of Aquinas's Trinitarian thought have pointed out, there is much reflection on the Trinity outside of the *Summa.* Without prejudice to the fine work done by Bruce Marshall, the most compelling and comprehensive treatment of Aquinas's Trinitarian thought is provided by Gilles Emery. See especially his *The Trinitarian Theology of St. Thomas Aquinas,* trans. Francesca Aran Murphy (Oxford: Oxford University Press, 2007).

64. For a lucid account of this, see Emery, *The Trinitarian Theology of St Thomas Aquinas,* pp. 338-59; also Emery, *La Trinité créatrice: Trinité et creation dans les commentaires aux Sentences de Thomas d' Aquin et ses précureurs Albert le Grand et Bonaventure* (Paris: Vrin, 1995).

behave. It is interesting that in this respect the gift designation *(donum)* of creation is not confounded with the grace that transforms nature in the incarnation and cross.

As I turn to examine briefly the extent to which Kelsey recalls the positions Aquinas takes in his theological anthropology — positions that presuppose a Trinitarian backdrop — it is apposite to remind that I am not suggesting that Kelsey intentionally recalls Aquinas specifically on these points, but rather finds agreeable traditional positions that have Aquinas as one of their major spokespersons. It is tempting to suggest that Kelsey and Aquinas mesh as perfectly in the area of theological anthropology as Kelsey and Rahner fail to mesh, but this is altogether too neat. On all four points where we saw significant disagreement between Kelsey and Rahner, there is, indeed, a decent element of correlation between Kelsey and Aquinas. Yet the level of correlation varies. I will begin with the two features where the level of correlation is stronger and then proceed to the two where the level of correlation is weaker. The emphasis in Aquinas's theological anthropology on embodiness is high. As is well known, here as elsewhere Aquinas avails of Aristotle to critique a tendency in Christianity toward a spiritualism that disregards the gift of the body and matter. Of course, the lingua franca for such spiritualism in the medieval tradition is Platonism, a role that Cartesianism plays in the modern period. Whatever might be the debits of the hylomorphic theory, it specifies the kind of finite creature human beings are as opposed to pure spirits (angels) who are also created and finite. One should not deny that Rahner also wants to make this point, and on a rhetorical level he does so in *Spirit in the World.* But it is also true that in Rahner's appropriation of Kant through Heidegger, what matters is more nearly finitude than embodiness. There can be no denying the intention to be faithful to Aquinas, but, arguably, embodiness belongs more nearly to the rhetoric than the substance of Rahner's deepest philosophical text.

So far we have illustrated a comparative, greater or lesser proximity of two Catholic thinkers to Kelsey, but not really made the case for real proximity. A serious challenge is presented by the fact that embodiness for Kelsey is much broader than a hylomorphic theory allows and suggests agency and vulnerability, public accessibility and accountability, and the value of practices and forms of life as opposed to interior states. Aquinas's texts may not prohibit such an extension, but neither does the extension seem logically entailed. Still, MacIntyre draws out of Aquinas something quite like what Kelsey has in mind without necessarily making a strong textual case for its probity.[65] Nonetheless, he does enough to suggest that an account of the virtues proves key, even as the historical, public, and institutional nature of the virtues ought to be highlighted. Kelsey would, undoubtedly, agree with MacIntyre's retrieval and his emphases, but would take the theological virtues out of the brackets where MacIntyre keeps them. For a theologian such as Kelsey, faith, hope, and love are not top-ups on the real and basic virtues but rather overlapping horizons for the practice of all virtues, and they also have a public and even political character.[66] Similarly, one can see a high degree of correlation between Aquinas and Kelsey when it comes to focusing on the quotidian, or given dimensions, of the human subject, which obviously involves embodiness and public accessibility.[67] Although the register is somewhat different, with Aquinas using the language of Aristotle to specify in a general way the horizontal dimension of the human person, and Kelsey in contrast pointing to the various contexts of a person's activities and practices, there is, nonetheless, a homology and most definitely a shared allergy to the fallacy of abstract concreteness in matters of religion and more specifically toward evacuating the prosaic reality of persons. One can easily infer from what Kelsey says that the relation between God and human persons becomes unreal, not only if God becomes an inference or a hypothesis, but also when persons are misdescribed by the search and finding of a non-quotidian area of religious talent or expertise.

Now, it is a more open question as to whether Aquinas does better than Rahner when it comes to unsubstitutability and understanding aright the level of analogy and disanalogy between the triune God and human being. It should be granted that one of the standard ways in which Aquinas secures the unsubstitutability of the human person, that is, in and through the notion of prime matter, which is the principle of individuation in the form-matter synthesis, would not be congenial to Kelsey. The objection would not be that unsubstitutability is not self-evidently secured by means of this conceptuality — such was the thinking of Bonaventure when he focused on incommunicability and Scotus on *haeceitas* — but rather that philosophy, rather than theology, is playing an adjudicative role. But this

65. Alasdair MacIntyre, *After Virtue: A Study in Moral Theory* (Notre Dame, IN: University of Notre Dame Press, 1984).

66. Kelsey, *Eccentric Existence,* pp. 197ff.

67. Kelsey comes very close to MacIntyre's translation of Aristotle's and Aquinas's treatment of the classical virtues when he talks of practices having their own intrinsic standards of excellence (Kelsey, *Eccentric Existence,* p. 197).

is not the only way in which Aquinas secures the identity of the selves. *Summa Contra Gentiles* (book three) implies an account of person as elected by God for sharing God's life. This puts Aquinas more nearly into the orbit of Calvin and Barth and thus more nearly into the orbit of Kelsey without in the slightest suggesting that there are not important differences between Aquinas and these other thinkers. It is crucial to Kelsey that unsubstitutability is not a metaphysical quality in a human individual, but an unrepeatable relationship established and sustained from the side of God.[68] When it comes to the kind of analogy supported by Aquinas, it is not self-evident whether Rahner or Kelsey is closer to him. What brings Rahner close to Aquinas is the presence of a strong Augustinian element in Aquinas's conjugation of the triune God under the aspects of knowledge and love;[69] what brings Kelsey closer to him is Aquinas's refusal to endorse fully the triad of memory, understanding, and will as the mirror in which the triune God can be seen.

Possibility for Engaging Catholic Theology

Although very much a concentrated exercise in Reformed systematic, we have seen that there is a modicum of engagement with Catholic thought in *Eccentric Existence,* negatively in the case of Rahner and positively in the case of Aquinas. Rahner, then, and to a lesser extent Aquinas, in significant respects define the actual engagement of *Eccentric Existence* with Catholic theology. But the more important question is, what are the possibilities of engagement? Needless to say, one asks this question with respect to all three inflections of the canonic narrative, and all three forms of Trinitarian taxis: the Father creating through the Son in the power of the Spirit; the Spirit, sent by the Father with the Son, drawing creatures to eschatological consummation; and the Son, sent by the Father, in the power of the Spirit, reconciling creatures.[70] One could, perfectly legitimately, stick to the first inflection of the canonic narrative and the first Trinitarian taxis and explore what is available in Catholic theology to deepen the conversation. It seems to me, however, that the greater good is served if one opens up lines

68. Kelsey, *Eccentric Existence,* pp. 272-78.

69. See especially Rahner's constructive account of Trinitarian economy in part three of *The Trinity.*

70. Kelsey, *Eccentric Existence,* p. 122.

of communication with forms of Catholic theology that represent one or other of the other inflections of the canonic narrative and one of the other two Trinitarian taxes. I select Hans Urs von Balthasar as an interlocutor, despite the fact that, as far as I am aware, there is not a single mention of Balthasar throughout Kelsey's two substantial volumes.

The general reasons for selection are easily stated: (i) Balthasar is a Catholic theologian with vast sympathies for Barth's uncompromisingly Christocentric theology and a well-publicized antipathy toward Rahner's transcendental program and fundamental theology in general. (ii) Throughout his vast triptych of *Glory of the Lord, Theo-Drama,* and *Theo-Logic,* the Christological center of the divine relation to the world and to human being has the triune God as ultimate horizon. (iii) Balthasar is intentionally a biblical theologian in the way few modern and/or contemporary Catholic theologians are. (iv) For Balthasar, the passion, death, and resurrection of Christ defines our ultimate context. This means that essential dialogue is between Balthasar's thought and part two of *Eccentric Existence.* (v) Even if the center of gravity in Balthasar's theology is incarnational in the broad sense deployed by Kelsey to include the passion, death, and resurrection of Christ,[71] Balthasar has very interesting things to say about consummation that rhyme in significant respect with Kelsey's articulation in the second part of volume one. I would like to draw out more extensively the affinities between *Eccentric Existence* and Balthasar's triptych on all these points, while also pointing to areas of tension, even if none of these tensions fundamentally deconstruct something like a shared space.

I begin with the overlap between Kelsey and Balthasar on the point of theological method. Formally, *Eccentric Existence* represents a type of non-apologetic apology, since it does not seek some neutral point outside of theology to mediate it to the broader culture and give credibility to its claims. In this sense, Kelsey's theology is in general line with the Reformation and more proximally in line with Barth, who rejected the drift of Protestant thought in the apologetic direction. To the extent to which *Eccentric Existence* decidedly favors Barth over Liberal Protestantism, Kelsey also is in line with his Yale colleagues, Frei and Lindbeck. Of course, for Kelsey, this does not mean that theology is hermetically sealed. Theology can and will engage in ad hoc apologetics; it will borrow from other disciplines to give a credible account of itself while being

71. Kelsey, *Eccentric Existence,* p. 609.

careful not to allow the borrowed items to dictate terms to theology. We suggested in section one, however, that Kesley is, arguably, more permissive than Barth and somewhat less permissive than Schleiermacher of the *Glaubenslehre* when it comes to borrowing from the discourses of culture. The relation between *Eccentric Existence* and Balthasar's triptych is close here. The triptych is self-consciously non-foundationalist, and it is obvious that from the beginning that Barth provides the clearest contemporary example of a way to do theology that does not end up in the apologetic cul de sac.[72] Here Balthasar's Barth book is pivotal,[73] since it shows the extent to which Catholic theology can reform itself in the light of Barth's non-foundationalism. Nonetheless, the modification has limits. One of these limits is set by Barth's highly negative view of the *analogia entis,* which, after his mentor Erich Przywara,[74] Balthasar thinks is based on a misunderstanding. On Balthasar's account, properly understood, the analogy of being does not function to set alien terms for theology that necessarily should have a Christological center and a Trinitarian horizon, but rather indicates that (i) the space of interlocution is much more extensive than Barth allows; and (ii) that practices and discourses that belong to culture enjoy a relative measure of integrity even as everything is ordered toward Christ. On the basis of what I said in section one, Kelsey could agree with (i) while leaving open (ii), for the real question would turn out to be how relative in the last instance is "relative" and what are the dangers of re-inscribing a fundamental theology?

We have spoken to the unique way in which *Eccentric Existence* elaborates a Trinitarian theology focused on, but not reducible to, the economy. It would be unrealistic to think that with theologies that have different confessional backgrounds and very different overall aims, they would match in every detail. One can stipulate a gross overlap between Kelsey and Balthasar with respect to Trinitarian conspectus to the extent to which both differ from Rahner and operate in a fundamental way in terms of premodern Christian grammar. Aquinas could function here a means of triangula-

72. See Hans Urs von Balthasar, *The Glory of the Lord,* vol. 1: *Seeing the Form,* trans. Erasmo Leivà-Merikakis (San Francisco: Ignatius Press, 1982).

73. Hans Urs von Balthasar, *The Theology of Karl Barth,* trans. Edward T. Oakes, SJ (San Francisco: Ignatius Press, 1992).

74. Throughout *The Theology of Karl Barth,* Balthasar argues that Barth's dismissal of Przywara's articulation of *analogia entis* is based on a misunderstanding. The analogy of being must be enfolded into the *analogia fidei* and enrich it. One can see that the entire trilogy represents a performance of this basic insight.

tion. But as a matter of fact Kelsey and Balthasar do overlap on a number of important points on Trinitarian schematization in excess of what can be adduced by availing of Aquinas to mediate. Here I will draw attention simply to a few examples of overlap in detail. In Balthasar — especially in volumes four and five of *Theo-Drama* and volumes two and three of *Theo-Logic* — the Trinity is not only encompassing, but absolutely regulative, with respect to other doctrines including theological views of the individual person and the community.[75] Again, similar to *Eccentric Existence,* Balthasar in the very same texts insists that all three persons of the Trinity are agential in each particular act of the economy, but that economic relations have to be thought of as grounded in relations in the immanent Trinity.

In addition, no less than in the cases of Kelsey and Barth, Balthasar is convinced that Trinitarian theology cannot do without a doctrine of election, although by the same token election cannot do without a strong sense of divine graciousness and delight in bringing into being and preserving what is other than the triune God. Thus, as one reflects on the triune God, given in gratuitous creation and solicitous preservation, this God is not best thought of by means of attributes such as omnipotence and omniscience, but rather of glory and holiness.[76] The root of the agreement between Kelsey and Balthasar is the attention they both give to scriptural language and how they honor its grain of sense. In Balthasar's articulation of theological aesthetics, glory and holiness are crucial ascriptions of God in Hebrew Scripture.[77] Interestingly — given Kelsey's elective affinity with Wisdom literature — for Balthasar, glory and holiness are as important in Wisdom literature as they are in the Pentateuch and the prophetic literature.[78] Obviously, in both theologies divine glory and holiness are refigured in the incarnation,[79] as this is rendered in Gospel narratives. Relatedly,

75. Hans Urs von Balthasar, *Theo-Drama: Theological Dramatic Theory,* vol. 4: *The Action,* trans. Graham Harrison (San Francisco: Ignatius Press, 1994); *Theo-Drama: Theological Dramatic Theory,* vol. 5: *The Final Act* (San Francisco: Ignatius Press, 1998); *Theo-Logic,* vol. 2: *Truth of God,* trans. Adrian J. Walker (San Francisco: Ignatius Press, 2004); *Theo-Logic,* vol. 3: *The Spirit of Truth,* trans. Graham Harrison (San Francisco: Ignatius Press, 2005).

76. Kelsey, *Eccentric Existence,* p. 77.

77. For Balthasar, see especially *Glory of the Lord,* vol. 6: *Theology: The Old Covenant,* trans. Brian McNeil, CRV, and Erasmo Leivà-Merikakis (San Francisco: Ignatius Press, 1991), especially pp. 31-86.

78. Balthasar, *Glory of the Lord,* vol. 6, pp. 344-64.

79. Hans Urs von Balthasar, *Glory of the Lord,* vol. 7: *Theology: The New Covenant,* trans. Brian McNeil, CRV (San Francisco: Ignatius Press, 1989), pp. 33-76.

love turns out to be the dominant ascriptor with respect to the divine considered in and through the reconciliation between the triune God and estranged human beings, brought about in and through the saving act of Christ. In this respect *Theo-Logic* 2 very much parallels *Eccentric Existence* 2. Finally, there is a far from insignificant overlap between Kelsey's and Balthasar's respective eschatological Trinitarianism. It is important for Kelsey to point to the different narrative logics and different Trinitarian schematizations of consummation and reconciliation, while underscoring that the same agent is the subject of both narratives and Trinitarian schematizations.[80] Balthasar proceeds somewhat down this road in *Theo-Logic* 2 and *Theo-Logic* 3 by demonstrating both that the Spirit is always the Spirit of Christ and that the Spirit's agency is far from being merely a function of Christ's saving action.

That theology has to be biblical on pain of not being theology functions as an axiom for both theologians. Without Scripture it is impossible to be sufficiently theocentrically and Christologically concrete, and this means in turn it becomes well neigh impossible to articulate a theological anthropology. As already indicated, there is agreement regarding the regulative function of the canonic narrative, which is formed in and through an interpretive process of the Christian community over time. In the case of both there is not, nor can there be, a zero-sum game between Scripture and tradition. Still, this does not mean that Kelsey would grant the theological tradition the same kind of scope as Balthasar. Neither can there be any disguising vast differences in style of biblical interpretation nor quite different perceptions about what texts of Scripture function as pivotal. Balthasar's exegesis is edifying and occasional in a way that Kelsey's is not. And even if Kelsey's exegesis is hardly beholden in a significant way to historical-critical method, it is quite evident that the measure of his acquaintance with its interpretive practices is considerably greater than that of Balthasar and that his exegesis is far the more disciplined and sustained. The measure of respect Kelsey accords the Wisdom tradition is perhaps unparalleled in modern Protestant systematic theology, which makes Balthasar's basically favorable comments in *Glory of the Lord* 6 seem pallid by contrast. Nonetheless, the major difference between Kelsey and Balthasar concerns the relative status of the Synoptic Gospels and the Gospel of John.[81] In line with Frei, Kelsey argues that the Synoptic Gospels

80. Kelsey, *Eccentric Existence,* p. 608.

81. Kelsey, *Eccentric Existence,* pp. 635ff.

have priority in that they render the unsubstitutable identity of Jesus.[82] By contrast, the Gospel of John represents a set of "theological remarks."[83] In *Glory of the Lord 7,* however, Balthasar thinks it a matter of principle to insist on the interpretive priority of the Gospel of John over the various narrative renditions of the Synoptics.[84] The contrast should not be made absolute. The secondariness of the Gospel of John in *Eccentric Existence* is not intended to delegitimate it; nor is the interpretive primacy of the Gospel of John understood by Balthasar to render redundant the Gospel narratives, which do indeed render Jesus' personal identity as the one who is constitutionally obedient to the will of the Father.[85] Rather it interprets precisely this personal identity, for personal identity is not constituted by some metaphysical principle of individuation, but by call and response. Moreover, for both, the identity of Christ is not simply relatively unique, but absolutely incommensurable. It is this very identity that is essentially shared by all other persons.[86] Balthasar is not embarrassed to use participation language that Kelsey so scrupulously avoids. Still, with respect to a Christological specification of the unsubstitutionable identity of persons other than Christ, both make a considered appeal to the Pauline symbol of "in Christ" *(en Christo).*[87]

With this we have already moved to our fourth point of overlap, which concerns the role and function of Christ in the economy of salvation. In *Eccentric Existence* Christ is not a type of human consciousness, but God's gift of Godself to an alienated humanity.[88] The backdrop is

82. Kelsey, *Eccentric Existence,* pp. 632-35.

83. Kelsey, *Eccentric Existence,* p. 639.

84. *Glory of the Lord,* vol. 7, p. 10. Balthasar writes: "Our concern is to make a synthesis; therefore the last theology of the New Testament, the Johannine theology, will always be the vanishing-point towards which we are travelling." To maintain the plurality of voices, however, Balthasar goes on to add, "though all the theologies of the New Testament remain open both forwards (into the mediation of the church which can never be brought to its end) and upwards (to God)."

85. John 6:38 (I have come down from heaven, not to do my own will, but the will of him who sent me) is as crucial for Balthasar as it is also for Maximus the Confessor, who is the inspiration here. See *Glory of the Lord,* vol. 7, p. 323. Of course, Luke 22:42 (Not my will, but thine be done) is also important.

86. Kelsey, *Eccentric Existence,* pp. 695-98.

87. Kelsey, *Eccentric Existence,* p. 698. For Balthasar's clearest statement of the church being 'in Christ,' see *Theo-Drama: Theological Dramatic Theory,* vol. 3: *Dramatis Personae: Persons in Christ,* trans. Graham Harrison (San Francisco: Ignatius Press, 1992), pp. 223-50, especially pp. 245-50.

88. Kelsey, *Eccentric Existence,* p. 620.

ineluctably Trinitarian: Christ is the Son sent by the Father with whom he is in eternal relation.[89] It is Jesus who interrupts and changes in a fundamental way our condition, which is that of being totally out of sync with the triune God. Christ enters fully into our condition and becomes sin for us, and however we describe Christ's death from a logical point of view, this death really is an exchange in which Christ's death enables us to live again. As with all other aspects of his theology, Kelsey feels his theological obligations are best served by not over-explaining. The biblical view of exchange is supported and Anselm's atonement theory not ruled out of court, while at the same time not being regarded as necessary.[90] The Trinitarian dimension to reconciliation, Christ's taking on the entire human condition even death, and the drama of exchange are key points in Balthasar's most sustained Christological elaboration in *Theo-Drama* 4.[91] Of the two, Kelsey is the more restrained, since he does not commit himself, as Balthasar does, to Holy Saturday, and probably would think that one could only do so by ignoring that there are two lines of completion in the Synoptic Gospels, the one that ends with the cross, the other that ends with resurrection.[92] Kelsey would likely quarrel also with Balthasar's projection of kenosis into the immanent Trinity. While the concept of Trinitarian mystery involves much more than an admission of epistemic humility with respect to describing the triune God, it involves no less.

Thus far, I have confined discussion of the strong overlaps between Balthasar and Kelsey to the reconciliation inflection of the canonic narrative and the Trinitarian taxis of the Son being sent by the Father in the power of the Spirit. But there is also a far from insignificant overlap when it comes to the consummation inflection of the canonic narrative and the Trinitarian taxis of the Spirit sent by the Father with the Son. First, as a matter of theological method, however much reconciliation and sanctification/consummation are distinguished, Kelsey admits a point that *Theo-Drama* 4 & 5 and *Theo-Logic* 2 & 3 perform, that is, a close connection between reconciliation and consummation is inevitable in theological articulation, even if neither is reducible to the other.[93] Second, when

89. Kelsey, *Eccentric Existence,* p. 618.

90. Kelsey, *Eccentric Existence,* pp. 642-46.

91. Balthasar, *Theo-Drama,* vol. 4, pp. 240-44 (New Testament), 255-61 (Anselm), 284-90 (Luther).

92. Kelsey, *Eccentric Existence,* pp. 620-21.

93. Kelsey, *Eccentric Existence,* p. 608.

Kelsey characterizes the Spirit as "obscure,"[94] he is saying something in excess of the attribution of "mystery" that applies to all three Trinitarian persons and their relations. The way in which the Spirit is given, that is, as subtly enveloping and empowering, or in Kelsey's language "circumambiently," means that one is denied even the kind of apparent fix that one might assume to have with regard to the Father and Son. Or in the language of the text: In contrast to the Father and the Son, in the case of the Spirit there is no identifiable Thou.[95] In *Theo-Drama* 5 and *Theo-Logic* 3 Balthasar sponsors an equivalent to Kelsey's "obscure" when he considers the mode of givenness of the Spirit as that of incognito, and he articulates an equivalent to "circumabient" when he speaks of the Spirit operating subjectively rather than objectively as in the case of the Father and the Son.[96] Although a copious book, *Eccentric Existence* is characterized by considerable discretion. Kelsey refuses to explain the superadded obscurity by appealing to the conditions in the immanent Trinity, which have to do with the specific hypostasis of the Spirit. With Bulgakov as a precedent, Balthasar makes suggestions as to what has to be the case at the level of the immanent Trinity,[97] even if these suggestions are best understood to be probative rather than categorical.

A third strong point of overlap is the positive way both theologians speak about apocalyptic. Kelsey is unembarrassed by the discourse of apocalyptic or apocalyptic rhetoric, which, he believes, finds broad expression in the Synoptic Gospels and in Paul.[98] Kelsey is not only siding with Ernst Kasemann over Rudolf Bultmann about the centrality of apocalyptic in the Bible in general and the New Testament in particular, but he is suggesting the necessity of such symbolic and mythic language is due not only the difficulty of describing the eschatological state, but the difficulty of rendering the agency of the Spirit and of Christ. Balthasar is fairly distinctive among modern Catholic theologians in being well disposed toward apocalyptic as

94. Kelsey, *Eccentric Existence,* p. 456.

95. Kelsey, *Eccentric Existence,* p. 506.

96. Balthasar's most sustained treatment is *Theo-Logic, vol. 3,* which tries to strike a balance between admitting that the Spirit is a person and not simply an energy and underscoring the peculiarity of the manifestation of the Spirit, which precisely is not to admit figuration.

97. I explore this aspect of Balthasar's thought in detail in my *The Anatomy of Misremembering,* vol. 1: *Balthasar and the Specter of Hegel* (Chestnut Ridge, NY: Crossroad Publishing, 2014).

98. See Kelsey, *Eccentric Existence,* pp. 456, 484, 508, 514, 524, 530, 532, 534 *inter alia.*

a genre,[99] even as he recognizes well its drawbacks, which tends to suggest real confidence about what the eschaton and judgment look like. Where this can be seen most clearly is at the beginning *Theo-Drama* 4,[100] in which he argues for the theological importance of the book of Revelation, as it is continuous both with the Gospel of John, but also with the "little apocalypses" of the Synoptics and the apocalyptic tendencies of Paul. Nor is the valorization confined simply to *Theo-Drama* 4; it is especially prominent in *Theo-Drama* 5, Balthasar's great text of eschatological Trinitarianism. Here again, however, Balthasar exceeds Kelsey in his affiliation to apocalyptic and in a sense styles theodramatic theology as apocalyptic theology. For both, however, the apocalyptic incidence in Scripture, which at the very least has to be acknowledged as an inexpugnable aspect of Christian hope, is not a matter of discourse only. For Kelsey, between the "already" of the reconciliation of human beings enacted by the triune God in the passion, death, and resurrection of Christ and the "not yet" of accomplishment of eschatological blessing history is "morally ambiguous"[101] and conflictual.[102] This is a major point with Balthasar in *Theo-Drama* 4 & 5. Yet in these texts Balthasar takes it up a notch in suggesting that after Christ the agonism escalates.[103] The positive overlap with respect to apocalyptic in both cases — if we allow for less exigent and more exigent forms — has as its reverse side a rejection of the theologies of hope that are evolutionary in principle or in fact. In an interesting move, Kelsey appropriates Moltmann's distinction between *futurum* and *eventus*[104] — only the latter being truly apocalyptic — to make a point against progressive or utopian forms of eschatology, only subsequently to turn the distinction on Moltmann's own exercises in eschatology.[105] The attack against evolutionary simulacra of Christian apocalyptic eschatology is a recurring theme in the triptych

99. The "apocalyptic" genre of Balthasar's theology receives extensive coverage in part 4 of *The Anatomy of Misremembering,* vol. 1. There I also discuss Johann Baptist Metz as a Catholic apocalyptic thinker and compare and contrast him with Balthasar. For a synoptic account, see my *Theology and the Spaces of Apocalyptic* (Milwaukee: Marquette University Press, 2009), pp. 45-52 (Balthasar), 78-82 (Metz).

100. Balthasar, *Theo-Drama,* vol. 4, pp. 17-69.

101. Kelsey, *Eccentric Existence,* p. 484.

102. Kelsey, *Eccentric Existence,* pp. 488-89.

103. See *Theo-Drama,* vol. 4, pp. 21-22, 56-58.

104. Kelsey, *Eccentric Existence,* pp. 452-53.

105. Kelsey, *Eccentric Existence,* p. 502.

with Balthasar going full bore at the theology of hope, which compromises hope by inscribing the future of God in the future of human being.[106]

Concluding Remarks

In the classical Greek tradition, *epiprepei* is a word for averbal or non-verbal action, behavior, or disposition that is appropriate or "seemly," and has as its Latin analogue *convenientia,* which had a fruitful career in theology and especially medieval theology with figures such as Anselm and Julian speaking to the congruence of incarnation and the cross. I want to reiterate the overwhelming sense of seemliness and convenience regarding the appearance of a truly polyphonic text characterized by amazing erudition and theological tact. *Eccentric Existence* excites precisely the doxological stance of gratitude and praise, which is a key ingredient in its theological articulation. It is impossible to do justice to such a capacious book and quite so masterly a theological performance. Accordingly, in my reading I restricted myself to three main aims, with the first providing a base for the other two, which were simply different sides of the same comparative coin. The fact that *Eccentric Existence* has already received quite a bit of commentary did not entirely obviate the task of a relatively adequate description of the text. While I do not purport to have said anything particularly novel, I judged it important to underscore the ecclesially specific nature of *Eccentric Existence* and to point to the ways Kelsey appropriates and develops the Reformed tradition, whose theological grammar is tied in the closest possible way to an interpretation of the canonic biblical narrative. A key feature of Kelsey's appropriation is his critical vetting and mediating between different modern appropriations of the classical Reformed tradition. The influence of Barth is conspicuous enough, both in its shape and in much of its content, to admit the label of "Barthian," but only with provisos, since there is much of Barth with which Kelsey is not comfortable, including the pivotal doctrine of election, which provides the key measure of organization in *Church Dogmatics.* What is more surprising is that the influence of Schleiermacher can also be tracked in the text, although this Schleiermacher most decidedly is not of "experiential expressivist" vintage.

Notwithstanding the importance of proper description, the funda-

106. See, for example, Balthasar, *Theo-Drama,* vol. 5, pp. 168-75.

mental drive of the essay is to provide a basic sketch of the actual and possible conversation between *Eccentric Existence* and the Catholic theological tradition. In section two I tracked the text's explicit and implicit engagement with Catholic theologians with a view to isolating what Kelsey finds congenial or objectionable in some of its major figures. I limited myself to one negative and one positive examplar, Karl Rahner and Thomas Aquinas respectively. The range of comparison could be extended in both directions. Although it is not Kelsey's problem, Kelsey would not likely approve of neo-Scholasticism, which places excessive weight on natural reason and pays almost no attention to the Bible and its narrative. Accordingly, Kelsey would approve of the kind of reaction found in Henri de Lubac, as he would heartily approve the broad outlines of de Lubac's treatment of nature and grace. As observed in passing, Kelsey embraces much of Catholic Liberation theology, especially the variety that one finds exhibited in Gustavo Gutierrez. With respect to Rahner, it is worth noting that he is criticized not as a Catholic theologian, but as a modern theologian whose horizon of thought is basically anthropological. If the critique of Rahner is explicit, the affirmation of Aquinas's construal of creation and its Trinitarian backdrop is implicit throughout part one of *Eccentric Existence.* There is no claim of genetic dependence here, even if Kelsey is far from ignorant of Aquinas. It may well be Kelsey's embrace of a premodern theological sensibility, which is characteristic of Calvin, gives something of a halo effect with respect to a medieval such as Aquinas, since the differences between these figures may well be less than between the classical Reformed tradition and some of that tradition's modern instantiations. The second and complementary aspect of the comparative dimension of the essay wanted to enlarge on the actual conversations between *Eccentric Existence* and Catholic theology by thinking of the possibilities of such conversation.

Section three constructed one such conversation, that is, a conversation between *Eccentric Existence* and Hans Urs von Balthasar, which has deep affinities with the theology of Karl Barth. The stress fell mainly on the positive correlations between Kelsey and Balthasar with regard to Trinitarian theology and theological anthropology as they previously fell on the negative correlations between Kelsey and Rahner on the same topics. In making the positive correlations, I took care to note differences between these theologians as the other side of their agreements. Clearly, I could have done more. For example, more attention could be paid to an issue that begs treatment: To what extent do Christian confessions themselves function grammatically with respect to fundamental orientation? In particular, does *Eccentric Existence*'s Reformed theology encourage a strong view of the Christian community, but a weak view of the church? Does the text suggest a somewhat exemplarist view of the eucharist? Would Balthasar find Kelsey's views here congenial? And again, Kelsey's emphasis on the quotidian rhymes well with Reformed insistence on the holiness of everyday life, whereas Balthasar is not uncomfortable with the notion that there are in principle special Christian forms of life that are to be valued even as they secede from the everyday practices and forms of life of Christian subjects in community. Given similar commitments to a particular inflection of the canonic narrative and a similar antipathy to anthropological models of theology, confessional allegiances count in terms of what theological commitments are adopted and what theological emphases are exhibited. This should not surprise. But even with a fuller conspectus of what the conversation would look like when differences are requisitely taken account of is to be at the beginning. And this is just as it should be, given the richness of *Eccentric Existence* and the texts to which it is being compared, but also keeping in mind that the capacious instances of Reformed and Catholic theology are themselves expressions in real time of generative and capacious theological grammars, which makes them at once truly new without being in any real sense novel.

Eccentric Ecclesiology

Amy Plantinga Pauw

I have known David Kelsey since I was a young child, and it is an honor to contribute to a volume engaging his magnum opus *Eccentric Existence.*[1] As fellow Presbyterians with long connections to Yale University, we were for a time a part of the same local congregation. Theological formation in congregations happens in unsystematic and often nonverbal ways. Still, I am convinced that the theological learning involved in shared communal practices can have a profound and lasting effect on *subsequent* efforts at systematic articulation. Given the overlapping "boundaries of our habitation," I find it fitting to focus this essay on the doctrine of the church, with particular attention to Reformed ecclesiological traditions.

Eccentric Existence is a deeply ecclesial theology that says little in any direct way about the church. Its approach to theological anthropology recognizes the importance of particular social and cultural locations in framing basic human questions. The questions of what and who we are and how we are to be oriented in the world are inseparable from the narratives of the particular communities to which we belong. Christian understandings of the triune God and God's irreducibly complex relations to all else form the narrative structure in which *Eccentric Existence* asks and answers the basic anthropological questions. Kelsey's entire project is based on the assumption that there are communities who "live with the writings of canonical Christian Holy Scripture in the practices that constitute their

1. David H. Kelsey, *Eccentric Existence: A Theological Anthropology,* 2 vols. (Louisville, KY: Westminster John Knox, 2009). Subsequent references to *Eccentric Existence* will be given in the text with page numbers in parentheses.

common life of response to God" (9). Challenging the modern assumption that relationship to God is anchored primarily in individual consciousness, *Eccentric Existence* roots its theological inquiry in the common life of Christian communities of faith by exploring the logic of the beliefs that shape the practices of these communities. *Eccentric Existence* demonstrates the communal Christian practice of reading Scripture throughout and reflects at length on various other practices as they shape and exemplify Christian communal responses of faith, hope, and love. In these and many other ways, Christian communities of faith are at the heart of Kelsey's anthropological enterprise. Yet there is little explicit reflection on the church. There is no "turn to the ecclesial subject" so prominent in certain streams of contemporary theology.

This ecclesiological silence is surely not an accidental oversight on Kelsey's part, but rather a deliberate theological decision. Rather than speculating on the various reasons for this decision or proposing a more ecclesiocentric theological anthropology, the rest of this essay will, on a very modest scale to be sure, explore two possible ecclesiological trajectories from *Eccentric Existence*'s "triple helix" structure of God's creative, consummating, and reconciling relations with all that is not God. I will call these trajectories *wisdom ecclesiology* and *supralapsarian ecclesiology*. In developing them I adopt Kelsey's experimental tone: "try looking at it this way" (9). No doubt many other ecclesiological trajectories could be charted, and the ones I have followed in broadly Reformed directions could be traced in other ways. My aim is to show the fruitfulness of *Eccentric Existence*'s three-fold structure for opening up another systematic locus.

Wisdom Ecclesiology

Kelsey notes that the doctrine of creation has done remarkably little work in modern systematic theology (259). Nowhere is this truer than in ecclesiology. The church is comprised of creatures, of course, so the doctrine of creation necessarily functions as a background belief for ecclesiology. But ecclesiology has tended to center its attention on what makes Christians different from other creatures, and even on what makes them less creaturely! When it comes to God's modes of relating to humanity, the emphasis in ecclesiology has been almost all on reconciliation and consummation, with the West stressing the former and the East stressing the latter. The primordial and ongoing graciousness of God's creative relations to humanity is virtually ignored in theological reflection on the church. As John Webster has noted in another context, "A doctrine of the church is only as good as the doctrine of God which underlies it." He warns against settling for "a selection of those divine attributes or acts which coordinate with a certain ecclesiological proposal."[2] By eclipsing God's creative mode of relating, ecclesiology generally operates with a truncated doctrine of God, and this has unfortunate theological consequences.

The church is a community of creatures, and "being continuously related to creatively by the triune God is an essential property of what creatures are" (828). This essential property needs to leave some mark on ecclesiology, even if anticipating the consummation of creaturely life or witnessing to creaturely reconciliation in Christ is deemed to be at the center of the church's mission. Christian life is a material life; it is a way of enacting bodily life in community *coram deo.* According to Christian belief, no area or dimension of life is bereft of God's presence, and no arena of human life and endeavor — social, political, bodily, artistic — falls outside the purview of faith. The church is where whole human lives are brought before God, with all their creaturely needs and strengths. Ecclesiology needs to reflect what Dietrich Bonhoeffer called "the profound this-worldliness of Christianity."[3]

Canonical Wisdom literature receives a lot of attention in Part One of *Eccentric Existence,* because it represents a strand in Scripture that is not concerned with God's drawing all things to consummation or with reconciling creatures who have become estranged. There is no assumption in canonical Wisdom literature that human creatures are destined for eschatological blessing. While human sinfulness is acknowledged, there is no presupposition of some original state of human perfection from which persons have fallen, and the theological focus is not on God's deliverance of sinners. The horizon of Proverbs, Ecclesiastes, and Job is creation. These books reflect on humanity's ongoing relation to God in what Kelsey terms the quotidian — the ordinary, day-to-day network of life-giving and life-orienting relations with the physical world and with various human communities.

2. John Webster, "The Church and the Perfection of God," in *The Community of the Word: Toward an Evangelical Ecclesiology,* ed. Mark Husbands and Daniel J. Treier (Downers Grove, IL: IVP Academic, 2005), p. 78.

3. Dietrich Bonhoeffer, July 21, 1944, letter to Eberhard Bethge, in *Letters and Papers from Prison,* Dietrich Bonhoeffer Works, vol. 8 (Minneapolis: Fortress Press, 2010), p. 485.

Until rather recently, the Wisdom books were often viewed by modern Christian biblical scholars as stepchildren of the canon, awkward presences whose concerns were largely alien to the center of Israel's faith. As John Bright put it in the 1960s, "some parts of the Old Testament are far less clearly expressive of Israel's distinctive understanding of reality than others, some parts (and one thinks of such a book as Proverbs) seem to be only peripherally related to it, while others (for example Ecclesiastes) even question its essential features."[4] Bright's discomfort with canonical Wisdom literature is understandable. Missing from these books are key elements in Israel's salvation history which have in turn supplied the crucial link to the New Testament portrayals of Jesus and the church: the covenant with Abraham, the exodus from Egypt, the giving of the law, the stories of the kings of Israel, the exile and return, and prophetic promises for future blessing. Canonical Wisdom is concerned with what makes for creaturely flourishing in the present and in general, not with what sets God's people apart from others, both now and eschatologically. Also missing in canonical Wisdom is attention to cultic purity and correct worship: the focus of faith's expression is not the worshipping assembly but the ordinary daily settings of home, field, and marketplace. Given the usual assumptions and moves of Christian reflection about the church, it is hard to think of a part of Scripture with less ecclesiological promise.

However, neglecting canonical wisdom is an ecclesiological mistake. God's ever-present creative blessing is the pedal point of the church's communal life and vocation. The Wisdom books are important for ecclesiology because they call the church, as a community of human creatures, to respond to God's wise agency as Creator with trust and praise, and to pursue creaturely wisdom in its own life. These books present human beings as utterly dependent on God for their very breath, and yet marked, in John Thiel's phrase, by a "gifted worthiness."[5] Biblical wisdom affirms human strength and responsibility before God even in the midst of sin. It encourages the church in the "long and meaningful middle"[6] of God's providence to take up its creaturely vocation to wisdom for the sake of the flourishing of its own life and that of its fellow creatures. This human vocation to

4. John Bright, *The Authority of the Old Testament* (Nashville, TN: Abingdon Press, 1967), p. 136.

5. John E. Thiel, "Methodological Choices in Kelsey's *Eccentric Existence*," *Modern Theology* 27, no. 1 (January 2011): 6.

6. Joe R. Jones, *A Grammar of Christian Faith: Systematic Explorations in Christian Life and Doctrine,* 2 vols. (Oxford: Rowman & Littlefield Publishers, 2002), vol. 1, p. 259.

respond to God's generous providence with thanksgiving and to work for creaturely flourishing would logically remain even in the absence of God's relating to bring creation to consummation or to reconcile creatures when estranged. And it does not disappear in the presence of these other modes of divine relating. The church's creaturely finitude is a reason for "doxological gratitude" (333), not for embarrassment.

Kelsey outlines some troubling consequences of not giving creation logical independence in theological anthropology. Starting with human need for redemption, and thus with human weakness and failure rather than with creaturely goodness, encourages "a theological anthropological denigration of human beings and a correlatively utilitarian and functionalist trivialization of God's relating to human beings" (113). Anthropologies that locate human actuality in consummation rather than in creation threaten the conviction that human beings before their eschatological fulfillment have the dignity and deserve the respect of ends in themselves, and not merely as means to our own ends (904). An ecclesiology that eclipses God's relating creatively to human beings is prone to ecclesial versions of both these theological mistakes, and opens the door to ecclesial triumphalism and escapism.

Denigrating the gifted worthiness of human beings as creatures invites what Karl Barth called "ecclesiastical docetism."[7] Docetic ecclesiology shies away from affirming the fully human character of the church, on the supposition that the grace of God's presence somehow lifts the church beyond the limitations and ambiguities of ordinary creaturely life; it denies the "this worldliness" to which Bonhoeffer called the Christian community: "living fully in the midst of life's tasks, questions, successes and failures, experiences, and perplexities."[8] An ecclesiology that neglects God's creative relating to the church in order to emphasize reconciliation can be tempted to demonize indigenous or secular culture by portraying human beings as worthless sinners in need of the church as the sacred site of God's redemptive power. An ecclesiology that emphasizes consummation to the neglect of God's creative relating can be tempted to portray the church as the community where God's eschatological blessing is already present in fullness, for example as a society of total peace in a conflict-ridden world.

Another dimension of ecclesiastical docetism can be seen in what

7. Karl Barth, *Church Dogmatics* IV/1 (Edinburgh: T&T Clark, 1956), p. 653.

8. Dietrich Bonhoeffer, July 21, 1943, letter to Eberhard Bethge, in *Letters and Papers from Prison,* p. 486.

James Gustafson has called "sociological reductionism" in Christian reflection on the church.[9] To affirm that the church is a creaturely reality means on the one hand to affirm that the church is intrinsically oriented toward the triune God, the source and sustainer of all creaturely life. The church is gathered and upheld by God and is called to serve God's creative purposes in the world. It means on the other hand to affirm that the church is an appropriate subject of historical and cultural analysis, patient of approaches that are used in examining other forms of human community. Kelsey makes a parallel claim about anthropology: "the internal logic of a Christian theological anthropology requires it to be open to conversation with and learning from atheological wisdom about what it is to be human" (6). To view the church as a field of the special presence and activity of Christ and the Spirit neither diminishes the church's creatureliness nor withdraws it from the realm of ordinary human processes. But ecclesiology has generally neither provided much conceptual space for social scientific analysis of the church, nor acknowledged the extent to which Christians have always theologized about the church with the moral and political tools their larger culture gives them.

Gustafson mostly portrays sociological and theological approaches to the church as parallel, not intersecting: sociological analysis of the church is affirmed as a complement to theological reflection on the presence of Christ and the Spirit in the church. He comes closer to a wisdom ecclesiology when he comments that his method is not to "move from the less theological to the more theological." "Perhaps," he muses, "God acts through the very processes of Church life that can be interpreted from the point of view of social theory."[10] Affirming God's creative relating to the church means that historical and sociological analysis of the church is an essential ingredient in any *theological* account of its reality. The ultimate context for the church as a community of creatures, as it is for all human communities, is God's ongoing creativity; the common life of the church is one of the proximate contexts in which God sustains and nurtures human persons in their concrete actuality. To analyze the church, as Gustafson does, as a human community, a natural community, a political community, and so forth, is also to reflect on a dimension of its God-relatedness.

Despite Barth's warnings about ecclesiastical docetism, he shared a

9. James Gustafson, *Treasure in Earthen Vessels: The Church as a Human Community,* 3rd ed. (Louisville, KY: Westminster John Knox, 2009), passim.

10. Gustafson, *Earthen Vessels,* p. 13.

wide ecclesiological reluctance to affirm the church's identity as a concrete, thoroughly historical community alongside other faith communities. Barth was concerned to disassociate the church from "all ideas of other human assemblies and societies which have come into being." Unlike other communities, which exist by nature or historical human decision, Barth insisted that the church exists uniquely "as a divine *convocatio*."[11] This theological move is ruled out by a wisdom ecclesiology. Even if one agrees with Barth that the distinctive purpose for which God has gathered the church is to be a witness to the reconciliation of the world as it has taken place in Jesus Christ (a debatable position, as the next section of this essay will argue), it does not follow that the church has no sociological commonalities with other communities. "Nature" and "historical human decision" are constitutive elements in the church's common life. Nor does it follow that the activity of "divine *convocatio*" is restricted to the church. According to a wisdom ecclesiology, it is part of the church's divinely given vocation to exist and work side by side with "other human assemblies and societies," like them to aim at "doing the relatively better relatively well"[12] in contributing to creaturely flourishing. As Thomas Merton insisted, "Our Christian calling does not make us superior to other [people]. . . . Our job is to struggle along with everybody else and collaborate with them in the difficult, frustrating task of seeking a solution to common problems, which are entirely new and strange to us all."[13] Part of the church's vocation is to share a vocation with others.

This essay has argued so far that a wisdom ecclesiology is needed as a complement to ecclesiological emphases on reconciliation and consummation to thwart Christian temptations to triumphalism, escapism, and the denigration of creaturehood. Thankfully, there has often been a disconnect between the church's practices and its ecclesiological self-understanding, with the former often surpassing the latter in affirming the blessing of finite creaturely life. However imperfectly, Christians have devoted themselves to the flourishing of creaturely life by feeding the hungry, tending the sick, and teaching the unlearned. In more recent times Christian communities have banded together with other communities of faith to address problems too big for any single faith tradition to handle, such as ecological degra-

11. Karl Barth, *Dogmatics in Outline* (New York: Harper and Row, 1959), p. 142.

12. Karl Barth, *The Christian Life: Church Dogmatics* IV/4: *Lecture Fragments* (Grand Rapids: Eerdmans, 1981), p. 271.

13. Thomas Merton, *Faith and Violence* (South Bend, IN: University of Notre Dame Press, 1968), pp. 142-43.

dation, poverty, and violence. The enormous medical, educational, and relief mission enterprises of the church are, despite their shortcomings and ulterior motives, enactments of Christian convictions about the goodness of finite creaturehood. Within their local fellowships, Christians have also affirmed the creaturely goodness of their common life: They have broken bread together, cared for each other in times of need, and mourned each other's deaths. Christian communities have done all these things, at least in part, as a faithful response to God's gift and sustenance of finite creaturely life. They have viewed neglecting or resisting these forms of creaturely care as a serious failing, highlighted in Jesus' parable in Matthew 25:31-46. Even when their ecclesiologies accounted for the existence and purpose of the church almost solely in terms of human salvation and glorification, Christian communities have cultivated practices that enact and affirm God's ongoing relations to the world as Creator. The communal practices of wonder, delight, and perseverance that Kelsey lifts up as appropriate responses to God's call to be wise for the well-being of the quotidian (345-54) have in fact characterized the church's life with some regularity. That is to say, the practices of Christian communities have in general reflected a more full-orbed doctrine of God than their formal ecclesiologies.

This inconsistency is not altogether surprising, because gaps between Christian belief and practice seem to be a steady-state feature of the church's life. In fact, the vigor of some Christian practices may be threatened by too much theological precision. As Kathryn Tanner notes,

> the more diverse the social group organized around such practices is (especially a community, such as the church, oriented around the ideal of universal membership), the greater is the pressure to keep the beliefs and value commitments involved in such practices undeveloped, ambiguous, or many-sided. In that way, the actions of participants remain coordinated . . . despite the fact that the participants do not precisely agree on what they are doing, or why.[14]

Practices such as feeding the hungry do not require much reflective depth in order to function. Some devoted Christians no doubt undertake such wise actions for the sake of creaturely flourishing simply "because Jesus

14. Kathryn Tanner, "Theological Reflection and Christian Practices," in *Practicing Theology: Beliefs and Practices in Christian Life,* ed. Miroslav Volf and Dorothy C. Bass (Grand Rapids: Eerdmans, 2001), p. 230.

did it." Others may justify the church's attention to creaturely flourishing as a means to what they regard as the proper ecclesiological ends of proclaiming and participating in God's reconciliation or consummation of humanity. For example, the rationale may be that hungry people cannot hear the gospel of God's reconciliation in Christ, so the church needs to feed them first; or, that orphans need the church's loving care in order for the divine goal of their creaturehood, eschatological consummation, to be actualized. However, the church's responses to the distinctive ways in which God relates to all else need not and should not be mutually exclusive. Feeding the hungry can be at once the church's wise response to a common human need, a public, bodily enactment of neighbor-love that proclaims human reconciliation in Christ (cf. Rom. 12:20), and an anticipation of the eschatological banquet at which all will be fed, because the unjust structures that perpetuate hunger will have been overcome.

Christian communities of faith will no doubt muddle along theologically while continuing to feed the hungry, and it is all to the good that the church does not wait until its self-understanding is clarified and well-ordered before it proceeds with its mission. Yet that does not mean that reflection on the church's creaturely relation to God is unimportant. A defective doctrine of the church suggests a defective doctrine of God. Moreover, ecclesiological defects such as docetism and theological denigration of creaturely life can have devastating practical consequences in the church. A full-orbed ecclesiology is practically as well as theologically beneficial. As David Cunningham notes, "without occasional attempts to devote some sustained thought to the meaning and significance of a particular Christian belief, the practices that embody that belief can become hollow, insignificant, and ultimately unpersuasive — even to those who undertake such practices with diligence and love."[15]

In developing a wisdom ecclesiology, the Reformed tradition's unsentimental realism about the church and its consequent searching for "an earthly form that takes into account as much as possible human infirmity and weakness"[16] is a good place to start. According to Reformed understanding, the church is not an island of heaven in the sea of earthly reality, but an earthen vessel (2 Cor. 4:7). As James Gustafson unpacks

15. David S. Cunningham, *These Three Are One: The Practice of Trinitarian Theology* (Oxford: Blackwell, 1998), p. viii.

16. Karl Barth, *The Theology of the Reformed Confessions* (Louisville, KY: Westminster John Knox Press, 2002), p. 105.

this Pauline phrase, it means two things: "The Church is *earthen* — of the stuff of natural and historical life. The Church is a *vessel,* it is useful."[17] The church is useful and valued by God precisely in its earthen character, not in spite of it. In the church, therefore, it is to be expected that ordinary human dynamics and limitations will be on full display.

This expectation is reflected in the cheerful Reformed acceptance of the inevitability of ecclesial conflict. "There have at all times been great contentions in the Church," declared the sixteenth-century Reformed pastor Heinrich Bullinger, "and the most excellent teachers of the Church have differed among themselves about important matters." Rather than repent of this fact, Bullinger confidently concluded that "it pleases God to use the dissensions that arise in the Church to the glory of his name, to illustrate the truth, and in order that those who are in the right might be manifest (1 Cor. 11:19)."[18] Internal ecclesial argument is not only a consequence of our sinfulness, as if there were some earthly place beyond conflict and contention that sufficiently sanctified Christian communities eventually reach. The need for argument is also a consequence of our noetic limitations, the narrowness of our grasp of God's gifting presence. This acceptance of ecclesial conflict points not only to Reformed understandings of polity and ministry but also to an underlying aesthetic about the church. This ecclesial aesthetic is rooted in a conviction that all creaturely reality is a theater of God's glory. God's glory pervades our ordinary activities and relationships; it is to be sought in the whole of life, not in separate religious places and objects. The church is not a heavenly space walled off from the rest of creaturely reality, but an earthly place where the divine glory that is present everywhere is acknowledged and praised.

Bonhoeffer wrote hopefully in a prison letter to his fiancée that "Our marriage shall be a yes to God's earth; it shall strengthen our courage to act and accomplish something on the earth."[19] A wisdom ecclesiology reminds the church that in its affirmation of God's creative blessing it too is to be "a yes to God's earth," not simply as a means to some other end, but as part of its authentic faithfulness. The church remains an earthen vessel:

17. Gustafson, *Earthen Vessels,* p. xviii.

18. Heinrich Bullinger, The Second Helvetic Confession, in *The Book of Confessions of the Presbyterian Church* (U.S.A.) (Louisville, KY: Office of the General Assembly, 1991), 5.133, p. 127.

19. Dietrich Bonhoeffer, August 12, 1943, letter to Maria von Wedemeyer, in *A Testament to Freedom: The Essential Writings of Dietrich Bonhoeffer,* ed. Geffrey B. Kelly and F. Burton Nelson (San Francisco: HarperCollins, 1990), p. 512.

the promise of consummation and the good news of reconciliation accomplished in Christ do not diminish the joys or make easy the ambiguities of its earthly existence, nor do they make moot the church's calling "to act and accomplish something on the earth."

Supralapsarian Ecclesiology

One of the striking features of *Eccentric Existence* is its distinctive ordering of the three ways in which God relates to all that is not God: "God actively relates to us to create us, to draw us to eschatological consummation, and to reconcile us when we have become estranged from God" (8). It is an order that is alien to most Western ecclesiology. By adopting this pattern, *Eccentric Existence* makes clear that while God's relating to us in creation and consummation is primordial and unconditioned, God's relating to us in reconciliation is, as Kelsey (following Calvin) puts it, "adventitious"; it is conditioned by the reality of our estrangement (432). Even in the absence of our sinful creaturely resistance and estrangement, God would still relate to us in Christ to bring us to eschatological consummation. Human sin does not negate the unconditioned character of either God's creative or eschatological blessing. Kelsey's shorthand for this supralapsarian view of God's relations to us in Christ is "Incarnation anyhow" (612). The shorthand for this section of the essay could be "church anyhow." Since God's relation to us in Christ is not contingent on the absurd and terrible reality of human sinfulness, the church's existence is not either. "Incarnation anyhow," and therefore "church anyhow."

A supralapsarian approach to ecclesiology is at odds with the dominant tendency to infralapsarianism in Western reflection on the church, according to which the church is a dimension of the divine response to human sin. In the words of the sixteenth-century Scots Confession, the kirk is founded on the "joyful promise" made by God to Adam following "the fearful and horrible departure of man from his obedience."[20] The common logic behind currently popular "purpose-driven" and "missional" understandings of the church is "sin, and therefore church." The argument of this section is that this logic warps theological understandings both of the church and of God's creative and eschatological blessing.

20. The Scots Confession, in *The Book of Confessions of the Presbyterian Church* (U.S.A.) (Louisville, KY: Office of the General Assembly, 1991), 3.04, 3.05, p. 34.

The church exists because God has gathered it, not because of any task it has been given. As Kelsey clarifies, communities of Christian faith are not "constituted by a purpose for which they assemble or have been assembled" (13). Yet, "having been constituted by God, they understand themselves to be sent in mission in and for the world" (13). The wisdom ecclesiology outlined in the first section left open the question of the church's mission in relation to God's consummating and reconciling activity. The claim was simply that God's creative blessing and the vocation to respond to it are nonnegotiable dimensions of the church's life. "Church anyhow" makes the further claim that, however important the good news of God's reconciliation of sinners is to the church's actual life and message, God's relating to reconcile does not define either the church's existence or its mission. The church's larger mission is to witness to and participate in what God has done and is doing in Christ.

Ecclesiology, of course, cannot avoid taking sin into account. Sin distorts all dimensions of humanity's relationship to God, and affects what is required for consummation. Since eschatological blessing presupposes that those who are blessed are not estranged from God, God's faithfulness to the promise of eschatological blessing entails God's deliverance of humankind from estrangement. Given the reality of human sin, the stories of reconciliation and consummation need to be told in relation to each other. But there are ecclesiological dangers in failing to respect the integrity of each story in the process.

These dangers are well illustrated in my little corner of the Reformed tradition, the Dutch Reformed. The early twentieth century saw pitched theological battles, both in the Netherlands and within the Dutch immigrant communities of North America, over the logical interrelations of eternal divine decrees. As Herman Hoeksema put it, "what in those decrees is conceived as purpose, and what as means? What is the main object in those decrees, and what is subordinate and subservient to that main object?"[21] Herman Bavinck, in a theological approach parallel to Kelsey's, insisted on "the manyness . . . of the decree."[22] There was for him an irreducible multiplicity in God's purposes. Thus to a certain extent, he thought, Christian theology has to remain unsystematic, refusing to achieve a tightly unified narrative of God's modes of relating by wholly subordinating cer-

21. Herman Hoeksema, *Reformed Dogmatics* (Grand Rapids: Reformed Free Publishing Association, 1966), p. 164.

22. Herman Bavinck, *The Doctrine of God* (Grand Rapids: Eerdmans, 1951), p. 385.

tain divine decrees to others. As Bavinck put it, "the history of the universe can never be made to fit into a little scheme of logic. It is entirely incorrect to suppose that of the series: creation, fall, sin, Christ, faith, unbelief, etc., each constituent is merely a means toward the attainment of the next, which as soon as it is present renders the former useless."[23] However for Hoeksema and his allies, the eternal divine decrees do have a "main object," and that is the manifestation of God's glory in the salvation of some and the damnation of others. The story of sin and deliverance completely dominates their understanding of humanity and God's relation to human creatures. Accordingly, Cornelius Van Til, a longtime apologetics professor at Westminster Seminary in Philadelphia, categorized humanity in terms of the "great antithesis" between believers and unbelievers, a chasm that renders largely irrelevant their common identity as God's creatures and nullifies God's promise of eschatological blessing, except in the case of the elect few. Hoeksema and Van Til questioned the validity of the notion of common grace, doubting whether human vessels of wrath whom God has made for destruction can be said to be recipients of God's grace at all. Hoeksema firmly rejected the notion; Van Til, while not completely denying that all human beings were recipients of common grace prior to the final separation of the elect and reprobate, regarded common grace as an earlier, diminishing grace that will fade away to nothing at the last judgment, when God's perfect hatred towards the reprobate and special grace towards the elect are consummated.[24]

This industrial strength Calvinism has dire ecclesiological consequences. By making the reconciliation of the elect the "main object" of God's eternal purposes, to which all else is "subordinate and subservient," Hoeksema and Van Til's theology drastically and permanently compromises God's creative and eschatological relating to human beings. Indeed, in their view human sin occasions the eternal estrangement and punishment of most of humanity, striking a blow from which God's gracious purposes toward human creatures never recover. Their ecclesiology shrinks the cosmic scope of God's eschatological promises to a consideration of the ultimate blessedness of a small number of human individuals. Within their theological framework, the purpose of the church is to be a small reconciled remnant, a very partial remedy for the devastation caused by

23. Bavinck, *Doctrine of God,* p. 391.

24. Cornelius Van Til, *Common Grace and the Gospel,* repr. ed. (Phillipsburg, NJ: P&R Publishing, 1995), pp. 24-33.

human sin. The remnant is even smaller than the boundaries of the visible church, because being in the visible church is no sure indicator of being reconciled with God through Christ. What finally counts is being part of the invisible church, its membership past and present determined by God's special election. But membership in the invisible church is simply another way of denoting who is saved in Christ and therefore headed for consummation. The dogma *extra ecclesiam nulla salus* thus becomes a tautology in their ecclesiology. In the end, as Brian Gerrish notes, it seems that pastors in the visible church are called to be more benevolent than God, for not all who have been ardently preached to and prayed for were from eternity chosen by God as members of the invisible church.[25]

Milder infralapsarian views of the church put more theological weight on the visible church, recovering the Reformed insistence on the importance of the ministrations of earthly communities of Christian faith. But since sin is still the choke point that divides redeemed and unredeemed humanity, emphasis on the visible church creates an ecclesiological temptation to justify the existence of the church by shifting to what Kelsey calls "the logic of coming to faith." On this view, the visible church exists to assist the transition from unfaith to faith, a transition that all human beings need to undergo because of sin. By this ecclesiological logic, "the movement from outside to inside communities of Christian faith can be exhibited as the change in subjectivity that is precisely what one undergoes through the process of actualizing or constituting oneself as an authentic, flourishing subject" (85). From sacraments to evangelism, infralapsarian reflection on the church "becomes focused on and systematically structured by the practical problem of how to overcome human sin and make human beings morally acceptable" (118). This form of infralapsarian ecclesiology, like the strong Calvinist version, risks denying the goodness of humanity's common creaturehood, and relegating consummation to a largely individual, post-mortem condition.

A "church anyhow" supralapsarianism does not rule out a central place for the reconciliation of sinners in Christ in Christian communal self-understanding and mission. As Bonhoeffer insisted, given the reality of human sin, the church must be "precisely that community of human beings which has been led by the grace of Christ to the recognition of guilt toward Christ. To say, therefore, that the church is the place of the recognition of

25. B. A. Gerrish, *Grace and Gratitude: The Eucharistic Theology of John Calvin* (Minneapolis: Fortress Press, 1993), p. 171.

guilt is nothing but a tautology. If it were otherwise, it would no longer be the church."[26] However a supralapsarian ecclesiology is concerned that the church's proclamation of the gospel in the face of sin does not lead to reductionist views of God and triumphalist views of its own life. In particular, it seeks to avoid what may be called *trickle-down ecclesiology,* the notion that all God's relating to consummate and reconcile human creatures flows through the church.

A supralapsarian ecclesiology affirms that God relates to reconcile all humankind universally. It rejects what Barth ridiculed as "pious egocentricity" in reflections on the church, according to which Christians rejoice in being the recipients of an "indescribably magnificent private good fortune, permitting them to obtain and possess a gracious God, opening to them the gates of Paradise which are closed to others."[27] Instead, the church is that portion of humankind who know, witness, and celebrate the good news of God's reconciliation and promised consummation of all things. The reconciliation that Christians seek with God and neighbor is not bounded by the community of the church. As the church lives out the good news of God's reconciliation in Christ, the church's passionate desire for communion is not with a God defined as the "God of the church," but with the God who relates to the whole of reality other than God. The church "precisely as church" seeks solidarity as well "not just with fellow church members, . . . but with all estranged fellow human creatures" (719).

A supralapsarian ecclesiology also insists that "God relates to draw all that is not God to eschatological blessing" (484). The church is a vanguard of the life of the new eschatological age inaugurated by Christ's resurrection, a community where eschatological blessing is recognized and celebrated as God's promised future for all creatures. While eschatological blessing takes place in a special way in the church, it does not follow that the mission of God in the world is "limited to the more or less intimate, inter-subjective community of the church," nor that the Spirit is "primarily located in the church and is only in the wider world by derivation from the church" (482-83). The communal practices that celebrate the inauguration of eschatological blessing are not narrowly ecclesial practices: "Such practices are not restricted to what the [Christian] community does when gathered. . . . They are the community's practices, and they are enacted

26. Dietrich Bonhoeffer, *Ethics,* in *A Testament to Freedom: The Essential Writings of Dietrich Bonhoeffer,* p. 362.

27. Karl Barth, *Church Dogmatics* IV/3.2 (Edinburgh: T&T Clark, 1962), pp. 567-68.

communally, but they may just as authentically be enacted by society that is host to the community" (520). A supralapsarian ecclesiology, like a wisdom ecclesiology, affirms that the church's vocation is in part shared with other human communities.

As in the case of a wisdom ecclesiology, it is helpful to recall Reformed realism about the church. Christians cannot claim that in their communal life "there is no longer any not-yet" (583). The church lives on time borrowed from fully actualized eschatological blessing. Kelsey rejects "sentimental" communal practices (characteristic of "utopian sectarian churches") that identify a particular type of community of faith with "the triumph of God's eschatological kingdom" (583). Kelsey also rejects the "ecclesial ontology" proposed by Stanley Grenz, following John Zizioulas, for the way it reduces God's relating to a single narrative of actualizing eschatological consummation, and may suggest that the only actual human beings are those "in the *ecclesia* — that is, only 'Christians' " (904). Rather, Christian communities of faith understand themselves to be, in T. S. Eliot's words, "torn on the horn between season and season, time and time, between hour and hour, word and word, power and power. . . ."[28] Alongside other human communities, they stand awkwardly "at the juncture and overlap" between the old world and the new (488).

The church is not the end of the ways of God. As the Second Helvetic Confession acknowledges, God has always had friends in the world outside the commonwealth of Israel.[29] A supralapsarian ecclesiology, like a wisdom ecclesiology, declares that the church witnesses to and participates in something much bigger than itself, a giftedness and hope that far exceed its own vision and understanding. Both these forms of ecclesiology are eccentric, because they refuse to position the church at the center of Christian self-understanding. That place belongs to God.

28. T. S. Eliot, "Ash Wednesday," accessible at http://www.msgr.ca/msgr-7/ash_wednesday_t_s_eliot.htm.

29. Bullinger, The Second Helvetic Confession, in *The Book of Confessions of the Presbyterian Church* (U.S.A.), 5.137, p. 128.

A Trinitarian Grammar of Sin

Joy Ann McDougall

In his 1993 essay "Whatever Happened to the Doctrine of the Sin?" David Kelsey provided a dramatic interpretation of the sea changes that had swept over the doctrine of sin in twentieth century theology.[1] Having lost its traditional moorings in the doctrine of creation, the doctrine of sin, Kelsey argued, had not disappeared from sight as some suspected. Rather the doctrine had migrated elsewhere in contemporary theology, finding new doctrinal loci in which to drop anchor. In particular, sin had been reinterpreted in three distinct ways: as the distorted relationship to oneself and failed self-actualization in the theological anthropologies of Reinhold Niebuhr, Paul Tillich, and Karl Rahner, as pervasive distortions in socio-political structures and individual denial of divine liberation in political and liberation theologies, and finally as a "willful disrelatedness" to the resurrected Christ in Karl Barth's *Church Dogmatics*.[2] Each of these migrations of the doctrine brought seismic shifts in the conceptual shape of the doctrine, shifts that in turn had profound theological, political, and pastoral consequences.

For example, defining sin in terms of an individual subject's estrangement from herself rendered sin as a form of failed self-actualization. This

1. David Kelsey, "Whatever Happened to the Doctrine of Sin?," *Theology Today* 50 (July 1993): 169-78.

2. Kelsey, "Whatever Happened to the Doctrine of Sin?," p. 177.

This essay was originally published in *Modern Theology* 27, no. 1 (January 2011): 55-71 and is reprinted in a slighted revised version with permission.

approach had the advantage of relieving original sin from being a fate to which one is subjected and held unjustly responsible; at the same time it threatened to equate human finitude itself with the state of fallenness and to psychologize sin to such a degree that it dissipated one's objective guilt before God. So, too, the migration of the doctrine of sin to that of redemption and liberation led to a prophetic re-interpretation of the state of sin in terms of socio-political forms of oppression and of actual sin as the individual's refusal to oppose such oppression through concrete action. Yet, Kelsey reminded his readers, social and political analyses of sin also brought along with them significant risks. They could justify the use of violence to liberate the oppressed, or else utterly demonize the oppressor, not to mention place undue confidence in Christian communities' ability to discern with certainty the structural distortions in society. Third and finally, Barth's Christological proposal had the puzzling consequence of at once magnifying the objective reality of sin and its serious consequences, while at the same time declaring sin's consequences ultimately null and void in the resurrection. Rather than despair over her sinfulness, the believer strikes a tone of "cheerful hilaritas" as she goes about her everyday existence, living in confidence and gratitude that her sin is truly overcome.[3]

Written in measured tones, Kelsey's early essay was more a diagnosis of the theological state of play than a prescription of the best way forward for a contemporary account of sin. After weighing carefully all the options, he concluded his essay without siding conclusively with any of the new trajectories of the doctrine. Instead, he queried whether each in the end were not "too complexly dialectical" to have much practical import on the preaching, pastoral care, and catechetical practices of communities of faith.[4] Furthermore, Kelsey mused whether the real reason for the loss of a meaningful sense of sin-talk in contemporary faith was the demise of a notion of divine wrath without which sin-talk bore little serious existential hold on contemporary believers.

Eccentric Existence: A Theological Anthropology is Kelsey's long-awaited response to these seismic shifts in modern theologies of sin.[5] While he follows Barth's lead in lending his doctrine of sin a Christological core, Kelsey significantly expands his Reformed predecessor's vision

3. Kelsey, "Whatever Happened to the Doctrine of Sin?," p. 177.

4. Kelsey, "Whatever Happened to the Doctrine of Sin?," p. 178.

5. David Kelsey, *Eccentric Existence: A Theological Anthropology,* 2 vols. (Louisville, KY: Westminster John Knox Press, 2009). All future references to the work will appear in the body of the text abbreviated as *EE,* followed by volume and page number.

by developing a *Trinitarian* grammar of sin, one that at once critiques and also incorporates key insights from the other two twentieth-century trajectories into his account. Throughout Kelsey's guiding commitment is for a genuinely *theocentric* anthropology, that is, one in which God's dynamic relationships toward the world govern the constitutive features of what, how, and who we are as human creatures. On this point the author follows Calvin's lead in subordinating all claims about humankind to our claims about God (*EE* 1:8). For Kelsey, such theocentricity is implicit in the logic of Christian faith, which testifies first and foremost to the human creature's utter dependence on God for the gift of its existence. As finite creatures, human beings live what Kelsey dubs an "eccentric existence," one that finds its ground and goal outside itself in the gracious, self-donating triune life of God.

Kelsey takes his cue for his theocentric anthropology not only from predecessors in his Reformed tradition, but also from premodern theology, in which anthropology had no privileged locus of its own; rather, claims about the human person were "scattered among discussion of how God relates to all that is not God" (*EE* 1:29). What complicates the God-world relationship is that for Christians "the One with whom we have to do" is not singular but "a communion in community of three perichoretic hypostases," Father, Son, and Holy Spirit (*EE* 1:120). On this point, Kelsey directs his readers to the scriptural witness. Rather than telling a single monolithic story, the Scriptures depict a God who relates to us "in three complexly interrelated but distinct ways: to create us, to draw us to eschatological consummation and when we have alienated ourselves from God, to reconcile us" (*EE* 1:5). While God acts self-consistently in these three relations, each form of God's relating has its own distinctive telos that cannot be subsumed or conflated with the others. God's forms of relating indeed occur simultaneously, but these relations follow a certain logical order: "God's relating creatively to us is ontologically prior to and logically independent of God's drawing creatures to eschatological consummation and reconciling them" (*EE* 1:121). Stated differently, stories about God creating do not require the story of reconciliation or of consummation, or the graciousness of these latter relationships to us could not be sustained. So, too, the story of eschatological consummation and reconciliation are distinct but inseparable from one another, since both are "concretely enacted in the selfsame story of Jesus Christ" (*EE* 1:121).

If the triune God relates to humankind in three distinct but intertwined ways, Kelsey proposes there must be a corresponding threefold pattern to how human beings fail to respond appropriately to the manner in which God relates to them. These forms of inappropriate responses to God's agency constitute the myriad forms of human sin. While Kelsey is not after systematizing all varieties of actual sin in his work, he does devise an architectonic Trinitarian grammar of sin through which one can identify how human lives characteristically "miss the mark" of God's creating, consummating, and reconciling ways of relating to us. To trade on an image borrowed from his former teacher Robert Calhoun, Kelsey stakes out the "buoys that mark the channels of the deep" (*EE* 1:565), so as to assist his readers in identifying the nature and the concrete implications of humankind's distorted relations to the divine, and to help them to steer their lives through the power of the Spirit toward wise practices aimed at the well-being and flourishing of their fellow creatures along with themselves.

Even though Kelsey borrows loosely the structure for his theological anthropology from that of premodern theology, his approach is by no means antiquarian. On the contrary! A central mandate of Kelsey's work is to reform problematic aspects of premodern Christian theological anthropology, most notably its "value anthropocentrism" that elevates human beings at the expense of other aspects of creation and that prioritizes the "rational soul" to the neglect or denigration of the physical body (*EE* 1:30). Beyond these overarching correctives, Kelsey directs his reforming impulse most clearly toward the notion of a primeval fall into original sin. Given the lack of any scientific and historical evidence for a calamitous fall event, Kelsey urges that contemporary theological anthropology should break with tradition and forgo any such genealogical account of sin. If one wishes to affirm the notion of original sin as a pervasive and intractable human condition (which Kelsey surely does), one must reconstruct this notion on other grounds that are compatible to contemporary views of the origins of human existence, notions of moral responsibility, and personal identity formation.

In this essay I survey Kelsey's Trinitarian grammar of sin, highlighting how the dynamic patterns of God's agency toward the world provide coordinates to chart the appropriate responsive attitudes of the Christian life — faith, hope, and love, and their fundamental distortions — misplaced faith, hope, and love. I do so with two aims in view. First, I seek to demonstrate that Kelsey's hamartiology is focused not only on how human beings "miss the mark" in responding to the graciousness of God, but also on how these wrong responses are manifest in a host of destructive practices in their proximate contexts, that is, in violations of their neighbors, themselves, and the rest of creation. Rather than focusing on the interior psychology of sin, Kelsey sets his sights on how the distortions of sin become manifest in the public and social practices of individual Christians and communities of faith that fail to support the well-being of creation. In so doing, he provides a Trinitarian grammar of sin that seeks to inspire the formation of Christian identity and to guide persons of faith in a pattern of Christian life led on behalf of their fellow creatures in everyday life-situations. Second, I pose certain queries to Kelsey's language of sin and the work's theological style to signal areas where further development might be in order.

I. Sin as Misplaced Trust

Arguably the most original aspect of Kelsey's Trinitarian theology of sin is how he situates his doctrine within a newly refurbished doctrine of creation. Kelsey works tenaciously to overcome a tendency in modern theology to present the doctrine of creation in a "terminally abstract" manner that has little impact on the other dimensions of Christian theology (*EE* 1:160). Kelsey puts creation on more concrete footing by rooting it in the Wisdom literature (in contrast to Genesis 1–2), where he discerns a vibrant notion of "God's being present to creation in hospitable generosity, free delight and self-determining commitment" (*EE* 1:163).

Humankind's appropriate response to God's relating creatively is first and foremost the recognition that as finite creatures we live out of this glorious gift from God. We must acknowledge, writes Kelsey, that we are not self-made men and women, but we "live on borrowed breath" (*EE* 1:202). In the author's preferred terminology, our existence is *eccentric,* in so far as we are absolutely dependent on our triune Creator for our ongoing existence. Integral to our eccentric existence is that we are called to delight and take pleasure in what Kelsey refers to as the "quotidian" or our everyday world: "the society of creatures instituted by God's self-commitment to their being and well-being in kind" (*EE* 1:213).

Building on his theocentric approach, Kelsey structures his initial analysis of sin according to the threefold pattern of what, how, and who we are in relationship to God relating creatively to us. In simplest terms, sin appears as missing the mark of what, how, and who we are most truly created to be. Sin is a distorted response to God manifest in everyday evils that diminish the well-being of one's fellow creatures and oneself. Again and again throughout the pages of his work, Kelsey describes the sinner as an individual living "cross-grain" to him or herself, engaging in destructive and self-destructive practices that "inflict on the sinner a distortion of its life" (EE 1:412).

Rather than offering a catalogue of actual sins, Kelsey describes three existential "hows" through which human beings respond in a distorted fashion to the delight, wonder, and perseverance with which God addresses creation. For example, sin takes the form of a distorted delight that falsely idealizes one's fellow creatures and leads to a sentimental attitude toward them (*EE* 1:413). Similarly, sin manifests itself in distorted wonder, when fellow creatures are no longer respected in their "concrete particularity," but become "instances of stereotypes," be they racist, classist, sexist, or otherwise (*EE* 1:415). Finally, sin expresses itself in distorted perseverance, in which the quotidian is viewed in wholly negative terms as having no future. For some, this can lead to postures of resignation — for others to desperate measures of self-preservation; in either case the result is the same: one becomes "utterly indifferent to the well-being of the quotidian for its own sake" (*EE* 1:417).

Note that in each of these existential scenarios, Kelsey does not pinpoint a fundamental root or motive for sin, but keeps his eyes trained on the array of distorted relations that display our warped loyalty to the triune God. In so doing, he attests to the fact that sin's presence in the world ultimately defies all rational and genealogical explanation. Sin is and remains for Kelsey a "negative mystery," an intruder on the scene of God's good creation, an "ab-surd fact that cannot be factored into contributing causes, a surd all the way down" (*EE* 1:411). So, too, his analysis affirms the parasitic nature of sin. Sin is not a thing in and of itself, but feeds off the goodness of created reality. As such, sin does not destroy what we are, even when it disfigures our creaturely reality so that we become a "parody of that identity" (*EE* 1:422).

Kelsey's initial description of sin culminates in a portrayal of three archetypal forms of distorted personal identity. Although Kelsey himself doesn't invoke the term idolatry to describe the root of these distortions, each of these personal identities could aptly be described as succumbing to just that. The first distortion arises when some dimension of the quotidian supplants God as the ground of our reality and value. A second is the converse of the first: placing one's ultimate trust in God but without any loyalty to God's creaturely project. Here the distortion lies not simply in a lack of regard for one's ordinary circumstances, but that one ultimately trusts in "something other than the triune God" (*EE* 1:429). A third form of distorted personal identity rejects both trust in God and loyalty to God's creatures and has faith only in oneself. According to Kelsey, this distorted personal identity is "in bondage to the deepest self-delusion," namely, that through their own powers they can secure their own reality and value (*EE* 1:432).

Although this doesn't become explicit until the conclusion of Part One of *Eccentric Existence,* Kelsey upholds all the central features of the traditional notion of original sin with the crucial exception of the notion of an original (first) sin as a genetic account of how humankind came to be in this binding predicament. Kelsey affirms five other features of the classical doctrine of original sin. First, he defends sin's "adventitious" nature; it is an accidental rather than essential property of human creaturehood (*EE* 1:432). Second, Kelsey upholds the radical nature of original sin as a self-imposed bondage from which human beings are incapable of liberating themselves. Third, Kelsey defends the universality or solidarity of all humankind in sin; no one escapes the bondage of original sin. Here he replaces the traditional grounds for this claim, monogenism, with a social theory of the inheritance of sin. Every personal body is born into a morally ambiguous world. Fourth is humankind's personal guilt for sin, which Kelsey affirms but again in a qualified way. We do bear moral responsibility for sin, but only for those distortions that we incur ourselves through our participation in social practices with our fellow creatures. Furthermore, Kelsey questions whether guilt is the best term to describe the kind of violation that we perpetrate in our relationship with God and with our fellow creatures. Instead, he describes our status as one of "impurity before God" in order to highlight the objective consequences of sin when we live cross-grain to God's creative project (*EE* 1:436). The fifth and final feature of the classical doctrine of original sin that Kelsey upholds but in an ingeniously reconstructed way is that death gains a greater power over human existence than it otherwise would have. Note this is *not* to claim that the wages of sin are death, since death and mortality are inherent and natural features of our creaturely existence. Rather, sin lies in how mortality assumes an exaggerated and false power in our distorted personal identities.

II. Sin as Eschatological Hope Gone Awry

Kelsey's second analysis of sin appears in Part Two, "Consummate Living on Borrowed Time," and it trades on the same theocentric and relational structure that he introduced in Part One. Kelsey sets the stage by illuminating how the triune God draws creation toward eschatological consummation. Then he addresses "how we ought to be or live" (our existential how in appropriate response to this consummating agency); second, "who we are" (our identities as personal bodies as those elected for eschatological consummation); and third and finally, "what we are" as glorified creatures.

Kelsey describes the drawing of all creation to eschatological consummation as a work of the triune God, but one in which the Holy Spirit is the primary agent. Noteworthy is the author's emphasis on the Spirit as "circumambient" among human beings as a deliberate corrective to the modern tendency to privatize and atomize the Spirit's presence as interior to individual believers. What renders the Spirit's activity eschatological is that it relates to creation in the here and now as the triune God ultimately will in the end time.

While the Spirit takes the lead in drawing all things to eschatological consummation, it is the Son who lends this eschatological blessing its particular shape. Kelsey describes Jesus' resurrection as the "advent of promise," by which he means that in his bodily resurrection creation's promised eschatological blessing appears proleptically — ahead of time in history (*EE* 1:450). Critical here is that this promised future is not the fulfillment of possibilities inherent in the old creation, but rather the final judgment on and end to that history and the beginning of a new creation. This promise places human beings in the peculiar situation of living in the overlap between their own created time and that of eschatological blessing — what the author describes poetically as "living on borrowed time" (EE 1:480). For Kelsey, "living on borrowed time" is a potent expression of our personal bodies' eccentric existence — that our existence is ontologically grounded outside of oneself in the triune God's gracious gift of new creation.

In terms highly reminiscent of Barth, Kelsey describes the appropriate response to the Spirit's gift of new life as one of "joyful hopefulness" or "cheerful confidence" that what has already begun in the world, namely, "a good and desired transformation of our quotidian contexts" will "be fully actualized" (*EE* 1:502, 501). The social practices that witness to this eschatological communion are those that seek to liberate one's fellow creatures from oppressive power relations, be they based on economic, gender, ethnic, or other finite criteria. Note on this point Kelsey builds creatively on Barth's notion of the church as a parable of the kingdom, and incorporates into it new insights won from political and liberation theologians. Persons "living on borrowed time" join in "liberating movements of social change" not with the mistaken aim of ushering in the kingdom of God through their own actions, but rather as "signs of hope, parables of eschatological community-in-communion marked by justice and peace" (*EE* 2:1030).

If the posture of joyous hopefulness is the believer's appropriate response to the Spirit's drawing us to eschatological consummation, sin manifests itself as inappropriate or distorted responses to the Spirit's agency — what I term eschatological hope gone awry. Kelsey categorizes hope's distortions in two ways: distortions in how we respond to the "not yet of eschatological blessing" and distortions in how we respond to its "now," its present inauguration. Believers respond distortedly to the "not yet" of eschatological blessing when they invest themselves in a range of well-intentioned efforts to overcome injustices in the world, but they do so without any joyful recognition that God's eschatological blessing has already been inaugurated in the world. Note that human beings' distorted response to the "not yet" of eschatological blessing can just as easily assume a passive profile — a quietist waiting on one's eschatological blessing, seeking escape from everyday existence rather than in its transformation.

The pendulum of distorted eschatological hope swings just as easily in the opposite direction, manifesting itself in dispositions that are oriented toward the actual inauguration of the eschatological blessing in the here and now, and which disregard its "not yet" character. Here Kelsey charges that believers can become overly optimistic about their current state of affairs, expecting through their own exertions to realize the kingdom of God on earth. Such optimism turns very quickly to pessimism under the mounting pressures of the moral and ontological ambiguities of the quotidian (*EE,* 1:582). Here, too, Kelsey points to passive expressions of such distorted hope either in triumphalist accounts of communities of faith as manifestations of the kingdom come, or insofar as a person sentimentalizes her present circumstances and blinds herself to the numerous real injustices in her midst.

The personal fallout from eschatological hope gone awry appears as three distinct ways of living cross-grain to our basic personal identity. Each represents a self-imposed bondage to a false identity from which the individual is incapable of rescuing herself — in short, the condition of original sin. The first is a fundamental distortion of one's personal identity insofar as the person acknowledges her election *not* to eschatological consummation, but instead to a certain role in society — either of her own choosing or to which one has been assigned — and through which she seeks to accomplish social or cultural change. We live in bondage to such finite social roles, argues Kelsey, once our identities become dependent on their success or failure. The second is the converse of the first: a person acknowledges a positive judgment on herself, but without acknowledging her election to eschatological consummation. Here the person succumbs to a false optimism about her own proximate contexts and resources, again placing ultimate hope in these rather than in God's eschatological blessing. Kelsey describes this form of distorted personal identity as a "bondage to some theory about the dynamics of moral and social progress in history" (*EE* 1:599). The third type of distorted personal identity is one in which a person acknowledges God's election, but misconstrues it as a negative final judgment on herself and her proximate contexts. Rather than looking with cheerful confidence on the eschatological consummation already inaugurated in the resurrection, a person defines her identity negatively in terms of "the reality of the moral and ontological ambiguity of the creaturely here and now" (*EE,* 1:601).

III. Sin as Distorted Love to God and Love as Neighbor

Kelsey takes up the problem of sin for a third and final time in Part Three of *Eccentric Existence,* where he places it in a soteriological context as humankind's distorted response to God's reconciling humankind in the person and work of Jesus Christ. In contrast to the other two relations of creation and consummation, reconciliation is not a primordial or fixed relation that God establishes with creation, but one in which the triune God relates to us "in terms set by the resistance of creatures" (*EE* 2:607). Kelsey describes the Son's sending by the Father in the power of the Spirit as a responsive self-giving love that exceeds God's hospitable generosity in creating and consummating creation; it is God's "persistent generosity extended to those who resist and reject what God shares with them" (*EE* 2:621). This persistent generosity delivers us from our violent resistance with "a nonviolent resistance" that at once frees and judges us (*EE* 2:619). Here Kelsey sounds a familiar note about the nature of divine judgment. It does not entail a penalty or punishment of one's deeds, but rather a full and clear disclosure of our self-imposed bondage to sin. Confronted with the reality of God's grace, we understand most fully the depths and the foolishness of human sinfulness.

Kelsey describes humanity's reconciliation in the classical terms of a divine-human exchange: our estranged existence is exchanged for the Son's perfect relationship with his Father. Jesus enacts this exchange by entering into the endless vicious cycles of violence and oppression that human beings perpetuate and undergo, and embodies therein his perfect relation to his Father through interactions of perfect self-giving with other human persons (*EE* 2:642). While Jesus' solidarity with humankind begins with his incarnation, it culminates in the crucifixion, where God assumes the ultimate consequence of our estranged existence. Through cross and resurrection Jesus takes on the full consequences of our living death, Godforsakeness, and gives us in exchange a share in God's life of perfect giving and receiving. Through the work of the Holy Spirit we become the "adopted brothers and sisters of Jesus" (*EE* 2:699), and by participating in the Son's relationship to the Father, our estranged existence is set right within the communion of God.

Although Kelsey emphasizes the objective character of humankind's reconciliation in Christ, this does mean that the estrangement of our proximate contexts disappears from sight; indeed, our quotidian existence continues to be distorted by vicious cycles of violence and oppression that draw us inevitably toward disintegration. In classical Reformation terms, we exist in the quotidian as *simul justus et peccator,* at once justified and sinful.

The proper response to God's reconciling agency toward humankind is a twofold love to God and to one's fellow creatures, which indirectly reflects and witnesses to the divine agape manifest in Jesus Christ. If we are called to respond to God's reconciling our estranged existence through practices of love to God (primarily prayer) and love-as-neighbor, we plunge into sin whenever we exercise one of these loves in the absence of the other or simply conflate the two. To engage in practices of prayer to God without exercising love-as-neighbor is to "miss the mark" of Jesus' reconciling agency toward humankind with whom he has entered into solidarity and assumed the consequences of their estrangement. In other words, to sever love of God from that of neighbor distorts the persons who do so by breaking faith with the community of fellow creatures on whom they depend and who depend on them for their thriving and flourishing. To exercise love-as-neighbor in the absence of prayer is an equally distorted response to God's reconciling estranged humankind. Here one genuinely responds to the deep needs of one's fellow creatures but does so divorced from their ultimate context, the love of God. Without reference to their ultimate context, enactments of love-as-neighbor lack the right measure: "adequate basis for critical distance from other human creatures and for self-critical distance from their own enactors" (*EE* 2:855). An equally significant distortion of human love is one in which personal bodies conflate practices of prayer and of love-as-neighbor as if they were one and the same. When love-as-neighbor is equated with the practice of prayer, prayer loses its defining character as a response to the particular ways in which the triune God relates to humankind. Conversely, if practices of prayer become interchangeable for love-as-neighbor, one's fellow creatures and their concrete needs actually disappear from sight.

Finally, Kelsey characterizes three archetypal ways in which personal identities become distorted through a false construal of what makes their life worth living. First, human beings can distort their self-identity by denying altogether that they are in need of reconciliation or forgiveness. This leads to a host of different strategies of self-justification of one's worth, for example, by seeking to exercise power over others or else by demonstrating some form of "superior conformity to a moral social order" (*EE* 2:867). A second form of distorted personal identity emerges when human beings genuinely recognize at some level the need for structural reconciliation in their finite contexts, but treat reconciliation as a "wholly future" goal to be achieved by social, political, or cultural movements in human history rather than something already accomplished through God's actions (*EE* 2:875). Here one builds one's worth on the basis of active engagement in social and cultural movements that are expected to remedy the estrangement of the proximate world. A third form of distorted personal identity occurs when a person recognizes the call to practice forgiveness, but does so without recognizing that structural reconciliation is already a gift guaranteed by God. As a result, such persons seek to earn their self-worth through their own moral actions: "who I am, who we are is constituted by our doing what we morally ought to do, including forgiving my enemies" (*EE* 2:882). The common denominator in all three distorted forms of personal identity is a form of works-righteousness: the futile effort to justify the worth of one's life by fulfilling the good works of the moral law.

IV. Contributions and New Frontiers: Where do we go from here?

As has become evident from my detailed parsing of Kelsey's Trinitarian grammar of sin, *Eccentric Existence* has an extraordinary scope. In its pages, one discovers a tremendously complex and analytically rich description of the predicament of sin and one that is etched across nearly the full length of his more than thousand page work. This makes distilling Kelsey's theology of sin — not to mention assessing it — no easy task! That notwithstanding, let me conclude by identifying three contributions of Kelsey's proposal for the doctrine, and by raising three clusters of questions and critical observations intended to spark further debate.

The first major contribution lies in the originality with which Kelsey develops the foundational claim of his work, namely, to have his Trinitarian concept of God govern the various claims of his theological anthropology. While one can easily name a host of different theologians who purport to have their doctrines of the Trinity substantively structure their theological anthropologies (e.g., Pannenberg, Moltmann, LaCugna, Grenz, to name just a few), Kelsey is unparalleled in rigorously pursuing how the distinctive patterns of the Trinity's agency in the world illuminate the distorted ways in which human beings respond to their God, themselves, and the world around them. One positive consequence of this Trinitarian approach is that it drives home the way in which sin affects human lives *in toto*. Sin is not a denial of one singular aspect of God's creative, providential, or reconciling activity or else a failing or defect to be lodged in a particular faculty of creatures. Rather, it is living cross-grain to God's dynamic intentions that penetrates the depths of human existence, twisting all of our faculties, actions, and practices — how we interact daily with our fellow creatures, how we understand God's election and judgment operative in our lives, and how we understand the reconciliation accomplished through Jesus' life, death, and resurrection.

A further positive consequence of Kelsey's rigorous Trinitarian approach is that it enables him to sustain a clear conceptual distinction between the problem of sin and moral evil; sin is an inappropriate response to God's creative, consummating, and reconciling agency toward us, while moral evils are violations of other creatures' integrity that fail to support their well-being. Note that while Kelsey insists on this categorical difference between sin and moral evil, he does not succumb to a perennial temptation that I often detect in theocentric approaches, namely, to have an individual's alienation from God loom larger than the particular ways in which human beings do violence to one another. Instead Kelsey logically interweaves the realities of sin and moral evil in such a way that the ways we are called to respond to the triune God in faith, hope, and love include per definition ways of living in and responding to one's proximate context properly. So, for example, faith requires that we live in our proximate contexts trusting God as the ground of our being and value, and expressing loyalty to God's project with creation. While God may alone ground our identity, the very nature of that God, a God who delights in the well-being and flourishing of all creatures, calls us to respond in wise practices for the well-being of the quotidian. To do otherwise is not only to violate the dignity of one's fellow creatures, but to distort one's faith in God.

A second key contribution of Kelsey's theology of sin is that it provides a fundamental course change from modern theology's anthropocentric paradigm of sin as an individual's estrangement from oneself. As I have highlighted earlier, Kelsey challenges the starting-point of modern theological anthropology, namely, that relationship to the divine is anchored primarily in individual human consciousness, and only derivatively in social embodied actions and practices, and the sphere of creation. For Kelsey, God's hospitable generosity and creativity stretches across the entire finite context into which we are born — from our social institutions to the nitty-gritty dimensions of our embodied existence. Therefore, human beings' appropriate responses to God in faith, hope, and love do not occur in a cordoned off interior realm of the spirit, but are always and everywhere embodied responses manifest in wise actions in our situated quotidian existence. Against this backdrop, modern analyses of sin that focus solely on failed self-actualization or acts of self-transcendence lose a great deal of their explanatory power, insofar as they bracket the ways in which our personal identities are constituted in and through social institutions, networks of relations, and practices — all of which are equally implicated in the distortion of sin. On similar grounds, Kelsey puts a question mark against neo-orthodox efforts to root sin narrowly in human pride and the self-arrogating will to power. Besides assuming a measure of power and agency that most human beings do not possess in their everyday existence, such a narrow definition of sin (even if it is complicated by notions of sloth, sensuality, or a failure to be a self) cannot do justice to the complex and often banal ways in which we violate and do violence to the well-being of others in our quotidian existence.

A third major contribution of Kelsey's work is that it offers a plausible and in my view salutary reconstruction of the notion of original sin. Key to its plausibility is that Kelsey deftly sets aside that aspect of the Western understanding of original sin that appears both morally troubling and scientifically indefensible to contemporary audiences, namely, the notion that there was a calamitous fall event, a first sin in which all of humankind has become morally implicated. Rather than explaining sin's presence in the world by positing a catastrophic fall from perfection, Kelsey looks to the witness of Wisdom tradition and particularly to the Book of Job to anchor his claim that sin is an absurd and mysterious fact that radically and universally distorts our quotidian existence. Insofar as each of us participates from the moment of our birth in a social network of giving and receiving among creatures, a network of relationships, practices, and institutions that are already profoundly twisted by sin, sin is a continuous corrupting force that reaches down to the depths of our personal identity formation. We are always and everywhere both subject to, and the subjects of sin, its victims and its perpetrators. This sociality and human solidarity in sin does not mean, however, that we don't bear personal moral responsibility for our own actions. Insofar as human beings are those who are created with the capacity to respond to God's generous hospitality toward us, we truly enact our own sins and distort our identities through engaging in a range of foolish actions that fail to serve the well-being of others, ourselves, and our proximate contexts.

Particularly salutary about Kelsey's account of original sin is that instead of burdening human beings with paralyzing guilt, it strives to awaken them to the magnificence and intimacy of God's grace. As Kelsey illuminates throughout this work, human beings are truly locked into disparate and desperate strategies of securing our flourishing, for example, through achieving excellence in our professions, or being elected to a given role in society, or else placing our absolute trust in a particular ideology or social movement. All such strategies for securing one's self are ultimately self-defeating, since they displace ultimate faith, hope, and love from God's steadfast loving agency to finite surrogates that cannot furnish us with the flourishing that we demand from them. Kelsey's portrayals of the imprisoning character of this human predicament are not, however, meant to incite the fear of judgment or to elicit despair, but rather to prompt us to acknowledge the radical eccentricity of our existence, our participation in the being in Christ. Since our reconciliation has been secured objectively in Christ's work, Kelsey reminds his readers, we need not live anxiously awaiting an ultimate judgment on one's life's worth. Rather we receive the gift of justifying freedom to live in joyful thanksgiving over God's graciousness, and the sanctifying grace to re-direct our life energies, our compassion and courage toward the well-being of our fellow creatures.

If these are three strengths of Kelsey's theology of sin, let me raise three clusters of questions and critical observations to prompt future conversation of his work. The first concerns how Kelsey's three distinct analyses of sin relate substantially to one another: Are they three snapshots taken from different angles of the same fundamental predicament of sin, or are they intended to mark the conceptual range of distorted responses to the triune God's agency, any one version of which human beings might fall prey to in the span of a given life? In other words, does Kelsey envision that the person who responds inappropriately to one aspect of God's relating begins to tumble down the slippery slope of sin and distorts his or her responses to the other distinct dimensions of God's relating? Or can we fall prey to just one of these sorts of distortions and not the others?

In keeping with Kelsey's instruction that creation, consummation, and reconciliation should not be taken as a temporal sequence of God's agency in history, but as simultaneously operative relations whose dynamic unity he likens to the three strands of a triple helix, my inclination is to think that Kelsey envisions his three analyses of sin as coincident distortions of a personal identity. If we fall prey to one, we fall prey to the others. But if that hunch is indeed correct, it begs the further question whether there isn't an unspoken root paradigm of sin running through Kelsey's three analyses of sin that unites them as one. To trade mischievously on Kelsey's Trinitarian grammar of his sin-talk, are these three truly one?

While as far as I can tell Kelsey does not address these queries directly in his work, let me venture the hypothesis that his three distinct analyses of sin can be read as different expressions of the root problem of idolatry — most simply understood as humankind's capacity to displace its ultimate faith, hope, and love onto a range of finite entities and, in so doing, imprison itself to false gods of its own making. If that is correct, namely, that idolatry is truly the fundamental dilemma of human existence, it prompts for me a different set of exciting questions about Kelsey's Christology: Does the uniqueness of Jesus' personal identity (who the author reveals in the first coda to his work to be the only true image of God; human beings are "the image of the image") lie in him being the sole human agent who does not succumb to idolatry? Is Jesus the only one who responds in perfect faith to his Father, absolute loyalty to his creative project, acts out of eschatological hope in the kingdom come, and enacts perfect love of God, self, and neighbor? What New Testament texts might support well this claim, for example, the temptations of Jesus in Luke 4? What other passages might demand nuanced interpretation, e.g., the Gethsemane scene in Mark 14:32ff., in order to defend such a claim? Finally, how might such a view of Jesus' true humanity, namely, as the only one who does not fall prey to the distortions of idolatry, help illuminate how Jesus' life, death, and resurrection accomplish human redemption?

My second question concerns Kelsey's use of the language of impurity and stain to describe the distorting effects of original sin upon personal identities. To recall, Kelsey proposes that this central biblical metaphor of stain replace the language of guilt in order to describe the fallout of original sin — our objective status before God as creatures who have violated our relationship with God whether we are cognizant of it or not. Following Ricoeur's lead, Kelsey reminds his readers that he doesn't intend the language of stain in a literalistic way to connote filthiness, but rather to symbolize the human being's condition in being born into sin, that is, becoming implicated in a dynamic movement away from God. The language of stain, he argues, can help us to envision the ontological and moral ambiguity of the human condition, namely, that while we remain good in our finite creatureliness, at the same time our distorted personal identities are truly offensive to God and require purification in order for them to reflect God's glory.

While I agree with Kelsey that the metaphor of stain displays the objective reality of sin (sin is not a mere illusion afflicting our consciousness but a reality that we cannot remedy ourselves), the language of stain and impurity has had a deeply troubling history of gender effects in Christianity. Feminist historians and theologians have challenged that the language of pollution or defilement for sin has provided a potent "rhetoric of otherness" in the church that reinforces dangerous gender stereotypes about women that diminish their agency or else scapegoats them as the source of sin's transmission.[6] The metaphors of impurity, pollution, and dirtiness have often been invoked to treat women's "embodied sexuality" as a "principal site of sin" to be ashamed of, feared, and controlled.[7] Now I am not suggesting by any means that Kelsey seeks to reinforce such sexism in his theology of original sin. Indeed as I noted earlier, he identifies gender stereotypes as a classic example of sin's failure to respect the genuine otherness of one's fellow human beings, by overlooking and exploiting their concrete particularity for one's own purposes. Moreover, in other stretches of his work that I have not addressed in this essay, Kelsey swims

6. Serene Jones, *Feminist Theory and Christian Theology: Cartographies of Grace* (Minneapolis: Fortress Press, 2000), p. 96.

7. Jones, *Feminist Theory and Christian Theology,* p. 120. For an elegant analysis of this problem with respect to Calvin's account of original sin, see Jones, pp. 108-24.

hard against a strong current of the Christian tradition that devalues the body, by affirming unequivocally the goodness of physical bodies and sexuality as unqualified gifts of God. And yet I am not fully persuaded that these efforts alone can neutralize the risks of the rhetoric of stain or impurity in the doctrine of sin to feed into women's shame or other persons' denigration of their bodies. At the very least, I would like to ask whether other embodied metaphors for sin, for example, those of wounds or being maimed by sin, might be in order here so as to expose and to redress the dangerous gendered history of effects of stain and impurity imagery and to prevent its idolatrous misuse.

My final query is less about Kelsey's theology of sin per se, but about the theological style of *Eccentric Existence* as a whole. Anyone who dips into just a few pages of this work can't help but notice that Kelsey has chosen a demanding style for his theological anthropology. This is a highly analytical work, which relies on elaborately wrought typologies, an exact parsing of the grammar of terms, and complex dialectical arguments to commend its proposals. In many ways these volumes are vintage Kelsey, reminiscent of his groundbreaking work on *The Uses of Scripture in Modern Theology,* in which he relied there too on a finely tuned typology and precise linguistic distinctions in order to shed fresh light on a highly vexed theological issue. And yet, Kelsey's analytical style for his theological anthropology genuinely surprised me. For one, I couldn't help recalling the author's own cautionary words from his earlier essay about the creative reconstructions of the doctrine of sin in modern theology: Might not all these efforts be too "complexly dialectical" to have practical import on the preaching, pastoral care, and catechetical practices of communities of faith? Stated differently, how might the theology of sin set forth in *Eccentric Existence* be turned to practical-critical effect to edify Christian believers and the life of the church toward which this work is directed?

I was also struck by Kelsey's analytical style in this work because it was a conspicuous departure from his genre-breaking decision in his other most recent work, *Imagining Redemption,* to pursue a "systematically unsystematic theology," that intentionally blurs the styles of pastoral and systematic theology.[8] Of course, there, too, Kelsey provides his readers with an analytically rich and linguistically precise account of redemption, but he anchors his conceptual work in a concrete narrative — the story of an

8. David Kelsey, *Imagining Redemption* (Louisville, KY: Westminster John Knox Press, 2005), p. 86.

ordinary family caught in a horrendous and complex tale of inexplicable evils undergone, innumerable wrongs committed, and lives undone. On my reading of *Imagining Redemption,* Kelsey's turn to narrative is much more than a rhetorical gesture; rather, it signifies a profound methodological commitment, namely, that if the theologian is to speak meaningfully about redemption, there can no "one size fits all" presentation, but rather one has to risk getting caught up in the messiness of human lives and particular narratives.

With those pastoral and methodological concerns in view, I wonder what might be at stake in choosing a decidedly more abstract style for this work. Why don't concrete narratives and dramatic human portraits figure prominently in these two volumes on theological anthropology, especially given its outright commitment to the quotidian, and its urgent call to pay attention to the concrete particularities of human lives? More pointedly, what might be lost about the human predicament of sin by diagnosing it apart from the very lives that it parasitically inhabits, distorts, and ravages in often catastrophic ways?

While I am eager to hear Kelsey's reflections on this question, let me close by offering a few conjectures of my own. First, I wonder if the theological style is dictated in part by the author's deep aversion to the psychological mindset in which theological anthropology has been cast in the past few centuries. Clearly Kelsey is profoundly suspicious of any and all efforts to sculpt an inner psychological landscape of human beings, as if the theologian has the tools to penetrate behind the concrete acts and practices of individuals and communities of faith in order to expose and dissect the internal workings of human consciousness or the human heart. If I read Kelsey on this point correctly, offering dramatic portraits of sin might not only psychologize sin to such a degree as to threaten its objective nature, but such portraits might defy the fundamental epistemic and ontological mystery of basic personal identities — one of the key claims about the human condition to which Kelsey tellingly returns in the closing line of his work.

Second, I attribute the scarcity of concrete narratives in *Eccentric Existence* to the fact that Kelsey intends this work as a *theocentric* anthropology, one in which the triune God's dynamic being is not only its organizing principle but remains to its final pages its primary subject — its most dramatic character. In other words, I take the genre of this work itself to be a performative act, gesturing to the eccentricity of human existence that relentlessly points beyond itself to what Kelsey calls "the One with whom we have to do" and to whom we are called in every moment of our lives to respond. Dwelling too long on the concrete distortions that afflict human lives and institutions would risk undermining Kelsey's overarching theological aim.

Finally, I take the conceptual style of this work as indicative of how its author wishes his proposals to be taken up by his contemporaries and by future generations. As Kelsey pointedly writes in the opening pages of the work, he intends neither to lay down absolute foundations nor to make apodictic pronouncements about how Christian theological anthropology must be done. Rather, his theological proposals are cast in the "hypothetical mode," that is, in the mode of "here is an important theological question; try looking at it this way" (*EE* 1:9). In other words, Kelsey's numerous proposals are meant to offer a conceptual compass to his readers to take along the way and to help keep Christian theological anthropology on a steady course. To return to the felicitous metaphor of his teacher Robert Calhoun, *Eccentric Existence* has carefully set buoys down in the deep waters of theological anthropology — not to dictate the only path ahead, but to provide some expert help in steering future generations on their theological way. For that sort of practical wisdom and theological humility that has been so characteristic of Kelsey's work throughout his career, I along with generations of readers to come will remain gratefully in Kelsey's debt.

For God's Own Sake: *Eccentric Existence* and the Theological Education Debate

Barbara G. Wheeler and Edwin Chr. van Driel

In the 1980s, David Kelsey took an excursion into territory well off the main roads of academic theology. It began with a series of day-trips. Kelsey was asked to monitor a project of the Association of Theological Schools that came to be known as Issues Research. The aim of the project was to stimulate serious reflection on the aims and purposes of theological education in North America. The project made grants to scholars to write monographs and convened conferences to discuss the written work. Kelsey's assignment was to read the books and articles, sit in on the conferences, and write periodic reports on the proceedings.

The project lasted more than a decade and generated scores of publications, including articles by Kelsey that chronicled the discussion, analyzed it as it developed, and suggested needed clarifications and possibly fruitful lines of future inquiry.[1] The whole Issues Research effort was highly unusual. In the decades before it began, most North American writing and talking about theological education had been produced by seminary presidents and church officials.[2] The focus was usually pragmatic: how to

1. In his work as evaluator of the Issues Research conversation, Kelsey was usually joined by Barbara Wheeler. They published several reflections on the project, among them: David H. Kelsey and Barbara G. Wheeler, "Mind Reading: Notes on the Basic Issues Program," *Theological Education* 20 (Spring 1984): 42-54; David H. Kelsey, "Reflections on Convocation '84: Issues in Theological Education," *Theological Education* 21 (Spring 1985): 116-38; David H. Kelsey and Barbara G. Wheeler, "Thinking About Theological Education: The Implications of 'Issues Research' for Criteria of Faculty Excellence," *Theological Education* 28 (Autumn 1991): 11-26.

2. A notable exception is H. Richard Niebuhr, in collaboration with Daniel Day

rearrange the pieces of the theological curriculum, the items in the faculty job description, or the accountability structures that linked theological schools and religious communities to better effect. When larger themes came into play, it was often in polemical volleys — seminary leaders making inflated claims about the effectiveness of their schools' programs, countered by church leaders leveling charges they could not fully document about the seminaries' failures.

Issues Research recruited a different set of participants: theological school professors, most of them from the fields of theology, philosophy of religion, and church history. The focus was on "basic" issues of purpose rather than practical problems, and the writing and speaking had a different tone. It was conducted in a scholarly mode, theological teachers and writers using the methods of their academic specialties to inquire into their educational and institutional practices at greater depth. Though there was plenty of strenuous argument, generally there was also more fruitful interchange, with one entry building on another, than there had been when most discussion was conducted in stump speeches and articles of opinion.

Before long, the conversation became rich and spirited. Not surprisingly, Kelsey was drawn from his role as observer and reporter into full participation. The tracking reports continued, but he also began work on his own proposal for how to understand "basic issues" in theological education and how to address them. In the early 1990s, he produced two books, *To Understand God Truly: What's Theological About a Theological School* and *Between Athens and Berlin: The Theological Education Debate.*[3]

Kelsey's contribution to the Issues Research conversation was twofold. He became its principal expositor. In both his books (briefly in *To Understand God Truly* and at considerable length in *Between Athens and Berlin*), he summarized the major contributions of others in language that made them accessible to the mixed audience of persons interested in theological education. He noted convergences among the works, uncovered presuppositions on which they rested, and outlined the differences and conflicts in their framing of questions and use of terms. His account of the theological education debate of the late twentieth century is the definitive one. If deliberations on the aims and purposes of theological education

Williams and James M. Gustafson, *The Purpose of the Church and Its Ministry: Reflections on the Aims of Theological Education* (New York: Harper, 1956).

3. David H. Kelsey, *To Understand God Truly: What's Theological about a Theological School* (Louisville, KY: Westminster/John Knox Press, 1992); *Between Athens and Berlin: The Theological Education Debate* (Grand Rapids: William B. Eerdmans, 1993).

were to resume today, the ways Kelsey has posed the issues would be the best basis for beginning again.

Kelsey's account of the discussion begins with its widely acknowledged starting point, Edward Farley's *Theologia: The Fragmentation and Unity of Theological Education.*[4] In this and a subsequent volume, *The Fragility of Knowledge,* Farley observed that contemporary theological education is almost universally experienced as fragmented, even incoherent.[5] Despite repeated attempts to "integrate" the segments of the curriculum, this is rarely achieved to the satisfaction of students, teachers, and sponsoring churches. Theological "theory" has proved perennially difficult to apply in "practice." As a result, theological education has been widely judged as inadequate preparation for professional ministry.

In order to discover what developments might have created these conditions, Farley plumbed the history of the theological course of studies, focusing especially on the origins of the four-fold pattern of fields (Scripture, theology, history, and practical or ministry studies) that in one form or another structures the curricula of all Christian theological schools. At the deepest level (because of Farley's focus on structure, his project was often compared to an archeological dig), he located *theologia,* theology conceived in the late Middle Ages and early Reformation as a profound personal wisdom that disposes the knower to God. Theology in this sense had literatures — Scripture, doctrine, the history of God's dealings with the church, and polemics — but it was a single unified thing, a *habitus,* a "way of being," rather than "a body of knowledge with separable parts."[6] In the later Reformation, the divisions of *theologia* were arranged in proper Protestant order: Scripture at the top, theology derived from it, history tracing the development of doctrine, and then application of sacred teachings to Christian life. In the nineteenth century, the first three divisions increasingly took the form of separate academic disciplines; meanwhile, Friedrich Schleiermacher, in an effort to justify the presence of theology in the modern German university, proposed a new purpose for the fourth division: the derivation and teaching of rules for ministry, which he deemed an indispensable social practice. Twentieth-century Americans gave ministry studies a distinctly functionalist cast: "Professional" ministry was now

4. Edward Farley, *Theologia: The Fragmentation and Unity of Theological Education* (Philadelphia: Fortress Press, 1983).

5. Edward Farley, *The Fragility of Knowledge: Theological Education in the Church and the University* (Philadelphia: Fortress Press, 1988).

6. Kelsey, *Between Athens and Berlin,* p. 104.

defined by the items in the clergy job description, and a sub-specialty, each with its own body of theory (psychology for pastoral care, for instance) was developed for each clerical function.

The legacy of these developments, Farley showed, is a jumble. The four fields, once unified by *theologia,* a conception of theology that no longer animates theological education, are now "holding pens" (Kelsey's phrase) for disciplines among which the relationships are far from clear.[7] The implicit top-down order, with application or practice at the bottom, still holds, though few theological thinkers today would argue that thought-action relationships are unidirectional. The functionalist picture of ministry toward which the whole endeavor is now oriented introduces its own confusions about what body of theory supports those functions. Is it the so-called classical disciplines or, rather, the additional bodies of social science theory that are referenced when the practice of ministry is taught? In short, the course of theological studies is a catch-all of structures, concepts, and intentions that were never part of any single larger whole. No wonder "integration" and the "application of theory in practice" are so hard to achieve.

Farley told this story of how theological education became so badly fragmented. Kelsey reformatted the account, as he has done so often throughout his teaching and writing career, organizing its themes and questions related to them in what someone once called "architectonic" ways that might help those who want to propose constructive responses to figure out where to start.[8] Kelsey raised sympathetic but critical questions about Farley's primary focus on the four-fold structure of studies. Granted that the current divisions are fossils of a once-vibrant conception theology, Kelsey questioned whether, given the pluralism of theological education, any one more current conception of theology could provide a unifying structure for all.

Kelsey also highlighted dimensions present in Farley's account but overshadowed by the heavy emphasis on structure. One was the matter of the *movement* of theological studies. Reformation Protestants proposed an orderly progression from scriptural source through theological exposition to application in a holy life; the Enlightenment and later developments

7. Kelsey, *To Understand God Truly,* p. 233.

8. One member of the committee that guided the Issues Research conversation remarked that the confusions and ambiguities in the group's substantive discussions were usually resolved in Kelsey's crystalline summaries of the discussions.

kept the direction of movement but modernized the terms, so that the theory obtained in academic studies is now to be applied in professional practice. Kelsey agreed with Farley and many other critics: One-way vectors do not adequately describe what transpires in either theology or education. But, he asked, will any single choreography of the relationship between thinking and doing (or in his preferred terms, concepts and acts) unify the educational activities of a pluralistic group of theological schools?

Kelsey identified a third dimension of Farley's critique, one that, he argued, holds most promise for surfacing a remedy for curricular incoherence: the goal of theological study.[9] Kelsey heartily concurs with Farley: essential as it is that ministers be theologically educated, the "clerical paradigm" of clergy functions should not be the orienting goal of theological study — what shapes it and gives its parts their place and justification. Rather, Kelsey insists, what does — or should — make theological education and the schools in which it is housed theological (and what is more likely to make ministerial education powerful than direct attempts to accomplish that) is the goal of understanding God truly, first of all for God's own sake rather than any more proximate purpose, such as training church leaders. Only if theological schooling is oriented to this goal can the current curriculum, now a "clutch of courses" (a phrase Kelsey uses repeatedly), become a course of study.

How is such understanding to be achieved, if the current educational and institutional activities do not currently accomplish it? Kelsey puts forward his own proposal, but before he describes it he expands Farley's critique of the current incoherence of theological schooling and, based on that critique, develops criteria for the adequacy of any proposal, including his own.[10]

First, Kelsey endorses the goal of recovering the unity of theological education but argues also that it must not be achieved at the expense of very real theological differences between schools that stand in different religious streams. Therefore, proposals for re-conception or reform must take into account and be adequate to the theological pluralism of theological schools. Kelsey makes the case for pluralism on theological grounds. God cannot be understood directly, he argues, but only by way of some-

9. Kelsey, *To Understand God Truly,* p. 215.

10. The following list is a construction by the authors of this essay of criteria that Kelsey actually uses in both of his monographs on theological education. It corresponds to and expands a list Kelsey compacts into a single paragraph (Kelsey, *Between Athens and Berlin,* pp. 196-97).

thing else. Various Christian traditions have placed very different kinds of the subject matter (texts, tradition, experience, for instance) at the center of their efforts to understand God. Kelsey chooses for all of them a "placeholder" he borrows from G. K. Chesterton, "the Christian thing," and insists that proposals to understand God will be adequate only if they do justice to the "irreducibly different" ways the Christian thing is construed.[11]

Kelsey derives a second criterion for any new proposals from his masterful demonstration of how the assorted structural elements, multiple patterns of movement, and disparate goals in the present-day curriculum are for the most part dimensions of two powerful traditions of "excellent schooling," to which Kelsey gives the nicknames "Athens" and "Berlin": *paidaia,* which Kelsey characterizes as the "cultivation of the soul" through slow growth in and toward an understanding of God[12]; and *Wissenschaft,* preparation for professional practice by means of "orderly, disciplined, research."[13] These types or models, Kelsey claims, are deeply rooted in the history of education and inescapably woven into all forms of theological education in North America. The two traditions are very different, and according to Kelsey they cannot be simply "synthesized."[14] The unsurfaced tension between them is the root of the incoherence of theological schooling. An adequate proposal for the reconception and reform of theological education must either make a compelling case for one of the two approaches or, preferably, offer an alternative that creates a new, more coherent order and rationale incorporating dimensions of both.

Finally, Kelsey argues than any adequate proposal should suggest ways to restore the public character of theological education that was common to both *paidaia* and *Wissenschaft* in their original versions. *Paidaia* for the Greeks was formation in the virtues required for citizenship in the *polis;* for early Christians too it entailed formation for participation in society and culture as well as the shaping of Christian dispositions. Over the centuries, however, under Christian auspices, it became an intensely religious and interior pursuit. Likewise, the Berlin model, especially as revised by Schleiermacher, was ordered, disciplined inquiry for a social purpose: the exercise of ministry as an endeavor essential for the well-being of society. More recently the functionalist model of ministry, comprised of the series

11. Kelsey, *To Understand God Truly,* pp. 31-32.
12. Kelsey, *Between Athens and Berlin,* p. 9.
13. Kelsey, *Between Athens and Berlin,* p. 12.
14. Kelsey, *To Understand God Truly,* p. 75.

of tasks the religious community requires of its "professional" leaders, has become the point to which theological education is oriented.[15] Neither model, Kelsey suggests, is most powerful in its present individualized form, so new proposals will be stronger if they suggest ways to reorient theological education to public as well as religious ends.

On the way to proffering his own proposal, Kelsey makes judgments about those of several other writers.[16] Most of those proposals are inadequate by one or more of Kelsey's criteria. His most stringent criticisms are two. First, by continued reliance on the "clerical paradigm" as an orienting goal, on theory-to-practice patterns of movement, and/or on awkward oscillations between elements of *paidaia* and *Wissenschaft* (especially those elements that tend to privatize theological schooling), various proposals are not theologically more coherent than what is now in place. Second, most of the proposals seek theological unity by putting at the center a single way of construing the "Christian thing" (doctrine for Max Stackhouse; "the Christian story" for John Cobb and Joseph Hough; "an ahistorical and universally self-identical essential self" that reflects on faith and achieves sapiential knowing the same way in all times and places for Farley).[17] Thus they all fail the test of adequacy to the genuine and "irreducible" pluralism of Christian construals.

Only one proposal meets most of Kelsey's tests: Charles Wood's, in his book *Vision and Discernment.*[18] Wood defines theological education as two-sided inquiry into the validity of Christian witness, consisting of "vision," a general understanding, and "discernment," inquiry about things in their particularity. He sets three questions to structure this inquiry: Is a particular instance of Christian witness faithful to Christian tradition? Is it true? Is it fittingly enacted? The focus on instances of actual Christian witness lends Wood's proposal its pluralism; the horizon of questions about instances of witness sets its theological character; his definition of inquiry as an objective activity rather than as the formation of subjective,

15. Kelsey, *To Understand God Truly,* pp. 63-79.

16. Kelsey's constructive proposal in *To Understand God Truly* was published in 1992, a year before his analytical and critical volume, *Between Athens and Berlin,* but the logic of the two works strongly suggests that the scheme of the latter was worked out before the earlier work was written. Kelsey himself calls the books "non-identical twins formed in the same gestational period" (Kelsey, *Between Athens and Berlin,* p. viii).

17. Kelsey, *To Understand God Truly,* p. 238.

18. Charles M. Wood, *Vision and Discernment: An Orientation in Theological Study* (Atlanta: Scholars Press, 1985).

interior consciousness renders the proposal "public"; and by the same deft move, defining *habitus* as the disposition to the *activity* of inquiry, Kelsey suggests that Wood may have transposed the Athens/Berlin tension into a "new key."

Kelsey's own proposal in *To Understand God Truly* builds on Wood's. In line with Wood, but even more emphatically, he asserts in both his title and his text that the overarching goal of a truly theological school is "to apprehend God for the sake of apprehending God."[19] He adopts a set of questions very similar to Wood's as the horizon for inquiry into the things of God. He then adds features that make his proposal, while still, he admits, "Utopian," more concrete. He locates the witness into which theological schools should inquire in order to be truly theological in Christian congregations, communities that gather in Jesus' name to "enact publicly a more broadly practiced worship of God."[20] The pluralism of congregations, used neither as the site of learning nor the subject matter *per se,* but rather as a lens through which instances of witness present themselves to be inquired into, will, Kelsey argues, secure the adequacy of theological schooling to pluralism of Christian belief and practice. And Kelsey frames his ideas as pertaining to theological *schools* rather than the necessarily abstract notion of "theological education." He expands the notion of inquiry and explores its implications, painting a detailed picture of theological understanding as "conceptual growth" that is guided by God's peculiar ways of being present and that is, at the same time, self-critically situated in a religious tradition, society, and culture.[21] In making these moves, he claims, he has found a "way between" Athens and Berlin, more theological, more pluralistic, and more publicly accountable than either.[22]

Kelsey's proposal attracted positive comments from other participants in the Issues Research conversation, including some writers whose work he criticized along the way. Nevertheless, it is likely that Kelsey's increasing involvement in research, discussion, and writing about theological education was cause for concern among his theological colleagues outside the Issues Research circle. When Kelsey began work on the two books on theological education, he was already widely admired for his theological gifts. He was well known as a master at critical explication,

19. Kelsey, *To Understand God Truly,* p. 176.
20. Kelsey, *To Understand God Truly,* p. 134.
21. Kelsey, *To Understand God Truly,* pp. 175-79.
22. Kelsey, *To Understand God Truly,* pp. 227-51.

teasing out the structure, direction, and ramifications of an idea, text, or tradition of thought with a thoroughness and clarity that few other contemporary theologians have achieved. Even his earliest work had shown another strength, the ability to frame constructive proposals that make sense without either oversimplifying the complexities they entail or prematurely resolving the tensions and problems they address. No doubt his students and fellow theologians expected that he would bring his extraordinary capacities to bear on major theological topics. In the view of many, theological education did not qualify as one of those. Kelsey himself noted that the Issues Research undertaking was an extremely "fragile" one, with no status in the field of theological studies and no institutional structures committed to sustaining it over the long-term.[23] The more it absorbed scholarly attention and writing time, the more Kelsey's side trip into the theological education debate must have looked to others in his discipline like a worrisome detour from mainstream theological work.

The publication of *Eccentric Existence* should allay any fears that Kelsey would not return to "major" theological issues. The work is major in every sense — size, scope, and centrality of its subject matter. It has something to contribute to numerous active theological conversations and debates, as the number of conferences on and written responses to the work (including the present volume) attest. It may also have the potential to restart the dormant theological discussion of theological schooling. In one of the last publications in the Issues Research exchange, Kelsey and Wheeler noted that one reason that the basic issues literature had had such limited impact on the "conceptual environment" of theological education might be that there were conceptual gaps in the literature. "The most important unattended topic," they wrote, "is anthropology."[24] Despite general agreement that theological education "aims to shape persons," there has been little specificity about who those persons are. The essay goes on to offer a cryptic sketch of models of human personhood that are implied by the conventional rhetoric about theological education and in the Issues

23. Kelsey, *To Understand God Truly,* pp. 14-15. Kelsey was correct. The conversation and the flow of written products came to an end in the mid-1990s, when the Association of Theological Schools and the principal funder, Lilly Endowment Inc., focused their work on the improvement of theological education in other ways.

24. David H. Kelsey and Barbara G. Wheeler, "New Ground: The Foundations and Future of the Theological Education Debate," in *Theology and the Interhuman: Essays in Honor of Edward Farley,* ed. Robert R. Williams (Valley Forge, PA: Trinity Press International, 1991), pp. 181-201.

Research literature. The authors admit that the sketch is "stark," and that there is no room, in a short chapter, to say more about the theological status of the models or the larger frameworks from which they are derived.

In *Eccentric Existence,* Kelsey offers a vast theological framework and numerous warrants for one of the models mentioned in the earlier work: the bodied intentional agent. His anthropological method has deep resonance with the underlying and overarching theme of his work on theological schooling: Its goal is to understand God truly. God, Kelsey has steadfastly maintained through all his work, "is not to hand," and therefore, "we cannot hope to comprehend God. At best we can hope to apprehend God's presence precisely in the odd ways God is present."[25] In *Eccentric Existence,* Kelsey derives his picture of who, what, and how human creatures are from a description, drawn from canonical Scriptures, of the odd ways God is present, creating, drawing to eschatological consummation, and reconciling the creation to God. This methodological choice is based on Kelsey's conviction that we are, as the title of his book says, essentially *eccentric* beings: "Your personal identity is defined by God alone and not by any creature. It is eccentrically grounded and defined."[26] Here we suggest how Kelsey's extensive thought experiment about the eccentric nature of human beings might prompt theological educators to think again about what theological schooling might be like if it were, in its many different situations and contexts, carefully and deliberately conducted, in all its dimensions, for God's own sake.[27]

Our approach, in making these suggestions, is different from the one Kelsey took in his brief article. There he tried to surface and critique anthropological models implicit in the Issues Research literature. We will try to travel the same road in the reverse direction, looking for ways that Kelsey's now fully developed theological anthropology might potentiate earlier proposals. It goes almost without saying (because Kelsey has said it so emphatically about his "method" in *Eccentric Existence*) that our

25. Kelsey, *To Understand God Truly,* p. 166.

26. David H. Kelsey, *Eccentric Existence: A Theological Anthropology* (Louisville, KY: Westminster John Knox, 2009), p. 340. Cf. *Eccentric Existence,* p. 590: "Personal bodies' . . . basic identities are defined eccentrically. Theocentrically speaking, while my basic personal identity is most definitely my own identity that only I can live, it is finally not defined by me but is defined eccentrically by God relating to me. It is defined by its 'related-to-by-God-ness' — that is, by its orientation to the triune God — not by my particular mode of self-relating — that is, by its orientation to me."

27. Kelsey, *To Understand God Truly,* p. 256.

approach is ad hoc, in line with Kelsey's insistence that, in light of the singularities of the events that drive Christian theological conceptualization, all theological thinking needs to be systematically unsystematic. The purpose of these suggestions is simple: to see whether *Eccentric Existence* can help to make more memorable several compelling arguments in the literature about basic issues in theological education that have had almost no impact on either the practice of or thinking about theological education.

First, *Eccentric Existence* might help to amplify Kelsey's fundamental argument about theological education, that it is theological only if it is theocentric. In *Eccentric Existence,* Kelsey makes a reciprocal claim about all of human existence, as we have already noted: It is *eccentric*: Human lives are not primarily about "us" but about God. Therefore theological thinking, a human practice, should be primarily about God and not about us. Yet theocentricity, Kelsey argued pointedly in his as yet unpublished Warfield Lecture, "In Praise of the Useless Glory of God," is in short supply in contemporary theology. There he observed that "across the entire spectrum, at least of American Protestantism, from fundamentalist to evangelical to doctrinally conservative to doctrinally liberal to radical movements, the description given of the God that is to be praised takes the form that God is basically: One who is useful to us." Kelsey does not deny that God is a God who saves, who is "a very present help in time of trouble." However, "talk about God relating to us to redeem us or to reconcile us only makes sense if first we have grasped who and what God is as at once radically as One radically other than, and radically close to, us and then respond in appropriate praise of God's singular intrinsic glory."[28] The focus of theological thinking and education should turn away from humanity and toward God, and from God-for-us to God's intrinsic glory.

Kelsey made this point earlier in his books on theological education. It did not take. Some form of the clerical paradigm, constructed of clergy functions and features of ministerial character, remains the stated goal of almost all theological schooling. Perhaps Kelsey's earlier statements were too mild and mannerly. "Understanding God truly," on first hearing, sounds like an easy goal to embrace. *Eccentric Existence,* an anthropology whose principal subject is God, adds to the sharp edge of the comment in the Warfield lecture the heavy weight of hundreds of pages of theocentric reflection and more compellingly, we think, warrants the argument that

28. David H. Kelsey, "In Praise of the Useless Glory of God," Warfield Lectures 2010-11, unpublished typescript, pp. 18-19.

the fundamental reform of theological education requires first its reorientation to God.

Here is an example of how a theocentric perspective might be brought to bear on a perennial issue in theological schools: the purposes of worship services in and for the seminary community. For Kelsey, prayer and, more widely, worship in all forms, is one of the appropriate ways in which human creatures respond to the triune God's relating to them. In practices of prayer, Kelsey argues, "attention is wholly focused on the sheer reality of the love that is the triune life, focused on it for what it is in and of itself and not on what it could do for us or on what the act of contemplating it could do for us, is what makes them practices of pure contemplative adoration."[29] These practices of prayer are necessarily communal and public because they are engaged in by human personal bodies as psychosomatic wholes. They are public, as Kelsey averred in *To Understand God Truly,* because most worship forms are shared and widely practiced.[30] Their basic communal character is expressed in moments of self-reminder: one prays with "the communion of saints" or "the whole company of heaven and earth." Solitary individual acts of prayer are parasitic on communal and public practices of prayers because the practices enacted in such prayers are themselves socially established.[31]

These notions of worship as focused on the "triune life . . . in and of itself" and on its essentially public character are rarely in play when the relationship of worship to the theological curriculum is debated. In those debates, utilitarian arguments — what worship can do for us — dominate. The value of a chapel and a campus worship program is often defended for one or more of three reasons. Some regard it as a laboratory where future pastors and worship leaders can experience different forms of worship and experiment with these in a relatively safe and contained environment. Viewed this way, the goal of the program is primarily educational, helping students to develop "skills" in worship leadership. From another perspective, chapel is an environment of pastoral care for students and other members of the community. Theological education can lay huge burdens on students, challenging deeply-held opinions, world views, and beliefs while adding financial, time, and career pressures to the mix. Students do relate to home and "practice" congregations, but often the seminary chapel

29. Kelsey, *Eccentric Existence,* p. 749.
30. Kelsey, *To Understand God Truly,* p. 137.
31. Kelsey, *Eccentric Existence,* p. 750.

is the place where the unique stresses of seminary study are addressed in worship and prayer. A third perspective sees the theological school as a species of church and worship as its core, the locus, as in any congregation, for the spiritual formation of the members. Within the worship life of the school, students are trained spiritually the way they are trained academically in the classroom.

These three perspectives have two features in common. First, they conceive of the place and importance of chapel within theological education pragmatically. The chapel is there, on each of these views, to meet human needs, in this case, students' for training as future worship leaders, for pastoral care, or a place of spiritual formation, or some combination of these. Second, each is focused primarily on the individual student participant in worship.

If prayer and worship are some of the appropriate ways of responding to God's threefold relating to us, however; if in prayer and worship attention is focused on the triune life for what it is in and of itself and not on what it could do for us or on what the act of contemplating it could do for us; and if prayer and worship are essentially corporate and public practices, then a different starting point seems apposite: to imagine what worship would be like if God rather than students' needs were at the center, and to conceive of seminary worship as a corporate and public practice, one that the whole community would endeavor to conduct, purely for God's sake, and that all or most of its members might even attend! Worship so conceived and practiced would not be extra-curricular or peripheral; on the contrary, it would animate the whole school and its members. It would serve as a constant reminder that the whole enterprise of theological education is eccentric to what — or better, to Whom — is truly at its heart.

Seminary chapel worship as just described — a pure response to the triune God's peculiar ways of relating to us — is of course (to use a phrase of Kelsey's own) a utopian picture. *Eccentric Existence*'s trenchant accounts of finitude and sin remind us that human motives are likely always to be mixed. But worship of the kind described can be glimpsed in actual settings — those who have attended Easter week services in schools in Eastern orthodox traditions, for instance, might say that they have seen it as the whole community packs the flower-festooned chapel and stands for hours-long sung services; so might those who have witnessed the austerity of a very Reformed service in a largely undecorated seminary chapel, or the non-stop enthusiasm of a student-led service of "praise." And the very act of asking, as a community, what sort of worship is truest to God, without regard for our immediate needs, could help to refocus the whole range of the activities of a theological school.

Almost as easy to embrace and then immediately to overlook as the notion of understanding God as the goal of theological education was the consensus in much of the Issues Research literature that the means to the end of understanding God truly is neither cognitive knowledge nor skills in the usual senses of those terms but rather "wisdom." Many gave immediate assent to Farley's contention that theology should function less as an academic discipline and more as a deep sapiential disposition. That broad agreement about the importance of wisdom, however, did little to relieve the incoherence of theological study, because the literature did not adequately distinguish the numerous different ways that "wisdom" was being construed.

Kelsey supplies the missing analysis as he describes how God addresses human beings through the quotidian of creation. One of the driving theological intuitions of Kelsey's books on theological education is that God cannot be known directly but only in the "odd ways" in which God makes Godself present. In *Eccentric Existence,* the idea of the indirect knowledge of God is ingredient to the three-fold divine relating to all that is not God. Following canonical Wisdom's creation theology, Kelsey describes what God creates in terms of several broad types of practices, including "practices of teaching and learning."[32] These practices have the force of a vocation: They are not only the context in which humans find themselves, but they are also the means through which God addresses them: "God relates creatively as One addressing human beings in and through their public, every day world with a call to be wise, placing them objectively in a vocation to be wise; addressing them with a call that engages all that they are by actively, though noncoercively, seeking to seduce in them a desiring love of wisdom born of need; offering, if embraced, to be the ground of their creatively well-being."[33] The different practices humans are created in are subject to standards of excellence which in Proverbs is personified in the figure of Woman Wisdom, who calls creation to be "wise" in their human practices, both for their own well-being and for that of the quotidian.[34]

Kelsey contrasts canonical Wisdom literature's understanding of wise practices and their normative edge with concepts of wisdom in three other

32. Kelsey, *Eccentric Existence,* p. 194.

33. Kelsey, *Eccentric Existence,* p. 235.

34. Kelsey, *Eccentric Existence,* p. 194.

intellectual traditions: classical Greek and Hellenistic thought, philosophical idealist thinking, and the American pragmatic tradition. In classical thought "wisdom" is found in three forms of teaching and learning: *theoria, poesis,* and *praxis. Theoria* is a form of life contrasted to practical action and focused on the contemplation of what is eternally true and good, thereby generating *sophia,* wisdom. In contrast, *poesis* is a form of life focused on skillfully making things, for which it needs another form of wisdom, *techne,* practical insight. *Praxis* is a form of life situated between the other two as political action focused on actualizing the common good of society and guided by a third form of wisdom, *phronesis,* "a certain political know-how." None of these three classical concepts of wisdom lines up with biblical wisdom, Kelsey argues: Biblical wisdom is not a form of contemplation focused on the eternal and avoiding the distraction of action; rather biblical wisdom is practical and ad hoc. It is not morally neutral like *techne* but rather seeks the well-being of the quotidian. It is not focused primarily on political action like *phronesis* but rather on the well-doing and well-being of social and community life construed more broadly.[35]

In Western idealistic traditions, stretching from Kant and Hegel to certain streams of phenomenological and existential thought, an anthropology that sees human beings as self-consciously responsible for their own self-actualization, which is oriented toward increasing human freedom, situates the concept of "wisdom" in the interplay between *praxis* and *theoria.* In these traditions, *praxis* means a form of action ordered to the realization of human emancipation or liberation. This action needs *theoria,* a body of knowledge that explains the laws of change, as a moment of rational critical self-reflection, not in the least to help *praxis* avoid being co-opted by society's oppressive power arrangements. Conceived as such, Kelsey points out, *theoria* has similarities to biblical "wisdom" in that it presupposes socially and culturally embodied practices and is at once rooted in and corrective of these practices for the sake of social well-being. At the same time biblical wisdom is different from idealistic *theoria* both in that it is far more ad hoc than idealistic traditions allow and is not, like *theoria,* focused solely or primarily on the liberation of the human spirit.[36]

Finally, American pragmatist tradition, skeptical of idealist large-scale theorizing, sees wisdom as an ad hoc form of reflection that supports a form of human action focused less on the actualization of freedom than on

35. Kelsey, *Eccentric Existence,* pp. 194-95.
36. Kelsey, *Eccentric Existence,* pp. 195-97.

the enrichment and complexification of experience. Wisdom in this sense is guided by an aesthetic rather than a moral orientation. Kelsey points out that in its ad hoc and normative character pragmatic "wisdom" is akin to biblical wisdom, but it lacks the theocentric or moral orientation that protects it against being co-opted by the social and cultural status quo.[37]

Much clarity could be gained, we think, if the framers of theological curriculum were to use Kelsey's careful exposition of the different meanings and weights of the term wisdom from different periods to identify what is intended to transpire in the practices of teaching and learning of theological schools. In fact, all these intellectual traditions are alive and functioning, usually unsurfaced and uncritically promoted, in theological education today: *poesis* to produce *techne,* or skills for ministry; theology as *sophia,* as a form of contemplation of what is eternally true and good; theological study as *theoria* aimed at informing and norming liberation *praxis;* and theology as an ad hoc form of wisdom complexifying experience. Imagine a theological faculty, using Kelsey's intellectual history of wisdom as a *discrimen* (a favorite Kelsey term), analyzing the aggregate of educational practices that constitute a given curriculum and holding those practices up to the standards, as does Kelsey, of canonical construals of wisdom. Even if such an exercise made little immediate headway toward unity, much less uniformity, of educational procedure, collegial critical self-reflection might send a faculty on a common quest for practices of teaching and learning that flow more organically from and lead as directly as possible to the goal of understanding God.

Eccentric Existence offers extended accounts of what the dynamics of such wise practices should be, emphasizing repeatedly, as did Kelsey's earlier work, the power of concepts to shape thinking and embodied intentional action inseparably from each other. In addition, *Eccentric Existence* offers compelling examples of practices to be learned on the way to wisdom. Kelsey expands, for instance, on those that stem from doxological gratitude (practicing wonder to develop the capacity to apprehend, attend to, and be loyal to fellow creatures; practicing delight; practicing perseverance), helping to shape a "just and compassionate gaze" on all of creation.[38] Elsewhere, he outlines the cognitive mastery and its ingredient disciplines — affective as well as cognitive — that are grounded in hope.[39]

37. Kelsey, *Eccentric Existence,* p. 197.
38. Kelsey, *Eccentric Existence,* pp. 345-46.
39. Kelsey, *Eccentric Existence,* p. 515.

He also gives a compelling account of the practices of enacting "love-as-neighbor."[40] These typologies of lived and learned practices are not meant to be synthesized into a singular picture of Christian communal life; nor could they become the basis for a "unified" theological curriculum. That would contradict all Kelsey's claims about the irreducible distinctions in the triune God's peculiar ways of relating to all that is not God. What is most important and potentially salutary for the future of theological education is the fact that all these practices and the notion of conceptual growth that undergirds them do not break down into the usual binary sets that riddle thinking about the theological curriculum: theory/practice; academic/practical; "classical" disciplines/ministry studies. Each of Kelsey's practices, as well as the picture of conceptual growth at their core, is an example of a "single response to the singular glory of the triune God."[41] We think that such theocentrically singular conceptions of wisdom, more than any new overarching scheme, are what theological education most needs to become more coherent and powerful.

In both these ways — by pointing up again the theocentric goal of theological schooling and by displaying the unifying power of wisdom as canonically construed — *Eccentric Existence* could effectively restart the Issues Research discussion where it left off. The work also has potential significantly to expand serious discussions of theological education. Here we briefly suggest new directions the discussion might take.

First, the perspectives in *Eccentric Existence* pose a serious challenge to the intense and intensifying individualism of contemporary theological education. Practices of teaching and learning, Kelsey holds, are "existential" because they express a fundamental orientation in life. Existential responses are often taken to be radically free and solitary acts of decision. Christian anthropological thought modifies such understanding in several ways. Two of these modifications are of special interest for theological education. First, on Christian thought, human beings are not simply centers of consciousness, but "objective personal bodies with far more complex sets of powers than just those constituting 'consciousness,' complex as they are." Therefore, the practices that make up the "existential how" of faithful response to the divine relating cannot be conceived as being only "modalities of subjectivity," but they are "concrete ways of being self-situated in proximate contexts that involve all of a personal body's

40. Kelsey, *Eccentric Existence,* pp. 793-827.

41. Kelsey, *Eccentric Existence,* p. 329.

entire array of powers."[42] Second, even though individuals are "accountable in [their] onliness" for their response, these faithful responses are not responses shaped by individuals by themselves, but are rather always communal, because "personal bodies are always conceptually formed by the communities of which those personal bodies are members and by their traditions."[43] This communal, conceptual forming through "the faith community's shared practices of speech and action" is what allows human beings to respond faithfully to God's relating to them.[44]

By sharp contrast, the educational and evaluative practices of theological schools almost always assume that the object of teaching is free, self-determining centers of consciousness who will respond by individually retaining, memorizing, and actively and mentally engaging the content of what is taught. How might theological education be different, and more powerful, if theological teachers were, even more deliberately than some already do, to take as the object of their efforts the whole community of students, all of them together as well as each on her own? And what might be the salutary consequences if the evaluation of the "success" of theological education were to focus as much on the progress of the whole body of learners as on the achievements of individual star pupils and the failures of the weakest ones? Our sense is that such refocusing would have broad impact, sending into church communities leaders whose most basic motivation is the well-being of the whole religious community and the world it serves, rather than high individual achievement in the performance of the tasks of leadership.

Finally, there is the matter of bodies, the emphasis on which is a hallmark of the anthropology set forth in *Eccentric Existence.* The hottest current debate among theological schools is about the use of new communication technologies that facilitate learning among persons at a great physical distance from one another. Many promote online learning as a means of access for students who cannot leave work or families to study full time and live on a residential campus. Others see community life as essential to theological education. Kelsey himself wrote an essay contributing to this debate in which he aimed "not to argue against or for distance learning in theological education," but rather "to exhibit the fruitful difference it may make if analyses of proposed changes in Christian theological educa-

42. Kelsey, *Eccentric Existence,* p. 341.

43. Kelsey, *Eccentric Existence,* pp. 341-42.

44. Kelsey, *Eccentric Existence,* p. 342.

tion are framed in explicitly doctrinal theological terms so that discussion of their merits is conducted as a discussion of what is theological about theological education."[45] In the essay, Kelsey anticipates the emphasis on embodiment that later would shape *Eccentric Existence:* "The *theos* in theological anthropology delights in complex organic matter," and therefore "the theological anthropology that undergirds programs of theological schooling should focus on the implications of the view that what we are is not spiritual souls contained in bodies, not ghosts in machines, not even centers of consciousness floating somehow above brains, but extraordinary complex bodies with an extraordinary range of powers."[46] Based on this observation, Kelsey suggests that the question theological educators should ask is: "Do the proposed educational changes assume the validity of some version of human being as spiritual machine or some version of human being as personal body?"[47]

If human beings are best conceived of, as Kelsey suggests in the article and argues in *Eccentric Existence,* as personal organic bodies, this has important consequences for the means of theological education. On such anthropology, "our bodies are inherently involved in our efforts to communicate ourselves as persons. In that case, learning and teaching inherently involve the organic personal bodies of teachers and learners. If coming to understand God involves deep changes in personal bodies, then teaching and learning that aims at deepening understanding of God inherently involves the deep organic bodies of both teachers and learners."[48] Kelsey poses his observation only in the form of a question — does this mean that teachers and students must in some way be physically present to each other? — but it seems that the line of his thought poses major challenges to online learning: What can prevent it from becoming disembodied and thus, at least by Kelsey's standards, something less than theological? As we write this essay, the community of theological schools is considering new standards for accreditation that cautiously open the door to more education-at-a-distance, a move that some ardently embrace and others deeply deplore. Perhaps the currency of the debate offers a way back into the deeper discussion of what might make any form or format of theological schooling genuinely theological.

45. David H. Kelsey, "Spiritual Machines, Personal Bodies, and God: Theological Education and Theological Anthropology," *Teaching Theology and Religion* 5 (2002): 2-9.

46. Kelsey, "Spiritual Machines," p. 7.

47. Kelsey, "Spiritual Machines," p. 8.

48. Kelsey, "Spiritual Machines," p. 9.

David Kelsey builds original, even radical theological constructs on solidly orthodox doctrinal foundations. His ideas about theological teaching and learning, previewed in his earlier books and worked out in dazzling detail in *Eccentric Existence,* have this character, and thus they form a promising basis for reviving the Issues Research conversation and engaging a broad range of participants from across the pluralistic spectrum of theological schools. Even more, the spirit that infuses Kelsey's work might make a renewed conversation attractive and sustainable over the long haul. His writing is invariably appreciative of the contributions of others, always generous yet never uncritical. And in *Eccentric Existence* as throughout his whole career, he models the deepest kind of scholarly piety, a thoroughly rigorous reverence that is never mushy or sentimental. He shows as much as he tells us how much more we can achieve in theological education if all our strivings are, first and last and always, for God's own sake.

From Narrative to Performance?

Shannon Craigo-Snell

Introduction

Eccentric Existence is, among other things, a continuation of that area of theological conversation referred to as narrative, post-liberal, or Yale school theology. This is clear in the reliance on canonical narrative and the vision of communal interpretation of texts, as well as other elements. At the same time, David Kelsey's current development of this tradition also emphasizes the importance of embodiment and Christian practices, the role of larger cultural influences, and the formation of personal identity. In these ways, Kelsey's work resonates with contemporary ethicists and theologians who shift from a Yale school emphasis on narrative toward a focus on drama or performance, hoping to retain the benefits of the post-liberal tradition while also attending to lived, embodied reality. However, Kelsey does not specifically embrace the terminology or engage the theoretical aspects of performance. This tension between narrative and performance is the subject of this essay. Does Kelsey's emphasis on narrative, embodiment, and practices add up to a performance theology? Or does his avoidance of the terminology of performance reflect a real disjunction between narrative and performative theologies? The goal is not a clear classification of Kelsey's work, but rather a close examination of the compatibility and contrasts between narrative and performance theologies. Can performance theology serve as an extension of narrative theology that appreciates the importance of embodied, communal practices of Christian faith? *Eccentric Existence* serves as a case study in this exploration, as it is a *tour de force* of Yale school theology and it explicitly attends to issues central to performance, such as embodiment, practices, and identity formation.

To make this inquiry, I begin with a brief look at Yale school theology, including its history, its characteristic marks, and how Kelsey's theology fits within this tradition. I then move to the more complicated task of describing contemporary performance theology, including its history and characteristic marks, and query whether Kelsey's theology can be seen to fit within this emerging strain of theological conversation. Finally, I reflect more broadly on the relationship between narrative and performance in contemporary theology. I conclude that, while these two perspectives have considerable overlapping insights, there are also strong methodological tensions between them. There are obstacles to a smooth transition from narrative to performance theologies.

Narrative Theology

The theological tradition in which Kelsey participates is variously referred to as Yale school theology, post-liberal theology, and narrative theology.[1] Different members of this strand of theological conversation reject some of these names for various reasons. However, the nomenclature is common enough that I hope to make a few general comments without entering into the controversial particularities. These terms describe a range of theological views that emerged in the latter half of the twentieth century. It is a theology with a zip code, as it was developed by Hans Frei, George Lindbeck, and others associated with the wisdom and lore of Yale University in New Haven, Connecticut. However, given the numbers and quality of American Christian theologians who have been trained in Yale school theology, the geographic specificity of its origin does not correlate to a similarly small scope of influence.

In one way, the inverse relationship between specificity of origin and expansion of influence is quite appropriate to the content of this theological tradition. George Lindbeck articulated a vision of Christian theology in which the specificity of its origin allows for discussion and engagement across traditions. He offered a "cultural-linguistic" approach to religion, in which

1. William C. Placher, "Postliberal Theology," in *The Modern Theologians: An Introduction to Christian Theology in the Twentieth Century,* 2nd ed., ed. David Ford (Cambridge: Blackwell Publishers, 1997), pp. 343-56

> . . . a religion can be viewed as a kind of cultural and/or linguistic framework or medium that shapes the entirety of life and thought. . . . [It] is similar to an idiom that makes possible the description of realities, the formulation of beliefs, and the experiencing of inner attitudes, feelings, and sentiments. Like a culture or language, it is a communal phenomenon that shapes the subjectivities of individuals rather than being primarily a manifestation of those subjectivities. It comprises a vocabulary of discursive and nondiscursive symbols together with a distinctive logic or grammar in terms of which this vocabulary can be meaningfully deployed.[2]

On the one hand, this approach allows the truth claims and commitments of the community to be taken seriously. They can be analyzed in terms of coherence, historical development, ethical implications, faithfulness to communal practices, and so forth. On the other hand, Christian truth claims are recognized as the claims of a community (or communities), and therefore do not have to be regarded as either universally true or false based on some independent valuation of accuracy, such as history, science, or reason. Christian truth claims are not pitted against the truth claims of other religious traditions in a modern arena of competition, judged by a standard outside any particular religious community. One hope of this approach is that, relieved of the need for arbitration at some higher court, participants in various traditions can speak to one another in ways that acknowledge difference and respect location. Acknowledged specificity becomes the starting point for dialogue across religious traditions, in stark contrast to apologetic projects that build on common ground.

This already suggests why Yale school theology is also described as post-liberal. Liberal theologies, particularly liberal Protestant theologies of the nineteenth century, often imply or refer to a deep, universal truth in which Christianity participates. A specific Christian community or tradition is then one instantiation of human relationship with the divine, which takes place in multiple forms across time and space. Brilliant examples of such theologies include the work of Friedrich Schleiermacher, Paul Tillich, and Peter Hodgson. Liberal theology can also facilitate dialogue across traditions, yet here the basis for discussion is acknowledgment of a greater, shared reality.

2. George A. Lindbeck, *The Nature of Doctrine: Religion and Theology in a Postliberal Age* (Philadelphia: Westminster Press, 1984), p. 33.

Yale school theology is not post-liberal because it necessarily denies that there is a larger, shared, ultimate reality. Rather, it takes a Barthian view regarding how we can know such reality and a non-foundationalist view of human knowledge in general. Karl Barth emphasized that the glory of God and the sinfulness of humanity together imply that we cannot know God of our own accord. Furthermore, any and every attempt to do so will result in "religion," in a self-serving picture of the world in which an image of ourselves is projected onto the heavens.[3] Given this, Barth advises Christians to cling to Jesus, as proclaimed in Scripture, and to allow God to master us rather than try to master God. Barth saw great danger in nineteenth-century liberal theology and responded with an attempt to de-center humanity and refocus Christianity on God in Jesus Christ, as known in Scripture. Precisely because he recognizes the effects of cultural construction, Barth urges Christians to rely on God as revealed in Jesus Christ. Part of Barth's lasting legacy is a condemnation of modern anthropocentrism and a declaration that God — not humanity — is the center of theology.

Finally, this strand of theological conversation is sometimes called narrative theology because of the importance placed on biblical narrative renderings of Jesus as central to Christian faith. In *The Eclipse of Biblical Narrative,* Hans Frei argues that the meaning of the Bible lies in the narrative depiction of Jesus Christ rather than in moral truths or historical events to which the Bible points.[4] Frei's deep appreciation for the meaning-making capacity of narrative, and for the interpretive practices of Christian communities, has influenced many contemporary theologians. Furthermore, although Frei focused on the narratives within Scripture, Old Testament scholar Brevard Childs added to the conversation a view of the Bible as an authoritative canon, a whole that is interpreted first and foremost by Christian communities that regard it as Scripture.[5]

It is no surprise that Kelsey's magnum opus fits nicely into the Yale school I have described as Kelsey himself is one of the key theologians within this tradition. Let me briefly mention some of the ways *Eccentric Existence* continues and develops this strand of theology. First, Kelsey

3. Karl Barth, *The Epistle to the Romans,* 6th ed., trans. Edwyn C. Hoskyns (Oxford: Oxford University Press, 1933), pp. 37, 44, 230ff.

4. Hans W. Frei, *The Eclipse of Biblical Narrative: A Study in Eighteenth and Nineteenth Century Hermeneutics* (New Haven, CT: Yale University Press, 1974).

5. Brevard S. Childs, *Introduction to the Old Testament as Scripture* (Philadelphia: Fortress Press, 1979).

identifies his project as, "a Christianly particularist anthropology" (7).[6] His theology is located quite specifically within the self-understanding of Christian communities. This specificity of location does not aim to limit conversation, but rather to serve as a starting point from which Christians can dialogue with other religious and scientific perspectives (6-7). Kelsey asserts that in order to build a bridge between Christian theology and other discourses regarding the human person, it is useful first to articulate clearly the particularly Christian wisdom that is to be brought into dialogue. He seeks to identify the convictions of Christian faith that are "nonnegotiable in intellectual exchange with anthropologies shaped by other traditions," to analyze the architectural features of the Christian "abutment" upon which a bridge of dialogue could be built (7).

Second, as Lindbeck described theology as the grammar of a community, Kelsey situates his theological reflections within the common life of ecclesial communities (18). More specifically, he locates his project of academic theology as part of the community's self-critical reflection upon their own communal practices as responses to God's ways of relating to all that is not God, particularly involved in formulating the standards by which communities evaluate such communal practices (21).[7] In this book, Kelsey asks, "What is the logic of the *beliefs* that inform the practices composing the common life of communities of Christian faith?" (27, his emphasis). He notes that while he tends to use the word "logic" to refer to the patterns of relation among beliefs, others use the word "grammar" (28).

Third, Kelsey's focus on this particular question is in line with the narrative tradition's aversion to apology. Kelsey delineates three questions that "guide most projects of secondary theology" (27). The first asks, "what is the logic of *beliefs* that inform Christian communal practices?" The second asks, "what is the logic of *coming to belief* or of coming to faith in God so that one join" Christian communities and practices? The third asks, "what is the logic of *the life of Christian believing*?" (27). Kelsey argues against conflating these questions with a stunning analysis of the problems attendant to many modern theological projects that muddle the three together. The modern turn to the subject, in tandem with the theological practice of separating anthropology into a distinct locus, has influenced a

6. David H. Kelsey, *Eccentric Existence: A Theological Anthropology* (Louisville, KY: Westminster John Knox, 2009). References to this work will be given parenthetically in the text.

7. Kelsey writes, "The patterns of practices and thought that are handed on are more appropriately likened to the rules of a generative grammar or an informal logic" (4).

number of theological anthropologies that have a similar structure. This structure describes the human person as coming to fullness through a series of developments or stages, driven by an inherent desire for the good or tendency toward wholeness (82, 85). This picture of humanity is painted in terms and concepts that are not dependent upon a prior acceptance of Christian faith, and can thereby serve an apologetic function. If a reader of such theology finds the portrait of humanity compelling, she is already on the road to belief, accepting that becoming faithful is part of becoming fully human. In Kelsey's terms, "The stages from unfaith to faith are nothing else than the stages from potential subject to actualized subject, and vice versa" (85).

In Kelsey's analysis, such theologies systematically privilege human concerns in ways that lead to instrumental, functionalist, and trivializing views of God, nonhuman creatures, and Christian beliefs and actions (113). Conflating questions of the logic of belief with the logic of coming to belief encourages rampant anthropomorphic focus such that God and nonhuman creatures are seen primarily in terms of their utility to humans.

This leads to the fourth continuity with narrative theology, namely, that Barth's attack on Protestant liberalism and modern anthropocentrism echoes throughout this text. In both structure and content, Kelsey offers a theocentric anthropology. His theological anthropology is derived from God-centered doctrines of creation, salvation, and eschatological consummation, and the theological anthropology thus derived locates the defining center of humanity in God's activity.

Fifth, Kelsey argues that theological reflection of the sort that he undertakes in *Eccentric Existence* — which he refers to as secondary theology — should be "accountable to canonical Holy Scripture read as an authoritative set of texts that is a kind of whole" (148). In ways resonant with both Frei and Childs, he then identifies three narratives in the biblical canon (God's relating to create, to draw to consummation, and to redeem) that he regards as definitively shaping Christian theology. He further claims that each narrative has its own logic and exists in specific relationship with the other two. The logic of each narrative is granted significant authority in Kelsey's theology; each narrative is regarded as having its own internal coherence that ought to be respected by those who view the Bible as canonical Holy Scripture.[8] In each of these five

8. Kelsey describes what it means to view the Bible as canonical Holy Scripture in pp. 132-56 (see esp. 138 and 159). Regarding the authority of narrative logic, Kelsey states, "the

ways, Kelsey's work in *Eccentric Existence* is paradigmatic of the Yale school theological tradition.

Moving from Narrative to Drama and Performance

Post-liberal theology emerged in the midst of the linguistic turn, employing metaphors of language to understand Christianity and focusing on texts and textual interpretation. In the decades since then, there has been increasing awareness of the ways in which human persons and religious communities are shaped and formed not only by language, but also by non-linguistic aspects of culture. There has been renewed interest in embodiment, practices, and ritual. Although the founding metaphors were primarily verbal, many of the fundamental insights of narrative theology are deeply amenable to these developments in theology. There is room to explore and appreciate how communal interpretation of Scripture takes place in liturgy and worship as well as the reading of texts and how the "grammar" of Christian faith guides actions as well as words. There is ample space to investigate how the norm of biblical narrative shapes personal identity in whole-bodied ways — shaping not just conceptual and linguistic patterns but also patterns of behavior and aesthetics. Furthermore, narrative theology values external, enacted, or public religious and cultural forms as both indicative and formative of identity.[9]

A number of theologians and ethicists who have roots in the Yale school have incorporated notions of drama or performance in their work in order to push the narrative tradition further in its appreciation of embodiment and enactment. One example is ethicist Stanley Hauerwas, who brought Frei's emphasis on narrative into Christian ethics by articulating the value of Christian stories in guiding behavior and shaping identity.[10] In an essay titled, "The Gesture of a Truthful Story," Hauerwas writes: "As Christians, we are not, after all, called to be morally good, but rather to be faithful to the story that we claim is truthful to the very character of reality. . . . What it means to be Christian, therefore, is that we are a people

logic of the plot of the canonical Gospel narrative descriptions of who the image of God is — that is, the plot of Jesus Christ's narrative identity-description — guides and norms the way in which the Introductions to this work warrant, frame, and organize the project's anthropological proposals" (912).

9. Lindbeck, *Nature of Doctrine,* p. 34.

10. Placher, "Postliberal Theology," p. 349.

who affirm that we have come to find our true destiny only by locating our lives within the story of God. . . . It is the astounding claim of Christians that through [Jesus'] story, we discover our true selves and thus are made part of God's very life. We become part of God's story by finding ourselves within that story."[11]

In "Performing Faith: The Peaceable Rhetoric of God's Church," a later essay co-written with James Fodor, Hauerwas states, "Christian existence is first and foremost an activity — a performance, if you will."[12] The concepts of performance and improvisation help Fodor and Hauerwas focus on time and repetition in the living of Christian faith in ways that story and narrative do not.[13] Relying on performance, rather than story, as a primary lens to understand faith also has the important benefit of understanding Christian faith and action in a more embodied way.

Comparing the final sections of these two essays highlights this difference in emphasis on embodiment. Throughout the first essay, "Gesture of a Truthful Story," Hauerwas relentlessly emphasizes story: "There is no point that can be known separate from the story. There is no experience that we want people to have apart from the story. The story is the point, the story is the experience, and the story is the moral. The task of religious education, therefore, involves the development of skills to help us make the story ours."[14] Then Hauerwas raises the issue of mentally handicapped persons who might not be able to read the Biblical narratives or to understand the Christian story in an intellectual way. Hauerwas argues that such Christians "learn the story through its enactment as they feel and are formed by the liturgy that places us as characters in God's grand project of the creation and redemption of the world. They know that they, too, have a role in God's people as they faithfully serve God through being formed by a community that is nothing less than the enactment of that story."[15] Nicely de-centering his own scholarly enterprise, Hauerwas ends this essay on the desiderata of religious education

11. Stanley M. Hauerwas, "The Gesture of a Truthful Story," in *Christian Existence Today: Essays on Church, World, and Living in Between* (Grand Rapids: Baker Books, 1988), p. 102.

12. James Fodor and Stanley Hauerwas, "Performing Faith: The Peaceable Rhetoric of God's Church," in *Rhetorical Invention and Religious Inquiry: New Perspectives,* ed. Walter Jost and Wendy Olmsted (New Haven, CT: Yale University Press, 2000), p. 382.

13. Fodor and Hauerwas, "Performing Faith," p. 394.

14. Hauerwas, "Gesture of a Truthful Story," pp. 107-8.

15. Hauerwas, "Gesture of a Truthful Story," p. 109.

by acknowledging the limits of intellectual apprehension of narrative and highlighting enactment of the story. The second essay, "Performing Faith," also ends with an image of a mentally handicapped person, this time borrowed from Rowan Williams' account of a British documentary.[16] The image is of Chris, who learns to dance and performs with delightful grace. This performance, and the process of "apprenticeship" through which Chris learns to perform, is offered as a model of Christian pedagogy.[17] Putting the two essays side by side shows Hauerwas' movement from story to performance as a way to incorporate attention to embodiment and embodied knowing while retaining his basic commitments regarding biblical narratives.

Hauerwas' student, Samuel Wells, is another ethicist influenced by the Yale school who moves from narrative toward performance categories, more specifically toward improvisation, in part to emphasize the embodied actions of Christian communities. Proposing a distinctly ecclesial ethics, Wells argues that "If the community of faith is the primary subject of theological ethics, narrative becomes an inadequate category for interpretation."[18] Focusing on narrative alone runs the risk that it will be seen as secret and sufficient knowledge that need not be further embodied in community and action.[19] He thus asserts that Christian ethics is "appropriately regarded as performance."[20]

Theologian Kevin Vanhoozer also works in some continuity with the Yale school of theology while moving toward performance. Vanhoozer underscores the importance of script for Christian performance and chooses to portray biblical authority in a way less involved with how it is used in community (as Yale school theologians such as Frei and Kelsey describe it) and more reliant on the structure of the canon itself.[21] He finds performance language useful in emphasizing an appreciation of embodied practices and action that is already present in narrative theology. He writes:

16. The documentary, *Stepping Out,* is described in Rowan Williams, "My Dancing Day," in *Open to Judgement: Sermons and Addresses* (London: Darton, Longman, and Todd, 1994), pp. 72-75.

17. Fodor and Hauerwas, "Performing Faith," p. 403.

18. Samuel Wells, *Improvisation: The Drama of Christian Ethics* (Grand Rapids: Brazos Press, 2004), p. 45.

19. Wells, *Improvisation,* pp. 45-46.

20. Wells, *Improvisation,* p. 59.

21. Kevin J. Vanhoozer, *The Drama of Doctrine: A Canonical-Linguistic Approach to Christian Theology* (Louisville, KY: Westminster John Knox, 2005), pp. 17, 166-67.

> Thinking of doctrine in dramatic rather than theoretical terms provides a wonderfully engaging and integrative model for understanding what it means to follow — with all our mind, heart, soul, and strength — the way, truth, and life embodied and enacted in Jesus Christ. As such, it does justice to the cultural-linguistic turn and the concomitant emphasis on practice, and at the same time opens up interesting new possibilities for conceiving the relationship of Scripture (the script of the gospel) and the life of the church (the performance of the gospel).[22]

Finally, this movement from narrative to performance can be seen clearly in an essay on theological anthropology written by Serene Jones, a constructive theologian who studied and taught at Yale. Jones invites the reader to "think of Christian doctrine as a description of the theater of imagination within which Christians stand as they interpret their world and give shape to their thoughts and actions."[23] She explains, "Learning a set of doctrines means more than memorizing a set of statements; it involves receiving a whole array of stage props and scripts that shape how we interpret and participate in the ongoing story of our lives as we see them unfolding in the grand theater of God's continuing relationship with the world."[24] In the note at the end of this sentence, Jones states, "Note that I am expanding Lindbeck's cultural-linguistic account of doctrine."[25] Jones then incorporates Kelsey's insights about distinct biblical narratives into her own description of four "dramatic portraits" of humanity, roles that Christians "perform": "creatures, sinners, forgiven saints, and recipients of life eternal."[26] For Jones, the movement from narrative to drama is an intuitive expansion that embraces lived realities and embodied actions within the framework established by Lindbeck, Kelsey, and other theologians of the Yale school.

Given this movement toward performance by contemporary theologians and ethicists who have been influenced by the Yale school, it is notable that Kelsey does not turn in that direction. But could he have?

22. Vanhoozer, *Drama of Doctrine,* p. 16.

23. Serene Jones, "What's Wrong with Us? Human Nature and Sin," in *Essentials of Christian Theology,* ed. William C. Placher (Louisville, KY: Westminster John Knox, 2003), p. 142. Emphasis removed.

24. Jones, "What's Wrong with Us?," p. 142.

25. Jones, "What's Wrong with Us?," p. 395, note 4.

26. Jones, "What's Wrong with Us?," pp. 142-43, 396. Jones's article was published when *Eccentric Existence* was well developed, but not yet published.

Are the basic commitments and contours of narrative theology amenable to performance readings? The import of this question moves in two directions: (1) Can performance categories be used to integrate current appreciation for embodied, communal practices into narrative theology?; and (2) Can narrative theology function as an established theological framework within which the insights of performance studies can be brought into play?

Performance

To investigate this, we need a more specific understanding of performance.[27] This is a tricky proposition since the word functions in myriad ways in contemporary scholarship, including in the works I have just surveyed. Jones uses drama and performance as intuitive metaphors to illuminate the importance of doctrine in one place, and engages the more technical aspects of Judith Butler's theory of performativity in another.[28] Wells uses the term drama fairly loosely to designate narrative in communal interaction then moves to more particular formulations of what is involved in improvisation. Vanhoozer begins with theater as an intuitive metaphor and then develops it in quite specific ways, identifying the congregation as the theater company, the pastor as the director, and Scripture as the script. Along the way, he draws on the writings of theater directors as the metaphor opens doors to conversation.

The power of theater as a metaphor or analogy with Christianity can be both a blessing and a curse to a theological project. It has intuitive force, such that nearly anyone confronted with "theater" and "Christianity" together can start developing myriad connections and assigning various roles. The church is theater; creation is theater. Liturgy is drama; all of history is one unfolding plotline. God is director; God is playwright; the Holy Spirit is waiting in the wings. In a way, the spontaneous conversations that occur when the subject is mentioned testify to the deep connections between theater and Christianity. Yet, the intuitive and flexible

27. My discussion of performance here echoes several of my writings on the subject, most notably Shannon Craigo-Snell, *The Empty Church: Theater, Theology, and Bodily Hope* (New York: Oxford University Press, 2014) and "Theology as Performance," *The Ecumenist* 16, no. 4 (2008): 6-10.

28. Serene Jones, *Feminist Theory and Christian Theology: Cartographies of Grace* (Minneapolis: Fortress Press, 2000), pp. 31-33.

nature of metaphors between theater and aspects of Christian tradition can make the analogies too loose to be useful, too fanciful to carry theological weight.

The concept I think most useful to carry forward is performance. It is a broad category that encompasses many of the ways in which dramatic, theatrical, and artistic metaphors are used in theology, yet it has been developed enough in the discipline of performance studies to have outlined structural features. This does not mean that it is a simple concept, easily nailed down. Performance studies itself is an interdisciplinary field, with roots in anthropology, psychology, theater studies, and linguistics.[29] The term "performance" is described as "an essentially contested concept," meaning that part of what defines the term is the various disagreements about its meaning.[30] Another way of phrasing it is this: in its current academic use, "performance" does not delineate a single reality so much as a cluster of characteristics that are taken up in diverse ways. This fluidity is appropriately understood as part of the meaning of the term itself; "performance" is less a dictionary entry than an entry into ongoing conversations about what "performance" means.

I briefly describe the broad characteristics of performance as action, interaction, and doubleness. The first two characteristics are fairly clear. A performance is an action that takes place in a particular time and place. It is not a freestanding entity that can be understood apart from its context. Interaction refers to the relationality of performance. There is a performer and an audience as well as the culture that surrounds each of them. A performance both instantiates and responds to the culture in which it takes place. These interactions are constitutive of the performance. It is important to note that sometimes a performer can be her own audience (and even critic), such that the relation is internal to the self.[31]

The third characteristic, doubleness, is less familiar. Marvin Carlson writes that in performance an action is "placed in mental comparison with

29. Marvin Carlson, *Performance: A Critical Introduction* (New York: Routledge, 1996), pp. 9-80.

30. Mary S. Strine, Beverly W. Long, and Mary Francis Hopkins, "Research in Interpretation and Performance Studies: Trends, Issues, Priorities," in *Speech Communication: Essays to Commemorate the 75th Anniversary of the Speech Communication Association,* ed. G. M. Phillips and J. T. Woods (Carbondale: Southern Illinois University Press, 1990), p. 183. The authors are drawing upon the work of W. B. Gallie, *Philosophy and the Historical Understanding* (New York: Schocken Books, 1964).

31. Carlson, *Performance,* p. 5.

a potential, an ideal, or a remembered original model of that action."[32] This is easy to recognize in the example of an actress performing Juliet. The actress does not become Juliet — there is a gap there, a doubleness between the actress and the character she plays. Doubleness is also recognizable in the performance of social roles. Performing the role of a theologian requires me to have some sense of what a theologian is, some notion of how a theologian ought to dress and speak and behave. There are cultural rules and expectations, which I have learned in community, which provide a template for my performance of being a theologian. There is a model or ideal — in my mind and in my community — for what being a theologian looks like. I am conscious of how my own actions and interactions relate to this role I am performing. As complicated as being a theologian is, that is easy next to the performance of being a mother, a social role that is over-weighted with conflicting ideals and models. There is a doubleness between my being a theologian and my understanding of what it is to be a theologian, a doubleness between my being a mother and my own ideal of what kind of mother I want to be. Carlson describes this as, "the peculiar doubling that comes with consciousness and with the elusive *other* that performance is not, but which it constantly struggles in vain to embody."[33]

Theorist Richard Schechner highlights the temporal aspect of doubleness when he describes performance with the phrase "restored behavior." This means that performance is behavior that we have somehow learned before. When we play a game, we are repeating set patterns of play. When we perform a ritual or ceremony, we are likewise re-enacting prescribed actions that we have seen or done before. Similarly, Schechner argues, everyday life is composed of smaller segments of restored behavior — patterns we have seen or done before. He writes, "the everydayness of everyday life is precisely its familiarity, its being built from known bits of behavior rearranged and shaped in order to suit specific circumstances."[34] Schechner's description of performance includes the characteristics of event and interaction, while emphasizing the element of doubleness.[35] He writes: "restored behavior is 'me behaving as if I were someone else,'

32. Carlson, *Performance,* p. 5. Carlson is drawing on comments by Richard Baumann in "Performance," in *International Encyclopedia of Communication,* ed. Erik Barnouw (New York: Oxford University Press, 1989).

33. Carlson, *Performance,* p. 5. Emphasis his.

34. Richard Schechner, *Performance Studies: An Introduction* (New York: Routledge, 2002), p. 23.

35. Schechner, *Performance Studies,* p. 24.

or 'as I am told to do,' or 'as I have learned.' Even if I feel myself wholly to be myself, acting independently, only a little investigating reveals that the units of behavior that comprise 'me' were not invented by 'me.'"[36]

One of the implications of this view of human performance is that our actions are not nearly as original as we might like to believe. We are not the first authors of our way of being in the world. Consider, for example, the rebellious American teenager. Desperate to act out against societal expectations, she chooses to dress in an unconventional manner, to listen to non-mainstream music, and so forth. Now bring to mind a picture of a rebellious American teen from the 1950s, the 60s, the 80s. Even our non-conformity conforms to recognizable patterns. Our attempts to be original are neither wholly unique, nor exact reproductions, but rather negotiated new instantiations of former tropes and repertoires. At the same time, our revised repetitions of previous patterns are what sustain and continually re-create those patterns. Both our actions and the guiding norms that shape them come to be in ongoing, negotiated performances.

In addition to these three characteristics of action, interaction, and doubleness, two other points should be made about the term "performance." First, what determines whether or not an event is a performance, according to theorist Richard Schechner, is simply cultural standards.[37] Our culture says that a production of Shakespeare *is* a performance, along with a musical recital and many other events. Academics involved in performance studies look at many things *as* performances. This means they ask questions that focus on these characteristics: action, interaction, and doubleness.

Second, the very focus on performance is caught up with a claim that human performances are constructive of meaning and constitutive of identity. When scholars write about performance in relation to the identity of persons or communities, performance is seen as constitutive of that identity. For many scholars, the doubleness and restored character of performance highlight the plasticity of human identity and the ways in which human persons are socially constructed. Judith Butler draws on linguistics, particularly the work of J. L. Austin, and postmodern theories to develop the concept of performativity. Against the tendency to see human behavior as the outward expression of a stable, inner identity, Butler argues that outward behavior — formed and guided by cultural rules and expectations

36. Schechner, *Performance Studies,* p. 28.
37. Schechner, *Performance Studies,* p. 30.

— generates the appearance of a stable self. Butler is concerned particularly with the relations between sex and gender. She denies a conventional view that persons are in some sense hard-wired with a gender identity that then is expressed in behaviors. Instead, she argues, persons learn to behave within the regulative norms of culture.

The performances of normative gestures then sustain the appearance of a stable sex and gender identity. Butler writes, "There is no gender identity behind the expressions of gender; that identity is performatively constituted by the very 'expressions' that are said to be its results."[38] Put much too simply, while more conventional views claim that identity generates behavior, Butler argues that behavior generates identity. Butler's use of "performativity" falls within the broader definition of performance outlined above, while particularly emphasizing how performance constitutes identity. Scholars differ greatly in their assessment of the degree and extent of performative constitution of the self. There is room, within the conversation of performance studies, for a variety of positions, including views that see performativity as an exhaustive description of human identity and views that see performativity as one aspect of identity in relation to others.

Having given this broad description, let me try to fill it out with an example. Consider a book. It could be looked at as an artifact, static and unchanging. Someone engaged in performance studies, however, will look at the *writing* of a book as an action. In this action, the author interacts with her culture and her readers, and the meaning of the book comes to be in the relations between the author, her readers, and the culture(s) they inhabit. It simply does not make sense to ask what a book means without asking "to whom," "when," and "in what circumstances." Also, there is a doubleness between the author's vision of what a book is supposed to look like and the book she writes. A performance-oriented writer exploring a particular book would posit that the writing of it contributed to the identity of the author in various ways, inculcating certain physical habits in her body, altering her social status, or changing her ideas.

Alternately, a person engaged in performance studies might look at the *reading* of a book as a performance. In this action, a reader interacts with the author, with her own culture, and with the culture of the author.

38. Judith Butler, *Gender Trouble: Feminism and the Subversion of Identity* (New York: Routledge, 1990), p. 25. See also, Judith Butler, "Performative Acts and Gender Constitution: An essay in phenomenology and feminist theory," in *Performing Feminisms: Feminist Critical Theory and Theater,* ed. Sue-Ellen Case (Baltimore: Johns Hopkins University Press, 1990), pp. 270-82.

To answer the question of what the book means, in this scenario, would include asking what it means to this reader, in this time, place, and context. This reading will involve culturally received notions about what books are supposed to be like as well as culturally normative reading practices. There is, then, doubleness between this book and remembered or imagined ideals. Finally, a performance-oriented scholar inquiring about the meaning of this book would consider that the reader's identity might be shaped by this text.

Performance studies, like any theoretical lens, brings some things into view and obscures others. The book as artifact falls from view, while the writing of it, the reading of it, even the binding or collecting of it, become clearer. Indeed, the meaning of the book comes to be in these actions, and can neither be nor be understood in isolation from them.

While this overview of performance draws upon the field of performance studies and uses language quite distinct from theology, there are clear resonances with the Yale school tradition. Narrative theology does not use the term doubleness, but it acknowledges that persons are shaped by cultural and linguistic norms that provide the logic and grammar for human behavior. We are always speaking and acting according to norms and guides we learn in community. We are always acting "like" a theologian or a mother or a Christian, acting "as if" we are students or fathers or brothers. Within the logic of Yale school theology, human understanding and action can only happen within such templates learned in community. Without them, we cannot know or be. There is always doubleness between the act (of knowing or speaking or behaving) and the guiding norm for such acts (regulative communal ideals of knowing or speaking or behaving), which both shape the act and make it possible.

Similarly, performativity is not a term associated with Lindbeck's work, yet there are resonances between them. He writes, "the linguistic-cultural model is part of an outlook that stresses the degree to which human experience is shaped, molded, and in a sense constituted by cultural and linguistic forms."[39] He consistently emphasizes the importance of " 'external' religious and cultural factors" over that of internal experience.[40] Discussing religions, Lindbeck describes how his cultural-linguistic outlook turns conventional wisdom regarding identity inside out. The logic of his statement is remarkably similar to Butler's view of persons. Lindbeck

39. Lindbeck, *Nature of Doctrine,* p. 34.

40. Lindbeck, *Nature of Doctrine,* pp. 33-34.

writes: "Instead of deriving external features of a religion from inner experience, it is the inner experiences which are viewed as derivative."[41]

Such resonances are, I believe, part of the motivation behind the turn toward performance among contemporary theologians and ethicists who have been influenced by narrative theology. Even without the technical terminology of performance, the connections between the two are clear. However, having a clearer and more technical description of performance in hand can be useful in investigating just how compatible narrative and performative theologies truly are. Using *Eccentric Existence* as exemplary of narrative theology in contemporary context, I ask whether it is fundamentally open to the move toward performance or if there are theologically significant disjunctions between the two. Except for a few rare instances to be discussed below, Kelsey does not employ the concept of performance. Therefore, my narrative-performance experiment will take the form of trying to read *Eccentric Existence* within the contextual framework of performance. If it works — if the text can fit into the conceptual framework of performance — I take this to be an affirmation of the continuity between narrative and performance theologies. If it does not work — if the text does not fit into the conceptual framework of performance — the disjunctures may be informative regarding the areas of discontinuity between narrative and performance theologies. The question then becomes: Does the theological anthropology Kelsey forwards fit within the conceptual frameworks of performance?

Performing Eccentric Existence

God is clearly the central performer in Kelsey's theology. To speak of human performing first, rather than God's, would be to reject the basic, theocentric outlook of *Eccentric Existence:* the premise that our identity is constituted first and foremost by God's relating. With this theocentric view, the first characteristic of performance — action — is easy. God creates, consummates, and redeems. Kesley does not offer a theological anthropology based on static characteristics of human persons, but rather one based on the richness of God's threefold relating. Kelsey's theology requires more verbs than nouns; it is steeped in action. The second characteristic — relation — is similar. God's relating to us is constitutive of who we are,

41. Lindbeck, *Nature of Doctrine,* p. 34.

and God's relating to all that is not God is bound to God's own Trinitarian relating. The third characteristic — doubleness — is more complicated.

God's actions of creating, consummating, and redeeming do not fit the descriptions of doubleness discussed above. There is no "potential, ideal, or . . . remembered original model" of these actions.[42] These actions are not restorations of cultural norms God saw or learned in community. These are original, unique. Surely, one could talk about Jesus as performing, a human being in community whose actions and interactions are constitutive of his identity (see 906), yet the larger picture of God's triune relating is sui generis. God is not striving to embody a model of what such relating might look like. In Kelsey's theology, God's creating, consummating, and redeeming are definitive of those relations.

Fodor and Hauerwas do refer to God as performing. In "Performing Faith," they write, "Christians worship a God who is pure act, an eternally performing God."[43] The authors recognize that God's performing would have to be quite different from human performing, as they note, "only God as Trinity can perform in such a way as not to be alienated from what God is."[44] These statements by Hauerwas and Fodor are in service to a theological view somewhat resonant with Kelsey's. Referencing John Webster, they assert, "It may be that the Christian faith is 'primarily an account of divine action' and 'only secondarily an account of the believing subject,'" and go on to claim, "our God is a performing God who has invited us to join in the performance that is God's life."[45]

Kelsey also refers to God as performing in a way that invites us to perform. The context for his use of performance language is a discussion about the glory of God, and the conceptual background is J. L. Austin's speech-act theory. Under certain conditions, Austin asserts, language performs what it states.[46] His famous example, taken up and critiqued by Butler in her description of performativity, is of a married couple saying vows. To say "I do," under particular circumstances, is to marry someone. It is generative, not merely descriptive, of reality. With this Austinian understanding in play, Kelsey says that human beings are "constituted as personal living bodies by God's relating to us in speech that performatively

42. Carlson, *Performance,* p. 5.

43. Fodor and Hauerwas, "Performing Faith," p. 382.

44. Fodor and Hauerwas, "Performing Faith," p. 382.

45. Fodor and Hauerwas, "Performing Faith," p. 382.

46. J. L. Austin, *How to Do Things with Words,* ed. J. O. Urmson and Marina Sbisà (Cambridge, MA: Harvard University Press, 1962), pp. 5-6.

displays God's glory as Creator" (294). God's address, both direct and indirect, constitutes us as living and personal bodies (314). This means that in our "sheer existence," we reflect and express the glory of God (330, 316). Furthermore, "God's self-involving and performative creative address . . . invites creatures' own self-involving and performative responses" (312). When we respond appropriately to God's address, we glorify God (330). Kelsey describes the Christian statement "God is glorious" as "performing an act of acknowledgement" (312). In our own performances, we are part of the performance of God's glory (316).[47]

In this discussion of God's glory, Kelsey uses the term performance to indicate that God's address is profoundly generative and calls for our response. He echoes Austin to indicate that God's speech does something. It is constitutive, rather than descriptive, of reality. However, Austin claims that utterances are only performative because of, and in the context of, culturally agreed upon norms and expectations.[48] Saying "I do" only counts as marrying someone under particular circumstances in which the various parties involved acknowledge that saying these words in such a way in such a context have the effect and import of marrying. In other words, saying "I do" is an example of doubleness, of restored behavior. In contrast, the import and effect of God's address is not conditioned by human cultural norms. Kelsey's use of the word "performance" thus functions more on a metaphorical or intuitive level than on a technical one. I cannot see a doubleness in God's creating, consummating, and redeeming actions, as Kelsey describes them. Hauerwas and Fodor, engaging performance more as metaphor than structural description, seem to perceive the problem, but rely on God's own Trinitarian self-differentiation to solve it. While it might be possible, with more fancy theological footwork than Fodor and Hauerwas provide in their essay, to argue that God's triune nature allows for doubleness in some sense, the sense created would be significantly removed from that employed in performance studies. There is a distinction between viewing something as an *act* and as a *performance.* A critical part of that distinction is doubleness. God acts. Without an account of doubleness, it does not make sense to say that God performs. While other visions of God might incorporate doubleness into accounts of God's activity, God as envisioned by Kelsey and other Yale school theologians acts, but does not perform.

47. Kelsey also describes Proverbs as having "performative force." See pp. 222-23.

48. Austin, *How to Do Things,* pp. 14-15, 26.

Does this mean that Kelsey's theology is simply incompatible with performance? Perhaps not. Perhaps we could say that while God acts, God's activity calls us to performance. While a Kelseyian narrative theology finds the source of theological activity in God, perhaps the terms of performance could help articulate our appropriate responses to God's relating. This shall be the next step of experimentation. Do we perform?

We certainly act, and interact, and we do so in ways that are governed and guided by learned cultural norms. There is decided doubleness to our actions; our behavior is restored behavior. Further, our performances are deeply constitutive of our identity. In describing how human actions constitute human behavior in community, Kelsey gives an account of performativity comparable to Butler's. His account of quotidian personal identity is an account of performative identity construction:

> Through a prolonged maturation process, human creatures are profoundly formed by the quotidian proximate contexts into which they are born and in which they live. The social and cultural aspects of those quotidian worlds hand on already formed — traditional — ways of acting and interacting with other human creatures in community, the humanly constructed cultural and social dimensions of their proximate contexts, as well as with the nonhuman dimensions of their proximate contexts, and also traditional ways of interpreting and relating to everything that happens to them. This includes ways of appropriating racial, ethnic, gender, and sexual differences (382).

Kelsey's description of quotidian personal identity includes an account of repeating normative cultures in ways that are distinctive, even as they are restored. His description is deeply resonant with descriptions of human agency in performative identity construction. In Kelsey's words,

> A human being's quotidian identity is always a negotiated combination of a social construct or constructs provided by the quotidian proximate context and an original self-construct by the human being. . . . Moreover, the self-construct aspect of quotidian identities involves some degree of originality, however slight or subtle, in the peculiar ways in which a given human being concretely enacts the expectations its proximate contexts lays on it, the concrete ways it goes about playing the roles assigned it, and the concrete ways it occupies the status to which it is assigned (382).

In these ways, Kelsey's account of personal identity is consonant with the conceptual apparatus of performance. However, for Kelsey, quotidian identities are "included" in the larger context of the human creatures' "basic identity" (382). This basic identity is that of being created, consummated, and redeemed by God.[49] This basic identity is "given to living human personal bodies by God" (384). This basic identity is not something we work at, strive for, create, construct, actualize, realize, or develop. It is not even something we "may or may not appropriate in self-involving subjective acts that are existentially formative" (384). It is just who we are.

There is a deep Calvinist comfort offered here, notable when Kelsey's prose simplifies into personal language. He writes, "while I have my personal identity only in and through relations with other creatures of giving and receiving, my personal identity is not given to me by them in their assessment of me and it does not depend on their judgments of me. My personal identity is free of them, grounded elsewhere. I am radically given to directly only by the triune God. . . . Your personal identity is defined by God alone and not by any creature. It is eccentrically grounded and defined" (339-40).

Human performance as constitutive of identity is thoroughly affirmed by Kelsey as it concerns quotidian personal identity. Our basic identity, however, is constituted by God's relating, and is impervious to humanly performative constitution. Faithful Christian life includes acknowledging our basic identities and performing our quotidian identities in ways that are congruent with them. Kelsey writes, "The human creature's quotidian identity is not replaced by its basic identity. Rather its quotidian identity is taken up into its basic identity and, across time, is shaped by it" (385).

This means that human creatures' basic identities escape performative construction. They are not, finally, normed and shaped by the linguistic-cultural context in which human persons come to be, act, and know. Given the broader context of Kelsey's Yale school theology, this can be stated more precisely. He is reflecting on "the logic of the beliefs that inform the practices composing the common life of communities of Christian faith" (27), upon the standards by which Christian communities evaluate whether or not their practices are appropriate responses to God's relating (21-22). The larger anthropological claim, then, looks something like this: The practices of Christian communities — in and through which human

49. More precisely, Kelsey asserts human creatures' basic identity is, "who they are by virtue of God relating to them to create, draw to eschatological consummation, and to reconcile when they are estranged from God" (384).

creatures come to know, understand, experience, and respond to God's relating — are informed by a belief that the most basic aspect of human identity escapes being thus formed by communal practices and is grounded securely in the relating of God.

Kesley's careful articulation of the limited scope of performative identity construction does not represent a major conflict between narrative and performative theologies. There are various views regarding the degree and extent of performative identity construction. Thus, there is room within Kelsey's narrative theology to say we do, indeed, perform.

Narrative and Performance, Reconsidered

As mentioned above, viewing something as a performance means asking relevant questions about the three primary characteristics of performance: action, interaction, and doubleness. It is in beginning to address these questions that problems arise between Kelsey's narrative approach and a performance-oriented perspective. Actions occur in particular times and places, and cannot be understood in isolation from those contexts. Kelsey's sweeping unsystematic systematics consistently emphasizes contexts, both proximate and ultimate, but from a bird's eye view that does not engage their particularities. Kelsey's methodology begins with the practices of Christian communities. Yet the diversity and multiplicity of Christian communities cannot be apprehended in the text. Although Kelsey offers three narratives (of God's relating, consummating, and redeeming), they are still grand, accounting for all humans in all times and places with a generality that rubs against the specificity of action.

This results, in part, from Kelsey's approach to the Bible. He carefully explains that he encounters the text as "canonical," "holy," and "Scripture," deriving the definition of each of these from how Christian communities read the text. He then identifies three narratives within the Bible, each having an authoritative narrative logic that commands respect. There is a slippage, here, between the Bible as read and the Bible as artifact. At times Kelsey describes the Bible as if it simply *has* three narratives with particular, identifiable, stable meanings that are independent from the action of reading and the context in which reading occurs. The wildly diverse ways in which Christian communities engage biblical texts fall from view in preference for a more unified (even in its three-ness) overarching account of God's relating to humanity.

Similar problems arise when trying to attend to interactions within the narrative framework. Interactions are unruly. It is difficult to locate and enforce their boundaries. Kelsey is deeply aware of the ways in which Christian faith always takes place within larger contexts, such that Christian traditions of beliefs and practices are in "overlap" and "tension" with other traditions, and "the boundaries of Christians' habitations are multiple" (6). He does not naively imagine Christian theological wisdom in isolation from other cultural traditions and wisdoms. However, in keeping with the traditions of narrative theology, Kelsey structures his anthropological inquiries by attempting to separate out the specific wisdom of Christian faith. While acknowledging that more interactions are always in play, he seeks to articulate particularly Christian "nonnegotiable" convictions, in separation and distinction from other, non-Christian beliefs (7). He looks closely at interactions between God, human creatures, Christian practices, and Holy Scripture. He carefully draws a line around distinctly Christian communal practices and beliefs, and asks about the interactions within that delineated sphere.

At the beginning of *Eccentric Existence,* Kelsey identifies his current project as formulating the theological abutment needed before building bridges of dialogue with other religious and scientific views (7). The difficulty with this is that I have never yet found myself standing only on one side of that river. Christian practices and beliefs already take place in interaction with other religious, scientific, and social views. Furthermore, this has always been the case, including the creation, handing down, and ongoing reception of Scripture. We are always already involved in interactions far beyond the (quite permeable) boundaries of Christian community. We do not find our nonnegotiable Christian convictions before entering into intellectual exchange with other traditions. Rather, it is in the midst of that exchange, precisely in negotiation, that vital Christian convictions come to be. Kelsey knows and acknowledges all of this. Yet the patterns of narrative theology involve articulating the grammar and logic specific to Christian community, and Kelsey thus draws a theoretical boundary around Christian communities and investigates interactions within that sphere. From a performance-oriented perspective, the boundaries Kelsey draws around specifically Christian communal beliefs and practices seem arbitrary or illusory, contradicting his own acknowledgment of a much more fluid, multiple, and messy world.

This relates to another distinction of Kelsey's that is questionable from a performance perspective: among the logic of beliefs, the logic of coming to belief, and the logic of believing. While this distinction nicely combats a particular strand of modernist, anthropocentric apologetics, it does so at the cost of neglecting the embodied nature of Christian believing. The characteristic of performance I refer to as doubleness suggests that our coming to believe, our beliefs, and our practicing of such beliefs cannot be so neatly divided. Acting as if I were a theologian is part and parcel of how I become one; acting as if I believe is part and parcel of how I come to believe. Furthermore, it is only in the practicing of belief that I come to understand what those beliefs really are. It is in the living of them that the logic becomes apparent, and indeed that the logic comes to be. Finally, the continuing tradition of Christian beliefs is sustained and recreated through ongoing, negotiated practices of coming to belief and believing.

Kelsey acknowledges much of this and honors the interrelations of practices and beliefs, asking about the logic of beliefs that inform Christian practices. Yet, partly in keeping with the non-apologetic commitments of the narrative tradition, he theoretically separates beliefs from believing, coming to belief from living out belief. Throughout *Eccentric Existence,* Kelsey contends against expressivist views of human creatures that privilege inner subjectivity. However, in theoretically excising the doctrine that informs Christian practices from the practices themselves — the concrete practices of worship and faithfulness through which Christians continually come to believe in the acts of believing — Kelsey falls into the same trap.

It is difficult to attend to the elements of action, interaction, and doubleness within the theological anthropology of *Eccentric Existence.* The reasons for this are not, I believe, due to idiosyncratic aspects of Kelsey's work, but rather stem from methodological approaches common in narrative theologies. The desire to draw Christian doctrine from firmly within the boundaries of Christian communal faith and practice can be hard to reconcile with the concrete multiplicity of such communal actions. Furthermore, such boundaries drawn between Christian communal practices and larger cultural influences limit the scope of interaction considered. Finally, the anti-apologetic bent of narrative theology can prevent focus on the ongoing dynamic doubleness between becoming and being Christian.

Narrative theology cannot smoothly flow into performance theology, even though the two share overlapping insights. While there is room within the narrative tradition to recognize human performance, there are also methodological commitments that prevent closely attending to such performances. With its careful delineation of the nature of Christian claims, its acknowledged specificity of location and reliance upon a particular view of a holistic canon with stable narratives, Yale school theology is shaped by a desire for solid ground upon which to stand in conversation with external sources of wisdom. Performance studies calls this desire, and its presuppositions, into question.[50]

50. I am indebted to several colleagues for their comments and insights on this essay. I offer particular thanks to Luke Moorhead, reigning expert on *Eccentric Existence.*

David H. Kelsey Publications and Presentations

Publications

Books

The Fabric of Paul Tillich's Theology. New Haven, CT: Yale University Press, 1967.

The Uses of Scripture in Recent Theology. Philadelphia: Fortress Press, 1975. Unrevised second edition, *Proving Doctrine: Uses of Scripture in Modern Theology.* Harrisburg, PA: Trinity Press International, 1999.

To Understand God Truly: What's Theological about a Theological School? Louisville, KY: Westminster John Knox Press, 1992.

Between Athens and Berlin: The Theological Education Debate. Grand Rapids: William B. Eerdmans, 1993.

Imagining Redemption. Louisville, KY: Westminster John Knox Press, 2005.

Eccentric Existence: A Theological Anthropology. 2 vols. Louisville: KY: Westminster John Knox Press, 2009.

The Glory, the Kingdom, the Power: Reconceiving Divine Power. Forthcoming.

Chapters and Articles

"Jewish-Christian Dialogue and the Protestant Revolution." *Conservative Judaism* 20 (1965): 44-50.

"Appeals to Scripture in Theology." *Journal of Religion* 48 (1968): 1-21.

"The Bible and Christian Theology." *Journal of the American Academy of Re-*

ligion 48 (1980): 385-402. Reprinted in *Readings in Christian Theology.* Edited by Peter Hodgson and Robert King. Philadelphia: Fortress Press, 1985.

"Struggling Collegially to Think About Evil: An Interpretive Essay." In *Occasional Papers.* Collegeville, MN: Institute for Ecumenical and Cultural Research, 1981.

"Human Being." In *Christian Theology.* Edited by Peter Hodgson and Robert King. Philadelphia: Fortress Press, 1982.

"Protestant Attitudes Regarding Methods of Biblical Interpretation." In *Scripture in Jewish and Christian Traditions.* Edited by Fredrick Greenspann. Nashville, TN: Abingdon Press, 1982.

"Homosexuality and the Church: Theological Issues." *Reflection* (April 1983): 9-12.

"Doctrine of Scripture" and "Theological Method." In *Westminster Dictionary of Christian Theology.* Edited by Alan Richardson and John Bowden. Louisville, KY: Westminster John Knox Press, 1983.

"Mind Reading." Written with Barbara G. Wheeler. *Theological Education* (Spring 1984): 8-14.

"The Doctrine of Creation from Nothing." In *Evolution and Creation.* Edited by Ernan McMullen. Notre Dame, IN: University of Notre Dame Press, 1985.

"Theological Use of Scripture in Process Hermeneutics." *Process Studies* (1986): 181-88.

"Aquinas and Barth on the Human Body." *The Thomist* 50 (1986): 643-89.

"Biblical Narrative and Theological Anthropology." In *Scriptural Authority and Narrative Interpretation.* Edited by Garrett Green. Philadelphia: Fortress Press, 1987.

"Church Discourse and the Public Realm." In *Theology and Dialogue: Essays in Conversation with George Lindbeck.* Edited by Bruce D. Marshall. Notre Dame, IN: University of Notre Dame Press, 1990.

"Whatever Happened to the Doctrine of Sin?" *Theology Today* (July 1993): 169-78.

"The ATS Basic Issues Research Project: Thinking about Theological Education." Written with Barbara G. Wheeler. *Theological Education* 28, no. 1 (Autumn 1991); reprinted in abbreviated form in *Theological Education* 30, no. 2 (1994): 71-80.

"New Ground: The Foundations and Future of the Theological Education Debate." Written with Barbara G. Wheeler. In *Theology and the Interhuman.* Edited by Robert R. Williams. Harrisburg, PA: Trinity Press International, 1995.

"Two Theologies of Death: Anthropological Gleanings." *Modern Theology* 13, no. 3 (July 1997): 347-70.

"Charles Hodge as Interpreter of Scripture." In *Charles Hodge Revisited.* Edited by John W. Stewart and James Moorhead. Grand Rapids: Eerdmans, 2002.

"Spiritual Machines, Personal Bodies, and God: Theological Education and Theological Anthropology." *Teaching Theology and Religion* 5, no. 1: 2-9.

"Foreword." In *A Christian Critique of American Culture.* Julian N. Hartt. Eugene, OR: Wipf and Stock, 2006.

"Wisdom, Theological Anthropology, and Modern Secular Interpretation of Humanity." In *God's Life in Trinity.* Edited by Miroslav Volf and Michael Welker. Philadelphia: Fortress Press, 2006.

"Personal Bodies: A Theological Anthropological Proposal." In *Personal Identity in Theological Perspective.* Edited by Richard Lints, Michael S. Horton, and Mark R. Talbot. Grand Rapids: Eerdmans, 2006.

"The Human Creature." In *The Oxford Handbook of Systematic Theology.* Edited by John Webster, Kathryn Tanner, and Iain Torrance. Oxford: Oxford University Press, 2007.

"Response to the Symposium on *Eccentric Existence.*" *Modern Theology* 27, no. 1 (January 2011): 72-86.

"God and Teleology: Must God Have Only One 'Eternal Purpose'?" *Neue Zeitschrift fuer Systematische Theologie und Religionsphilosophie* 54, no. 4 (2012): 361-76.

"Response to Tom Greggs." *Scottish Journal of Theology* 65, no. 4 (2012): 464-70.

Review Articles

"Can God Be Agent without Body?" *Interpretation* 27 (1973): 358-62.

"Christian Sense Making: Hartt's *Theological Method and Imagination.*" *Journal of Religion* (1978): 428-35.

"Aesthetics and Theology." *Religious Studies Review* 19, no. 4: 312-15.

"Peter Hodgson's *God's Wisdom: Toward a Theology of Education.*" *Teaching Theology and Religion* 3, no. 2 (June 2000): 117-18.

"Theology in the University: Once More with Feeling." *Modern Theology* 25, no. 2 (April 2009): 315-27.

"Parting Conversation: Review of William Placher's *The Triune God.*" Published after Prof. Placher's death, with a response by Amy Plantinga Pauw, a eulogy by Raymond Brady Williams, and "Last Respects" by Stephen H. Webb. *Conversation in Religion and Theology* 7, no. 1 (May 2009): 115-19.

Presentations

Named Lectureships

Thomas White Currie Lectures. Austin Presbyterian Theological Seminary, Austin, TX, 1982.

Sarum Lectures. Oxford University, Oxford, England, Trinity Term, 1985.

Tate-Wilson Lectures. Perkins School of Theology, Southern Methodist University, Dallas, TX, 1986.

Taylor Lectures. Yale Divinity School, New Haven, CT, 2004.

Warfield Lectures. Princeton Theological Seminary, Princeton, NJ, March 2011.

Selected Papers

"The Very Idea of a Theological School." Presented at a Lilly Endowment-sponsored conference on research in theological education as the basis for extended discussion, New Harmony, IN, April 12-14, 1989.

"The Role of the Local Church in Theological Education for Ministry in the City." Theological Education and the City Conference, Yale Divinity School, New Haven, CT, October 29, 1992.

"On *To Understand God Truly*." Pittsburgh Theological Seminary, Pittsburgh, PA, September 2, 1993.

"Doing Theology in the Academy." Duke Divinity School Conference on Campus Ministry, Durham, NC, November 4, 1993.

"Post-Liberal Theology." Gordon-Conwell Theological Seminary, South Hamilton, MA, November 16, 1993.

"Between Athens and Berlin." Southern Baptist Theological Seminary, Louisville, KY, January 27, 1994.

"Two Theologies of Death." Duodecim Theological Society, February 25, 1994.

"Rethinking Theological Education." Plenary Address, Annual Meeting of the American Theological Librarians Association, Pittsburgh, PA, June 16, 1994.

"Values in Seminary Education: An Interfaith Exploration." Keynote Address, Skirball Institute Conference on Values in Seminary Education, Los Angeles, CA, February 24, 1995.

"Theological Education and Spiritual Formation." The Annual Priestly Ministry Lecture, Holy Cross Greek Orthodox School of Theology, Brookline, MA, February 13, 1997.

"Christian Theologies of Other Religions." Hope College, Holland, MI, April 3, 1997.

"Charles Hodge as Interpreter of Scripture." Charles Hodge Conference, Princeton University Department of Religion and Princeton Theological Seminary, Princeton, NJ, April 1997.

"Some Kind Words for 'Total Depravity.'" Inaugural Lecture for the Institute for Reformed Theology, Union Theological Seminary, Richmond, VA, October 1999. Also presented at the New Haven Theological Discussion Group, New Haven, CT, March 23, 2000.

"'Sin' in Paul Tillich's Systematic Theology." Faculty Seminar, Institute for Reformed Theology, Union Theological Seminary, Richmond, VA, March 6, 2000.

"Human Being: Theology and Science." Templeton Lecture, Albertus Magnus College, New Haven, CT, April 13, 2000.

"Spiritual Machines, Personal Bodies, and God." Plenary Address, Convocation of Eastern Cluster of Evangelical Lutheran Church of America Seminaries, Chicago, IL, September 23, 2000.

"Genesis and Theological Anthropology: A One-sided Conversation with Claus Westermann." Bible and Theology Section, American Academy of Religion, Nashville, TN, November 20, 2000.

"Seven Takes on the Love of God." Response to Seven Papers, Systematic Theology Section, American Academy of Religion, Denver, CO, November 19, 2001.

"Wisdom and Theological Anthropology" and "Theological Anthropology in Systematic Theology." Duke Divinity School, Durham, NC, April 10-11, 2003.

"Human Flourishing and God." Colloquy: God's Power and Human Flourishing, Center for Faith and Culture, Yale Divinity School, New Haven, CT, October 6, 2008. Also presented at the New Haven Theological Discussion Group, New Haven, CT, October 20, 2008.

"Picturing God in a Fragmented World." *Societas Homileticus,* Yale Divinity School, New Haven, CT, August 2010.

"The God of Abraham Praise" and "God's Power in Two Registers." Seminars, Institute for Theology, Philosophy, and Culture, Eberhard Karls Universitaet Tübingen, Germany, June 19, 2012.

"Why Must God Have Only One 'Eternal Purpose'?" Evangelisch-Theologische Facultaet, University of Tübingen, Germany, June 20, 2012.

Contributors

Shannon Craigo-Snell is Professor of Theology at Louisville Presbyterian Theological Seminary. Her writings include *The Empty Church: Theater, Theology, and Bodily Hope* (Oxford University Press, 2014), *Living Christianity: A Pastoral Theology for Today* (co-authored with Shawnthea Monroe) (Fortress Press, 2009), and *Silence, Love, and Death: Saying "Yes" to God in the Theology of Karl Rahner* (Marquette University Press, 2008).

David F. Ford is Fellow of Selwyn College and Regius Professor of Divinity Emeritus in the University of Cambridge. His publications include *Self and Salvation: Being Transformed* (Cambridge University Press, 1999), *Christian Wisdom: Desiring God and Learning in Love* (Cambridge University Press, 2007), and *The Future of Christian Theology* (Wiley-Blackwell, 2011).

Joy Ann McDougall is Associate Professor of Systematic Theology, Candler School of Theology, Emory University. Her publications include *The Pilgrimage of Love: Moltmann on the Trinity and the Christian Life* (Oxford University Press, 2005) and numerous essays on hamartiology, feminist theology, and women and theological education, both in anthologies and in academic journals such as *Modern Theology*, *Theology Today*, and *The Journal of Religion*.

Cyril O'Regan is Huisking Professor of Theology at the University of Notre Dame. He is the author of five books and numerous articles in systematic and historical theology and in philosophy of religion. His two most recent books are *Theology and the Spaces of Apocalyptic* (Marquette University Press, 2009) and *The Anatomy of Misremembering: Von Balthasar's Critique of Philosophical Modernity,* vol. 1: *Hegel* (Crossroad, 2014).

Gene Outka is Dwight Professor of Philosophy and Christian Ethics Emeritus at Yale University. He is the author of *Agape: An Ethical Analysis* (Yale University Press, 1972) and of *God and the Moral Life: Conversations in the Augustinian Tradition* (Oxford University Press, 2016). He is co-editor (with Paul Ramsey) and contributor to *Norm and Context in Christian Ethics* (Scribner's, 1968), co-editor (with John Reeder) and contributor to *Religion and Morality* (Doubleday Anchor, 1973), and co-editor (with John Reeder) and contributor to *Prospects for a Common Morality* (Princeton University Press, 1993). He was President of the Society of Christian Ethics in 2001.

Amy Plantinga Pauw is the Henry P. Mobley Jr. Professor of Doctrinal Theology at Louisville Presbyterian Seminary. She is the author of *The Supreme Harmony of All: The Trinitarian Theology of Jonathan Edwards* (Eerdmans, 2003), *Proverbs and Ecclesiastes* (Westminster John Knox Press, 2015), and *Church in Ordinary Time: A Wisdom Ecclesiology* (forthcoming). She serves as general editor for the theological commentary series Belief (Westminster John Knox Press).

John E. Thiel is Professor of Religious Studies at Fairfield University. He is the author of six books, including *Senses of Tradition: Continuity and Development in Catholic Faith* (Oxford University Press, 2000), *God, Evil, and Innocent Suffering* (Crossroad, 2002), and *Icons of Hope: The "Last Things" in Catholic Imagination* (University of Notre Dame Press, 2013). He served as President of the Catholic Theological Society of America in 2011-12.

Edwin Chr. van Driel is the Directors' Bicentennial Associate Professor of Theology at Pittsburgh Theological Seminary. After the publication of *Incarnation Anyway: Arguments for Supralapsarian Theology* (Oxford University Press, 2008) he worked on the new hymnal of the Presbyterian Church-USA, *Glory to God* (Westminster John Knox, 2013). He is now working on a book on Pauline exegesis and Protestant theology.

Barbara G. Wheeler is a researcher and consultant. She served for thirty years as President of Auburn Theological Seminary and was the founding director of Auburn's Center for the Study of Theological Education. She is a co-author of *Being There: Culture and Formation in Two Theological Schools* (Oxford University Press, 1997) and co-editor of and contributor to several collections of essays on theological education. She has directed ten studies of various facets of theological education and was principal author of reports on that research (http://www.auburnseminary.org/center-study-theological-education).

Charles M. Wood is Lehman Professor of Christian Doctrine emeritus at the Perkins School of Theology, Southern Methodist University. Among his publications are *The Formation of Christian Understanding* (Westminster Press, 1981), *Vision and Discernment* (Scholars Press, 1985), and *The Question of Providence* (Westminster John Knox Press, 2008).